New Burlington

New Burlington

The Life and Death
of an American Village

JOHN BASKIN

W·W·NORTON & COMPANY·INC·

NEW YORK

The photographs on pages 56, 71, 75, 151, 208, 215, 228, 229, 234, 246, and 260 are by Ken Steinhoff, and those on pages 63, 171, 186, 252, and 257 are by Dan Patterson.
The author offers thanks to the owners of the older, family photographs for kindly permitting their use in this book.

First Edition

Library of Congress Cataloging in Publication Data

Baskin, John.
  New Burlington.

  1. New Burlington, Ohio—Social life and customs.
2. New Burlington, Ohio—Biography. I. Title.
F499.N38B37 1976   977.1'74   75–43636
ISBN 0–393–08366–7

1 2 3 4 5 6 7 8 9 0

For Sarah, and the McIntires, who knew New Burlington
and for Dora, and my parents, who had only heard of it

Contents

Introduction

On a recent visit to my father's house in South Carolina I drove through Greenville behind a truck from the dairy which bought milk from our checkered herd, many of the cows once the idiosyncratic milkcows of widows who had at last given up to buy milk over the counter like any sane person. At that moment I thought *between then and now I have written a book which is a history of the distance between two points.* This did not come as any revelation but rather as a statement I made to myself which seemed, at last, *true*.

Let me go to the beginning. I came to New Burlington, Ohio, three years ago, by the accidents of my life. The villagers told me that before long they would be gone. The U.S. Army Corps of Engineers was building a reservoir over their village and soon children would waterski in 175-year-old cornfields. The people of nearby Cincinnati and Dayton would drive out in pursuit of images they would like to pronounce *healing*.

Full of complaint, I thought then I would become a carpenter; I would *restore* New Burlington. I would document the specific death of all the abstract deaths mourned by the sociologists in their bleak treatises upon the last rites of God and family, social custom, rural life, small-town morality, and the ordered universe. I would write the great American obituary. I perceived New Burlington as a *gift*: the world (engineers) crashes in to obliterate the past (the village).

This is a view which presupposes a villain and is therefore to be rejected. This is what I learned in the first writing. While we would all like to name the enemy and fight him hand-to-hand, it cannot be done. There are no more villains (in the sense of our archetypes, snake-eyed men in dusty streets), or in the event there might be, such should be regarded almost kindly, as antiquities. The modern condition of villainy is, I think, a manifestation of the circumscribed life. *Forgive us, Father, we know not which we do.* In this way, I came to see the army engineers as nothing more than a visitation of the villagers' interior life. This may be viewed in the political context: we deserve those we elect because they *are* us.

When I finished the final draft (such a thing is never finished, rather abandoned, put out on the waters in a bulrush basket with a prayer *Give the child a good home*), I was interested by the fact that the village life begins and ends with the presence of an engineer; a man is surveying the bottomlands for promise, in his terms. I did not do this on purpose, it merely happened, and it is significant mostly in its neatness. Today we tend to speak of people as *members*, as "He is a Republican" or "He is a Rotarian." The presence of the engineer reminds us that while he is an engineer he is *first* one of us, and reflective of us. (Some of my neighbors ask me what *New Burlington* will say about the engineers and the lake which will cover the village and I tell them: *nothing*. They turn away, disappointed.)

There is another presence in the material which I want to mention and that is mine, my presence. I am instructed by a short-story writer whom I regard as wise to carefully introduce what I am doing because I am writing nonfiction, a form she suggests has trained readers in noise and statement. So I point out to you my presence beside the two engineers. It is, I hope, a quiet presence and largely without statement but what it suggests in the form of this book is the necessity to understand choices. My own life between milkcows and a moment of recognition 15 years later is filled with the painful luxury of unwitting choices. And so *New Burlington* is a reconciliation with my leave-taking, at age 18, from a similar place and history.

I have reconstructed *New Burlington* to look impersonally at my time. My first belief about this time was a sentimental one. Now I believe there is nothing easy to say. I would like for any statement in *New Burlington* to come from the interaction among the villagers themselves, who are woven together by common things: themselves in the presence of each other, work, dislike, judgment, death. It is important to see that the villagers constantly contradict each other, that they refute and argue. I hope the villagers manifest some of the mysteriousness of being alive. If I believe in one quality of human-ness, it is its ambiguity (which arises from the unsettling fact that the world itself is both alive and dying). I am hugely interested in the interminable pause before resolution and in the spaces of *New Burlington* I have also intended for this pause to be examined over and over. I think I have led the villagers to reveal themselves in these ways. I hope that I have.

If I am guilty of bearing any messages one of them might be that once people had something to do and now they do not. I think we are all faced with two problems, and they are basic and countervailing: how to live honorably, and what to do to support an honorable life. Seldom do they occupy mutual ground. The assumption that they do is one of the great contemporary delusions.

Rarely now do I honor work. It is a hard pretense that all of it is honorable. I have come instead to honor intensity, and even that sly old dog, *intent* (the road to good intentions is paved with hell).

It is likely the reader will wish to look at *New Burlington* as a history. When I think of history, I think of a lady named Abigail Winas who said, "History is a drunk in the snow with his feet sticking out." I think of *New Burlington* as a book of stories and voices in which the characters ponder some of their time on earth. It could be said, then, that it is no more than a book about *loneliness*.

John Baskin

Wilmington, Ohio
November, 1975

Memory believes before knowing remembers.
Believes longer than recollects,
longer than knowing even wonders.

"God will provide," he said.
"Provide what? Dandelions and ditch weeds?"
"Then He will give us the bowels to digest them."

—William Faulkner,
Light in August

Acknowledgments

To George, Marjorie and Peach Lovett, who gave me a place to stay in New Burlington in that last year of its life; and to the Lane family—particularly Howard and Wanda—who provided me with another after New Burlington came down.

To Moselle Kimbler, now of the Aspen Institute, and William C. Pendleton of the Ford Foundation, who first liked the village material; and the Alicia Patterson Foundation; and, of course, Richard Nolte and Jane Hartwig.

To Harrison Salisbury for first publishing any of the New Burlington material.

To Carrie who loaned money and gave friendship.

To my friend Job Robinson who helped with the old photography, as did Axel Bahnsen.

To Connie who helped with the typing.

To all of these who helped with research of one kind or another: Cleetus Patterson, Bessie Linton, Mr. and Mrs. James Beam, Martha Beam Stanley, Dorothy and Paul Johnson, Marie Blair, Opal Jasper, Esther Mitchner, Ruth Haines, Margaret Haydock, Leona Graham, Mary Ames, Roy Reeves, Mrs. George Fletcher and her daughter, Mrs. H. M. Berley, Marjorie and Myra Haydock and Eleanor Larkin, Mary Snook, Carleton Smith, Elva Matthews, Raymond Braddock, Alice Haines, Betty Magee, the McMillans, Ray Taylor and Donald Ballard, Bill and Geneva Coe, and, of course, the McKays.

And to Wayne and Sue, for always being across the cornfield.

New Burlington

PROLOGUE
The People: A History

When someone said the word *history*, the old ones glowed translucently as if memory had been rekindled to light from within. They picked their way carefully through rooms like dense but uninhabited forests to where a glass-fronted bookcase was filled with Bible concordances, old volumes of sentimental verse, obtuse family genealogies and scrapbooks. And bent to retrieve the massive books called *local histories*. These books were next to the Bible and possibly as often consulted, both regarded as ultimate warehouses where truth lay sacked like grain for the winter. The *actual* truth was that one was essentially mysterious and truthful only if one cared enough to honor ambivalence, the other a blatant lie. "This is how it all was," they said. "This is what you need to know."

If the weight of truth were literal not metaphysical then these histories would be scriptural; the sober books caused shelves to warp and worried the joints of those who moved them into the lap where they pressed against the bones. They were books that told everything, and nothing.

Alpheus Harlan's township history would begin with geology: *New Burlington, Ohio, in the Paleozoic Era was very largely limestone, at the bottom of the sea. Later the ice came, so heavy it depressed the spine of the continent and after the ice, cranberry bogs prepared the ground for the great hardwood forests.* A mad march through time and a suggestion of infinite calendar leaves falling to curl on the floor of epochs. For twenty thousand years New Burlington, Ohio, would be traversed only occasionally: the ancestors of Indians pulled by the tides of moon and seasons. And before that, the patient motion of the shifting earth itself.

New Burlington, circa 1850

Then Anderson the surveyor will press through the overwhelming forest, stand where the land slopes a gentle mile from east and west, where two streams meet like a wishbone, and calculate through the surveyor's level the linear and angular measurements of the New Burlington, Ohio, countryside. This rich crust rising to expectation in the warm chambers of the mind: a judgment.

Anderson will squint at the surveyor's level. Imagine fields and men in the fields working. They will shove back the great trees. Plant grain on its newly domestic floor. And corn will grow in the twenty-thousand-year-old soil of the cranberry bogs. But for a time now Anderson's vision will lie fallow.

In 1798 the Northwest Territory consists of six future states and five thousand white men. Such vastness means a dearth of companionable noise; the ears strain in the vacuum of community. Large concepts offend and must therefore be broken into manageable proportions. A continental land mass under stress, the Northwest Territory divides and in 1803 Ohio becomes officially a state.

In this year the nine planets are aligned, an event which occurs once every 179 years, a sign of cataclysm. Such an event, it is said, may cause sun storms, change wind directions, effect 'the gravity of the earth. As though nature prepared to transfer its own upheavals into a social system: history would assume the politics of gravity and earth fault.

Six Indians squat in the bottomlands of Anderson's Fork roasting corn over a fire. From across the field David Mann watches them. It is his corn growing in the three acres he and his brother have cleared. Not understanding the evolving notions of real estate the Indians afterward become extinct. The Manns, new citizens of this monarchy of forests, prosper. They will be fecund even as the grass and the grain. Seed will be sown everywhere, around tree stumps across bottomland and in the wide furrows of silent uncomplaining wives. The fields will provide: farmers, mortgages, commerce, and widows.

The first men are dissidents and hold curious opinions. They are Revolutionists, mercenaries, Tories, abolitionists. They are moving west where they wish to bury their grievances in the dark and promissory soil. For a time politics is largely forgotten for such a stealthy craft does not thrive in the shade of sycamores which grow uncounted in the Anderson's Fork bottomlands. The men intend to remove the trees but it will take them over a hundred years and the perfection of efficient saws.

As late as 1844 when the tanner James Haydock walks to Dayton to hear Benjamin Harrison address a political rally, he returns home to announce that he was never out of the forest. Grandchildren of the settlers, however, will live to see the fields in every direction, corn being a seasonal forest of more manageable proportions. The land will be laid out like tile, sheets of earth fitted at field-corner, a flat and stormless ocean upon which farmers sail on tides of ear and stalk.

In the midwestern novels of Dreiser and Howe the characters say: "I feel a kind of chicken-raising mind to be dominant here." And: "I don't want to be like the people here for none of them are contented or happy; but I intend to be like the people who I am certain live in other countries." Sherwood Anderson writes that the pioneers, going into unvisited lands, must be very brave or very dull. But these are the reflections of men of great sensibility desiring a life of flavor and fine talk. This, too, perhaps as illusory as the indefinable sweats and humors of farmers pushing themselves across an entire continent to ram against the Pacific and curse its unnavigability by covered wagon.

The relatives write to Alpheus Harlan in New Burlington and tell him to leave. *Get away*, they say. *Go someplace else. Go west. Go anywhere.* But Alpheus, bound to his wife and his history, navigates only the alley between his notary public's office and the cobbler shop where the coal scuttle is. And buries himself in the musty family vaults of genealogy. Dreaming of roads pointed outward from New Burlington like the spokes of a wagon wheel.

Meanwhile the New Burlington, Ohio, countryside fills with people. Some are troubled by nothing more than the state of their mortal stomachs, such as the arriving Yorkshireman: "This be a main queer country for I have asked laboring folks along the road how many meals they eat in a day and they all said three and sometimes four if they wanted them."

Heavy timber crashes in the bottomlands. The straight seams of furrows burst with corn. John Grant builds a grist mill on Caesar's Creek. Above the mill Massie Spray's pear tree brought on horseback from Virginia will soon drop its fruit in three counties. Mr. Reeves puts a crease in his windowsill, marking a course across his bedroom so that he might sleep with his feet in Clinton County, the rest of him in Greene. And Teeny Reeves singing in the rain barrel to make her small voice large. A village grows between the two streams.

A social structure makes the people no less independent. They retain the right to marry their distant cousins, raise corn behind the house, allow hogs to wallow in the main street, and be mildly superstitious. In

1876, wounds of war healed, the village dead tucked with ceremony in the high ground to the east, New Burlington, Ohio, is: one sawmill, two churches, one school, one hotel, three groceries, one wagon shop, two dry goods stores, two doctors, one carpenter, one cobbler, one undertaker, three blacksmiths, and one chicken thief. Population: 275. Real estate: $16,281.

In the spring: gypsies, umbrella mender, lightning rod salesman, stove mender, junk man, rag man, peddler. Willy Hawkins meets the peddler in the covered bridge over Caesar's Creek and with a blacksnake whip makes him dance.

"I could dance better," says the peddler, "if I had my Jew's-harp."

"Then get your Jew's-harp," says Willy.

The peddler reaches into his pack and pulls out a pistol.

"Now, by God," says the peddler, "*you* dance."

And Willy Hawkins dances his club foot clattering against the wooden floor of the bridge a clumsy and furious dance.

In 1910 when Halley's Comet passes overhead Mrs. Murphy runs in the streets to warn her neighbors: the earth is finished. She and Pat pray for hours in the living room. Later Joshua Compton refutes the coming of electricity as an aberrant fever running unchecked in the walls. Mrs. Reeves, on her way into the village to sell eggs, fords Anderson's Fork on a pair of stilts. An old villager who deeds his land to a son perceived later to be ungrateful, retrieves the deed and throws it in the fireplace. Afterward he spits upon the floor. "Proves it's my house," he says.

Growth, too: The village begins its own telephone company, prompted by the news of Lincoln's assassination which does not reach them for 24 hours. Outside the village, the rich fields run on and on. They are seen as perpetual, like old guilt, irreverent thirsts, nameless dreams. The New Burlington girls make fine brides, with all God's earth as a handsome dowry: is not a woman more lovely standing on several hundred acres of her father's topsoil?

Adolphus Foland, poor but hardworking orphan, marries Martha Compton, daughter of well-off Ferris Compton, and says later in the cobbler shop: "There's no excuse for any able-bodied man to remain poor forever."

Neatly against its single street New Burlington, Ohio, is an axis around which the fields revolve. Decade after decade the same families go into the same fields. Although they have entertained fanciful notions, most of the young men do not go away until the first great war. When they return they seem restless and impatient, as though the fields and forest obscure a true vision which lies beyond. *Outside. Where they have been.*

Donald Haines, a young man himself, watches from the hillside above

Caesar's Creek where only two families have farmed since the Revolution: "The boys went away and they drove back to the village in the afternoons and said they would be back to the farm soon but then they were married and they never got back. They would leave out of here in the mornings like a caravan . . ."

In this century the forests seem tiny and managed. When they are seen through the heat of July they are like mirages shimmering behind the precise fields. They appear to be kept, as the village widows keep in windowpots tiny trees which bear scarce and bitter fruit.

Sarah Haydock Shidaker, wedding day, February 25, 1914

Family:
Sarah Haydock Shidaker, 82

Now that she is old, Sarah often finds herself telling the story of Grandmother Morris and the lamp. It is one of her favorite stories and although it happened many years before she was born she tells it as though she had been there, paying careful attention. When she tells it the story becomes like a parable. She has always been afraid of the dark, will always be. When she is past 80 she will place Edwin's hat and coat on the newel post in the front hall before she goes to bed. And sleep soundest after first light.

I think I am afraid of the dark because they told me to expect my mother's death. In 1897 and I was five. My aunts told me. I slept with mamma and edged my hand over to her to see if she was still alive. I could not stand the dark. I wanted to see her. To know she was alive.

Before electricity farmers went around with lanterns. The night shall be filled with music and the cares that infest the day shall fold their tents like Arabs and silently steal away. That is possibly Longfellow but certainly not Sarah Haydock. I am such a coward when it's lamplight time in the valley. I have such a lonely disposition.

When mother was five Grandmother Morris rode sidesaddle to John Grant's store in the village to buy a coal oil lamp. As grandmother prepared to strike the match she asked everyone to stand back. 'I've seen it done,' she said, 'but I don't know about it.' My mother cried. Then the match was scratched and the lamp lit up the darkness and they were all very happy.

I slept with a lantern on the staircase. How I have always feared the

*night. I cannot see out because of the dark and every week the news saying
there's robbery in the park. At night I imagine I may die. I will become an
angel or a fairy. Once a gypsy told my fortune. She took my right hand
and said, 'I see letters an inch high. They spell F-E-A-R.' I have never
disputed that reading.*

*I would dearly love to be superstitious but I don't know how to go about
it. I know you do not dream of losing your teeth nor of silver money and if
you dream of the dead you'll hear from the living. A team will not turn
around at noon. O I suppose they well might but it's an unwilling team. I
love superstition but my momma has no time for it. I put on my left shoe
first every morning however. My brother looks at the sun in the fields and
sneezes. When Aunt Sarah Harlan for whom I was named died an owl
screeched all night in the maple tree. We have never heard it since.*

James

James Haydock, bound boy unimpressed with apprenticeship, runs away.
Walking from New Jersey to Kentucky then up the Bullskin Trace into
New Burlington. Past buffalo wallows at the end of Cornstalk Road. Later
he will become his grandchild Sarah's first conscious memory: he is feeding an ear of corn to a horse. "Critter hungry?" he asks. "Critter hungry?"
What might a critter be? Sarah wonders. She must remember to ask her
mother.

James, who knows all of Tennyson, Whittier and Longfellow, teaches
Sarah about Maude Muller:

> *Maude Muller on a summer's day*
> *raked the meadows sweet with hay.*
> *Beneath her torn hat glowed the wealth*
> *of simple beauty and rustic health . . .*

Sarah, too, will soon know her grandfather's poets. Soon she will hide
Jane Eyre under her mattress.

James is a tanner working for hours in chicken manure and human
urine up to his elbows. On the path to the tannery is a sign inviting
villagers to contribute to the wastes James uses. Even after the tannery is
gone there is a great stain in the earth above Anderson's Fork. It will be
years before anything grows there.

James' first wife is Catherine Howe from Brimstone Hollow. Proud of
their firstborn she rides horseback to show the baby to her parents,

catches pneumonia and dies. The child is Sarah's great-uncle John. Until he is a grown man John does not know that Elizabeth, James' second wife, is not his real mother. Sarah remembers him as an old man with a white beard. She sees him weeping over his real mother who to him will be forever a young girl.

When James is very old he sits on a bench in the village and talks to Joab Stanley. They are both as deaf as tombstones. James watches Joab's face. When Joab stops talking James begins. It does not matter to them that the conversations are disparate.

His health dwindles and his mind begins to drift. Three days before his death James climbs a tree in his nightshirt. A neighbor comes to call.

Do you know me, Poddy?

Yes I know you and I never knew no good of you.

He is 92 years old and his ambition is to live into the twentieth century which he misses by two months.

Thomas

Thomas the tanner's son follows his older brother John to war. By running away in the night, hiding in Jesse Hill's cornfield, and lying about his age. He is fifteen. Miss Anita Weeks, of the neighborhood, says: "The pretty boys have all gone away . . ."

Thomas is sent to Johnson's Island in Lake Erie where he guards an aristocratic Confederate officer from Mississippi who cannot lace his own boots without the assistance of his manservant.

"He had the cream and knew nothing of the milk," says Thomas. On guard duty he almost freezes to death but Caspar Lutz takes off his own overcoat, wraps Thomas in it and covers him with leaves.

No shots are fired on Johnson's Island and in the final winter of the war Thomas is helping unload supplies when he finds a barrel of flour marked *John Grant's Store, New Burlington, Ohio.*

"I am now more homesick than otherwise," he writes home.

When the war ends Thomas returns to become the village cobbler. John, a blacksmith who shod army mules with the Second Ohio Heavy Artillery, is now deaf from the roar of the cannons. His wife writes him notes.

The men afterward remember the war as if it has been an extended leave from their real lives, or a vague and complex game. Pain, as a fixed

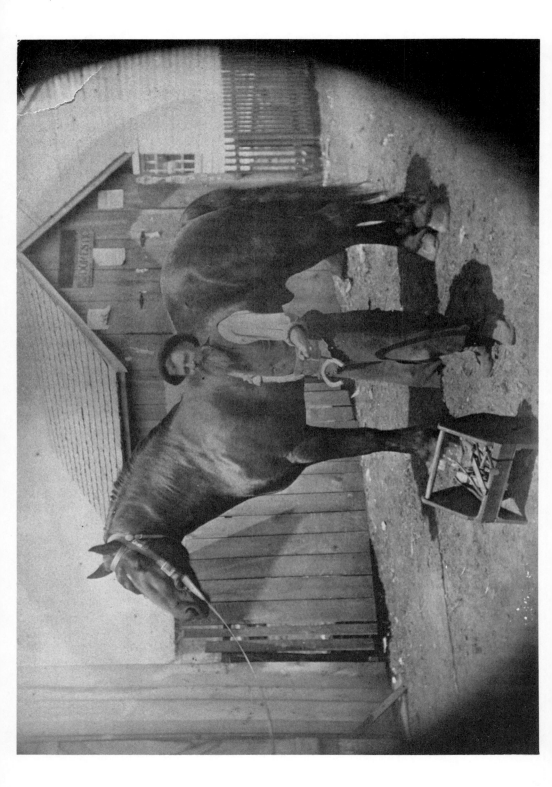

memory, seems to vanish even as the pain of disastrous seasons vanish before the next season when expectations are again high.

Forty years after Appomatox Frank Reeves will come out of Thomas's cobbler shop and run into Sarah on the sidewalk. "Awful goings on, Sarah," Frank will say. "I've fought the Battle of Gettysburg this afternoon and misplaced a regiment . . ."

Poor Frank, thinks Sarah. *He is completely exhausted.*

Thomas's shop is just down the street from his house. Village children like to visit the shop where they sit on his tools. "Over a bit, Freddy," says Thomas. "I need the awl." Thomas has a last for every foot in the village even Emma Mann's clubfoot.

From their kitchen Sarah and her mother can hear Thomas pounding. At night when he closes the shop they hear him coming by the rattle of his keys on a hook. The sounds are permanently inscribed into the background of Sarah's childhood. In a time to come the rattle of keys will startle her, as if her father's presence looms behind the sound.

Village

Sarah walks downtown under the October maples.

Isaiah and Eva Stanley live here. And have a harpsichord no one ever plays. The funeral home is where Black Jane came to pack ice around the corpse. She had magic in her hands they said. Some do. Some it is with mashed potatoes and some it is with art. I am hungry at funerals. When Mae Compton died she wore a beautiful white dress. I was more interested in the dress than the corpse. I was only fourteen. This is the church but I am not a cheerful giver when the plate goes by. I always think of candy. The installation of the Lord's work is not of such interest to me. It is very vague. Who made you? God made you. Who made God? Yes and who did Cain marry when it was just the four of them. Lots of mysteries.

The school is here and Etta Weir will bounce a piece of chalk off your head if you misbehave. Next is Aunt Ruth Morgan's house. Grandmother Farquhar is sitting with her and they are arguing about who is passing by in the street. This is their form of conversation. People say the man who lives there takes morphine. What can it be, morphine? What does it mean? I know some who use Jayne's Expectorant for colds because it is 50 per cent alcohol. Sometimes the cold has nothing to do with it. Uncle John says a blacksmith can't shoe a horse drunk. 'Why Uncle John,' I said, 'you or the horse?' Poppa's mother was very staunch in the WCTU. She prayed with saloonkeepers. Grandpoppa didn't think much of it. 'Where's grandmother?' someone asked. 'O,' he said, 'she's gone to Clarksville to fight liquor.' I had a drink of warm beer on a hot day and decided I didn't need any more of it.

And here I am at Trevor's store. Once Herman Jones said, 'I wouldn't have that Sarah Haydock on a Christmas tree. I'd much rather have Esther Powell.' Right in my bother's store and Herman Jones old enough to know better. Well, we are fearfully and wonderfully made. Men and horses too.

Trevor's father-in-law is Jesse Hawkins the Quaker minister. When he died, Mrs. Hawkins moved from the country into the village and each morning she hangs a towel on the screen door so we can look out and see that she is well. My nieces, Marjorie and Myra and Eleanor, took her into the fields to see a combine. She knew there was such a thing but she had never seen one. She used a cradle to cut the wheat. Marjorie and Myra and Eleanor live above the store and when Uncle Tom's Cabin came they could look from their bedroom window and watch the roustabouts driving tent stakes. At night they looked out and saw Little Eva dying.

Family

The Haydocks come from the farming country of Yorkshire, England. Their name comes from the docks of hay in their fields. They are related to the Howes who fought on both sides of the American Revolution. "Both the English lord and the riverboat captain but not the man who invented the sewing machine," say the Haydocks.

Sarah's great-grandfather, James Howe, fought at the siege of Yorktown for which service his widow received $12 every three months. She called it "the pension and the bounty," regarding it as payment for something unspeakably noble which occurred in the family. "She could neither read nor write," says Sarah, "but she could sew a fine seam."

Sarah herself does not talk of the sanctity of bloodlines. "Poppa's mother's great-uncle," she says, "was hanged in Oklahoma for stealing a horse . . ." But Sarah will always be a Haydock. When she is a young woman traveling by train to Cleveland for a convention of the Order of the Eastern Star she is mistaken for Zasu Pitts. At first she finds such a situation amusing then she does not. She begins to think: *What if I were to insist I were me and no one believed me. Men and women alike are turning to stare at me now.* She goes to the conductor and tells him she is not Zasu Pitts. "I am Sarah Haydock," she says, "my own father's daughter."

Momma is not poppa's first wife. His first wife was Ella Farquhar who went to the pump without an overcoat when it was raining. 'Let God's leather take God's weather,' she said. Then she died of the hasty consumption.

She was reading a novel when my half-brother, Trevor, was born. In the novel she found the name, Trevor. She pronounced it like this: Tree-vor. Everyone called him Toadie, though. It was because he hopped everyplace. One day he disappeared and poppa found him sitting in the garden eating onion tops.

My momma is Susie Morris who began teaching in New Burlington in 1880 where she met my father. At first Trevor refused to go to school. He said the school bell hurt his head. Finally he returned to school. He found it strange to go to school with his mother. She wanted me as a model scholar but I can tell you I loved her more as a mother than as a teacher. When momma was a little girl she went to stay overnight with the minister's daughters. They knelt to pray but she jumped over them into the bed. Upon noticing this the minister said, 'Susie, doesn't thee pray at night?' And she said, 'Only when it thunders.'

Her father was born two years before George Washington died. Once he shot a grizzly bear and sold the hide for $3 to Governor Trimble who was the third governor of Ohio. He shot the bear and wounded him then tracked him through the blood in the snow and found him in his den which was the rib cage of a cow. That was a few days and nights ago.

Poppa wanted a grandson so badly. But my brother Trevor had three girls. The first was Eleanor which poppa made into a 'him.' When I heard I ran down the street saying 'Trevor has a little boy and his name is Elmer!' She always sat at poppa's right. Once she was put in the wrong place and poppa stopped the proceedings. When Trevor's son was born poppa was so anxious.

He was so scared there would be no son to carry on the name. A name that is a good name should be carried through. What else do we know of immortality? A name is all the good things stood for over the years. People wish to leave it untarnished. If you cannot stay then leave your name and in good repair. At a Haydock reunion say 'Thomas' and half the family will stand up.

I was going to be named after momma's grandmother and poppa's

Trevor Haydock, worshipful master, New Burlington Masonic Lodge

mother. I was to have been Millicent Elizabeth Haydock which is some name any way you look at it. Then when Dr. Farquhar delivered me he said to momma, 'Thee has a little dishwasher.' And poppa said to her, 'Her name is Sarah Harlan Haydock.' I am glad because Sarah fits me best. I have always seemed to have been a Sarah.

My momma lived and died and never saw Port William. Poppa died in his easy chair. We never die of sickness, we Haydocks. My grandmother, Elizabeth Haydock, died at Mrs. Weaver's funeral. She and Aunt Margaret were viewing the body when Aunt Margaret felt her lean on her arm. She looked at Elizabeth and saw that death was present. Grandmother Haydock's father died while praying in church. Uncle John died while resting for supper. My poppa died while talking to momma. It was on a Sunday morning. Everyone was coming to dinner. They had taken Saturday night baths—you cannot get nearly as clean on any other night—and momma said, 'Thomas, aren't you going to change your clothes?' And he said, 'Susie Annie H., I'm changing right now.' He took off his shoes, leaned back and closed his eyes. That was all. That's the way we Haydocks die. Not sick half a minute, just close our eyes.

I thought I could never get over it. When we're in deep trouble, the Haydocks do not cry. I can choke nicely with a band around my throat but I've never been any hand to cry. We want to fight it out by ourselves. We have our characteristics. Never try to break the Haydock silence. You may tell me your joys and sorrows but I won't tell you mine. The words are not there. When we're sad we walk the floor and look out the windows.

When Aunt Deidamia was very old she held a petunia in her hand all day, offering it to guests. When she was very small she caught on fire and was burning nicely. Up the path behind the house. Grandmother Haydock grabbed her and stuffed her into the rain barrel. 'Visitations of fire and flood in one afternoon,' Aunt Deidamia says. At dinner she looked across the table at Aunt Margaret and thought she was looking into a mirror. And began fixing her hair.

Sarah and Hattie Mitchener

Edwin

At the school commencement in 1913 Sarah meets Edwin Shidaker. They have known each other forever but this time they regard each other differently. Edwin drives Sarah home in his buggy. She invites him in but he says no. "My horse is rather fractious and I should get him home," he says.

"He thought he'd come back on Wednesday," says Sarah afterward. "I knew, however, that he was down toward New Vienna on Sundays. He said nothing of Sunday. So I said to him, 'This won't do either of us any good.' So he quit New Vienna and took up with me. I often wondered why. I never asked, though. I was afraid I might be told. That was the spring of 1913 and I was never jealous. I didn't have time. I had to water the chickens."

Soon they are married and Sarah moves into the nearby country where Edwin farms on part of the Shidaker land. The land has come down from the Cherokee, Preserved Fish Dakin, a Shidaker forbear who received 2,000 acres for fighting in the Revolutionary War.

The Shidakers are very particular people. Edwin's grandfather allows no white chickens in his yard. He finds white feathers upon the green grass very untidy. Edwin's cousin, Edith Collett, has a club meeting and before it she asks Edwin if he will move the hogs from the field beside the house. And please not haul manure in the field across the road because the wind is from the south. Sarah is surprised. *Who would have thought of such a thing*, she thinks. *We are created free and equal but not just alike.*

The Shidakers are very positive and a little cold. I accept this like I would a sore toe but my Eddie is not like this. He is very handsome and his work is hard and honest. The Shidakers never whip a horse nor kick a dog nor nag their wives. God forgive me! Edwin lived down the road from Aunt Sarah Harlan for whom I was named. Our romance was by horse and buggy. I was never in an automobile with a young chap in my life. An automobile was the works of the devil. It was something new and frightened the horses. Walter Lackey had one with a rumble seat. Tain't no treat in a rumble seat all by yourself in the moonlight. The boys courted in buggies and if the horse was well behaved they could wrap the lines around the whip socket. The young men of my day didn't have Fords to get about in so they married who was handy.

After we were married my first biscuits did not turn out so well. So I took the dough and dumped it in the chicken yard. When Eddie came in from the fields at noon he found all the chickens with their feet stuck.

My but I loved the farm. I say there are just three things in life: animal, vegetable and mineral. They are all found in the country. Few of them grow under a city's concrete. They say a tree grows in Brooklyn. 'A' means one. One tree.

We planted corn after the grubworms hatched out and flew away. Then we knew it was warm enough. We planted clover seed under the dark of the moon in March when the ground was honeycombed with ice. Sow oats in the mud they say and wheat in the dust and plant beans when the moon is such-and-so or they'll be all vine and no beans.

The hired man was John Bell who was Negro. When my son Warren was a little rowdy John Bell could handle him. 'Come along, Warren,' he would say, taking Warren by the hand. 'Let's go to Africa, you and me, and leave the rest of them here.' Only John Bell could comb Warren's curly hair without making him cry. 'Be careful when you comb in the kitchen, John Bell,' Warren would say. He called the back of his head 'in the kitchen.' John Bell always said, 'Yes m'am sir.' He said that took in the universe.

Edwin was a born farmer. He would rather plow a furrow than anything. He was a prince in looks and action. We were 49 years and two months together. But right back here I had a little fear of Eddie. He was German, I think that was it. When he lost his temper it was gone. He was afraid of nothing but wind and lightning. He took no chances with hot horses pulling steel implements in the fields. His mother, Elizabeth, took the children and hid in the box stairs when it stormed.

O a lazy person should watch and not participate! There were no waterworks in those days and in the cold of winter perhaps we had a soapstone in the bed. We did not travel about because cows and hogs can tell time. At feeding time a hog is at the gate and so is the cow, standing by the hog. That was the way we lived. When the blueprint is before you, you yield. It was our way of life. I had my men and the loveliest things to cook with. There was Edwin and my three sons and John Bell, hog lard and cow butter. My kitchen was eighteen by twenty-one because I like space. I can do no big financial work but I can cook. I had one father, three brothers, one husband, three sons and three grandsons. I knew nothing of girls. When I was a girl I thought more of the mirror than anything else. I had no mother-in-law, no sister, no daughters. Only men and dogs. And I won only two things in my life: my husband and a chicken feeder.

I was satisfied. In spite of hog cholera, hail on the young corn and drought. Nice sun, adequate rain, boys in line, livestock well. This is all I asked for. This is true. But there were desperate heartaches too with the hail riddling the crops and the wind and the corn suffering for rain. How we prayed for rain only to turn around and pray for it to stop when we were in the mud. In December of 1934, 120 fat hogs died of cholera. The fertilizer truck came each day. They were piled at the front gate. Bertha Bailey stood in the yard and cried. We almost did not get over it.

During the depression men hung themselves in their barns. Lou Wolfe the gasoline man came just after we had butchered a beef and it was the fall of the year and temperatures dropping. Eddie was fearful the beef hanging in the barn might freeze. So he put an overcoat around it and buttoned it up. Lou passed up the barn the next morning, the door open just a bit, and he thought Eddie had hung himself. He came to the house and said, 'Sarah, where's Eddie?' I said, 'O he's here but I don't know where just at the moment.' He looked so queer. I thought: is it my fatal beauty? Then Eddie came around the corner of the barn from feeding the cattle. I thought Lou would pass out in the yard although I knew he didn't drink. He thought Eddie was out hanging in the barn with his overcoat on.

Well, times were hard and worry upon worry. We lived, however. Man proposes, God disposes. And the days followed the nights as they always have.

Light

In the Late Twenties electricity comes to New Burlington. A traveling man comes to do the wiring and boards on a nearby farm where he milks a cow to pay his keep. His work goes slowly because the cow kicks him and breaks his leg. Finally curious neighbors gather outside a lower New Burlington home and watch a porch light switched on. The bare bulb hangs from the porch ceiling on a long cord. When the light goes on the people think they see the darkness shaken as if it were dust settling.

Lights in the village make Sarah happy. Light dispels mystery and she too would have it. An old villager explains to her how it works: "You pull a cord," he says. "On and off, you see." For the Christmas of 1939 electricity lights the Shidaker Yule tree. Sarah buys lights for the tree, the table, the ceiling, a floor lamp, and a radio. When Edwin turns on the radio a voice is singing:

There's nothing left for me
of days that used to be . . .

Edwin and the boys laugh but Sarah is sad. "Well," she says, "it *is*
now a wonderful time to live. Who would go back to a coal oil lamp?
Circumstances alter cases. No farmer wants to turn his furrows with a
team and a housewife would rather have a Mixmaster than a crock and
spoon. We are living on the earth but in a different way and now everything is taken care of but death. We know how to avoid birth but we still
die. All things end, somehow or another."

Soon Edwin buys Sarah a freezer. When Frank Matson comes to
deliver it she looks inside and says, "Why, If I should die my Eddie could
lay me out in here and keep me forever . . ."

October

The fall of the year is my favorite time by far. O yes. Then it is time to
gather the crops of the field. It is the payment, you see. My favorite month
is October because I was born in October and my mother before me. She
and poppa were married in October and she died then too and when I lost
her I lost my best friend, there's no argument about that. If the Lord wills
I'd like to say goodby in October too.

Sometimes I sit and think when I am through thinking other things:
what would I be doing if I were now 16? I consider it a legitimate ques-
tion. I'd like to be young again just to see what I would do. I wish I had
gone to Vassar and majored in history. I remember dates because after all
they never change. Higher math? I couldn't be bothered. I read Shake-
speare and thought of myself as Portia. I did like astronomy. I have always
liked the stars. I was born under Libra. Justice, you know, is blind. And
erasers are on lead pencils to take care of the wrong we do. The signs have
an effect upon our dispositions. If the moon can change tides why not
dispositions?

My but I am old. This was once a dimple. Now it's a crack. I have
trouble with my feet and my conscience. First one pains me then the other.
My feet are barometers. They tell me when it will storm. I knew a lady
who lived to be 103. I find that mysterious. We are not supposed to live
that long. Threescore and ten and perhaps by reason of strength another
decade. Why that's it.

Isaiah Morris's widow celebrated perfect sight and hearing on her 87th *birthday. 'Isn't it wonderful,' she said to her guests, 'that a harp of a thousand strings should stay in tune so long?' But sometimes there is such a thing as living too long. I do not smoke, drink, or drive an automobile. There's nothing left for me to do but play the piano. Lay not up your treasures on earth where moth and rust corrupt. But if I married an old man I would want him to have $90,000 and a very bad cough.*

Turn backward O time in your flight and I'd live you differently! There are some things I'd omit and others I'd have just a little more of but I have no regrets of how I treated my momma and poppa. Now I am old and on stairsteps I show all the years of my life. Sometimes I don't wave at my nearest and dearest for watching my step which shows me the poverty of my feet.

I am the last leaf on the tree and I believe I am outliving everyone else. My love for my people has been very strong. I am root and branch New Burlington. Once I said, 'I wish my heart were as cold as cistern stone.' Jessie McGee was so surprised. On Sunday she visited the churchyard graves and afterward came to me and said, 'Yes, like stone.' Well, if wishes were horses beggars could ride.

I am alone in a strange world now. So many people work strange ways and there are no more Sundays and no more nights and I wonder: where will my grandchildren have their potato patches . . . ?

The old villagers are mostly gone now and Sarah's grandchildren study science in distant universities. A young man lives in the upstairs which she rents out. He is training to be a psychologist. Sarah listens carefully to his definitions. An interstate highway slices in front of the old Shidaker homeplace and she is the last of the family to own any of Preserved Fish's land. New Burlington itself is mostly gone. The rest waits for the waters of the new reservoir. Sometimes on Sundays friends drive Sarah to the village where she looks for familiar landmarks trying to recreate New Burlington on its vine-covered foundations.

I see the houses and I put my dear ones in the houses with their intimate stories and private thoughts. In my night dreams I go up and down the street and in the homes of my loved ones. O memories that bless and burn! Sometimes in my dreams I am no longer a woman of past 80. I am a young girl . . .

Perspective: John Pickin, 58

John Harlan Pickin's grandfather, Alpheus Harlan, studied tombstones in Pennsylvania for traces of his English ancestry. Obsessed, he worked for years on a genealogy; names and dates became a private geometry determining the shape of his universe. He had a stroke before he was finished. His son dropped out of college to help him. He lost his sight. He was partially paralyzed. Finally he died, in the middle of laughter from an intimate moment shared with his wife.

He stuck himself in that hole of a town, the family said. *His wife was a Haydock,* they said. *She wanted to stay. Not Alpheus. He was bright. He could have been somebody . . .*

John Pickin grows older in New Jersey now and the distance is ever more awesome. After his great-grandfather James Haydock walked from New Jersey to Ohio he worked in the tannery which left a great stain in the earth. In his own century, John looked upon the stain and imagined himself a pioneer. He grew older. His ancestors became vivid to him. He began to understand their lives and therefore his own. He, too, pondered his own history. Years later, miles away, he found himself unmistakably bound to a dying place to which he will never return.

New Burlington was like a medieval society. You were so close. Thrust together. Everybody watched everybody else. How could you possibly get out of line? One of the villagers saw a couple of little girls wading in Anderson's Fork. Two inches of water. 'I saw their ankles,' they said. 'Indecent!' But that life causes certain tolerances too. If you know all you

44

forgive all. You met these people every day, face to face. I suppose there was a great deal of hypocrisy. It did not occur to me. The people helped each other. When a neighbor died his survivors were deluged with cakes. Cakes fairly descended upon them.

I identify with that dirty hole in the ground. I belong there. From the age of two on I heard nothing but: *this is where we came to, came from. We know every inch of this place. We are of this place.* My aunt could name everyone within twenty miles. I have felt this in England where my father was from. I was there during World War II when soldiers were not well regarded. I asked for a place to sleep in a little village called St. Neots, 17 miles from Cambridge. It was the place of my father's ancestry. There had been a John Pickin in every generation for six generations. The innkeeper had no room. 'Anybody know John Pickin?' I asked in the bar. An old man of 80 said, 'I once knew a John Pickin . . .' Then I was placed into their middle. My people were Harlans and Haydocks so I was part of the community. It is all beyond rationalization.

My mother said that the first she remembered of the outside world was the Spanish-American War. There were new words like *Manila, Santiago,* the *Philippines.* Her boyfriend sent her back a piece of hardtack. My mother was a grown woman before she met a Catholic. She knew one Jew. He was a pack peddler who gave cheap cut glass for rags. His house frills were a feature of the village.

The woods crushed in on all sides of New Burlington. How dreary life must have been. There were no lights. No radio. A kerosene lamp flickers. It is cut off. There is darkness everywhere. You walk, or ride a horse. News? There is a telegraph three miles away at Roxanna. Mother remembers her aunt wringing her hands in the streets saying, 'Cleveland won the election! The country is finished!' Cleveland was the first Democrat in 25 years. He was considered wicked.

Everyone in the village had a descriptive name. There was 'No' Evans, who never agreed to anything. Pig-eye Blair. Guinea Noggle. It showed their Anglo-Saxon origins. The Anglo-Saxons took a person's worst feature and that became his name. The New Burlington settlers came and built houses flush upon the streets. Why, when they had the whole of Ohio, build a house right on the road? They had it this way back in New Jersey where they came from. What you have in the time of your youth you duplicate later. The county authorities once objected to the cup chained to the town pump. Unsanitary, they said. So the villagers took it off and hung it on the wall of the tavern nearby.

So how does a town succeed? New Burlington was Quaker, restrained and conservative. Perhaps that inhibited growth. In Dayton the college and the sciences were associated with the Germanic part of the community. The Anglo-Saxons were anti-intellectual. They stayed out and farmed.

The village people brought things up in conversation as if they were momentary. But they occurred *one hundred years* ago. All history was collapsed in upon itself. Into this tiny space were all events. Outside events were of . . . no interest at all. The world went by. The Civil War was the prime topic of conversation. It was refought frequently in Thomas Haydock's cobbler shop. Until well past 1900 they never talked of anything else. For over 40 years.

If they had had no Civil War they would have died of boredom. The Harlans became privates in the war to get away from the village. They heard about life somewhere else. *They would have it.* My grandfather Alpheus wanted to go but he was 13. So they kicked him off the train. You could talk out the news of the village in a very short time. It was old stuff quickly. But during the war they got around. They saw things. Life was dangerous but not dull. Those who didn't get their heads shot off enjoyed it, I think.

In the old house in New Burlington was an attic room. It was dark, filled with things. There was a sword in a scabbard hanging on the wall that belonged to one who never came back. There was a string of tent pegs from some encampment. On the wall were prints of battles and bits of uniforms and a sword cane that one of them had carried when he was down south after the war, during the occupation when folks still were not very friendly, especially after dark. A beaver hat. A uniform of a type we couldn't identify. And books, books of it all. The Civil War had been won by the Ohio Volunteer Infantry and the Army of the West. No one had ever heard of the Army of the Potomac. So I always felt close to that war, having sat in a room full of it while of impressionable years.

The Harlans had land but none of them wanted to farm. Anything to be in town. No matter how small. For a hundred years there had been a revulsion against farm life. It was too hard. They were leaving in 1800. They were still leaving in 1900. Grandfather Alpheus wouldn't plant a garden, wouldn't touch the soil. He didn't even like to go into the backyard. He refused to work with his hands. The people of the village were largely involved in getting their hands into the soil. Perhaps they disliked him for this.

Farm life was hard on everyone. There were horrible stories of people going through manure spreaders, of tractors rearing up and crushing the driver, ragged cuts that led to lockjaw. My aunt felt sorry for the women because they had no one to talk to. They spent their lives looking at the backside of a cow. She, of course, had the advantages of the village.

Farming was very rough. I saw their work. It was an endless labor. 'Well,' one said, 'I canned eight hundred quarts this year but it didn't match last year.' I remember the women as bigger. Bulkier. Svelte figures were not desired. There were no sex objects of course. Sex did not exist. The women made cakes in milk pans. Their recipes began: *take thirty eggs* . . .

Always you heard these things: *He went to Iowa. He went to California.* They told each other these things. *Get away. Go someplace else. Anyplace else.* In the last half of the century the intellectual character of the villages changed. At one time people were well-read. They congregated and held a reasonably high level of conversation. Politics. Philosophy. Religion. I saw their books. In lieu of notary fees sometimes grandfather Alpheus took books. The change was that people of ability moved on.

First there were only the villages. Then towns grew. There was a railroad. When places grew, people of ability went there. Those who stayed had lesser ambition. Lincoln grew up near Gentryville, Indiana, didn't he? But soon he left. Part of the Harlans did go west. They got through the pass just before the Donner party made it famous. If some of the Harlans had been there they would have been famous. They would have also been dead. There was a great urge to rove. *Someone got through the pass.* The word filtered back. They wrote to each other. Boxes of letters. Trying to get the ones at home to move. Make them dissatisfied. *Go west,* they said. *Go anywhere.*

What happened to those who left? Some of them married women who smoked.

Dickens came through here about the time great-grandfather Haydock was walking in. He did not think much of James Haydock. He found the country cut off, by no means neat. There were no hedgerows. The fields were not laid out well. Dickens' biggest complaint was that they made him drink ice water. They gave him nothing civilized to drink. They were boorish. They spit. They were rough, he said, and I expect that was so.

There were the Quakers midtown and the Methodists uptown. The difference was trifling, of course. My mother was the first to play a musical instrument in the Quaker church. It was a pump organ. Before that it had been considered wicked to have any instrument. My aunt went to church and came back saying, 'Why does the Lord always move *her?* Why is *she* always moved?' She wasn't moved too often in church herself. She *was* moved to tell people what was wrong with them. For their own good. This made her very popular. She said, 'Never forget the golden thread that ties everything together.' She was very independent. 'Consult the inner light,' she said. To hell with the president, anybody. 'Consult the inner light.'

Aunt Maude, grandfather Alpheus' daughter, was quite content with New Burlington. She wanted to be at home. Everything held her to that assumption. She would die in the village. She loved the creeks and the fields and read *David Copperfield* every year. She made salt-rising bread without yeast or baking powder and mailed it to me in New Jersey. She knew the creeks and the runs, little churches and abandoned schoolhouses and forgotten burial grounds. She knew who lived where and who had lived where back and back. She was afraid of only two things: fire and flood. In 1959 the water went to the upper end of the village. It was the worst flood they ever had. Aunt Maude was seriously sick by this time but she would neither go to a doctor nor have one in. When the water came she refused to leave her house. She was finally carried out under protest.

Two days after the flood crested I flew out and by then the water had subsided and a hard frost had crusted the coal pile. Aunt Maude had gotten back in the house, had a fire going, and could not be moved. In March, two months later, she took a turn for the worse. She was near death and an ambulance was called to take her to a hospital. She was placed on a stretcher and halfway through the door she held her arms out straight and they couldn't get her out. They brought her back in and laid her on the couch and she was content. And she died, but in her own home and on her own terms.

The Builders

It is late in the nineteenth century. Buildings rise from the landscape like gigantic blooms of wood and stone. Their weight and symmetry are pleasing to the eye. Such building, for a time, may be seen as piety. Only the devout still adhere to the intractable disciplines of mortise and tenon, eight-by-eight sills, slate and brick. In such architecture is possibly enough weight to anchor a family's moody generations in one place for yet a few more years.

If the old Quaker builders considered religion to be the ecumenical name for all discipline then such a thing not only renounced darkness it also held up stone walls and slate roofs. Even the barns of New Burlington, like the architecture of ancient churches, had buttresses, arches, naves, and aisles.

In the eastern edge of New Burlington is a huge round barn. The Quakers said it was built round "because there was no corner for the devil to hide in." The Methodists, more earthy, told neighborhood newcomers that a man once died in the round barn. When pressed for details the newcomer is told: "Fellow ran himself to death trying to find a corner to piss in."

Methodists, sighed the Quakers. Methodists had organ music and liked loud sermons.

But if some asserted religion was the underpinning of such a barn then others said simply that a round barn used less timber and gave more space. The owner, who may have considered all these things, built it, finally, to impress a lady. The lady was impressed and they were married.

Logging in New Burlington

No one knew the religion of William Wood yet no one doubted his devoutness. There were those who thought religion was *practice* and William Wood the most saintly of all. He came each spring, walking from Virginia. In the hot New Burlington summers of the nineteenth century he built barns of all sizes, the least of them elegant. They were cut from nearby hardwood to rise one bent at a time and mark the landscape with character.

William Wood was a surgeon with broadax and adze, attending the joints of mortise and tenon, accuracy his anodyne for the pain of sloth. The barn carpenter lived in a room—he called it his martin's box—above the kitchen of the maiden McKay sisters, Abigail and Sarah. Cutting sill and plate twelve-by-twelve from oak under a fierce sun, he wiped his face with a clean pair of drawers he kept in one pocket. He cut his tenons an eighth of an inch shy and drove an oak pin through the mortise to pull a two-foot thick walnut swing beam into place forever. No one had a clearer eye for chamfered scarf joints, king posts or purlins.

When the barn carpenter got older he no longer followed the starlings back to Virginia in the autumn. He stayed on in New Burlington surrounded by the fields held in place by the weight of his barns. He stayed in his room in the winter, keeping the maiden ladies company. As the Ohio winter closed bitterly in at the end of the year he sometimes stopped his neighbor, Johnny McGee, and said, "Mr. McGee, the cold is closing in and would you get me a bottle of whiskey when you're next in town?"

Johnny McGee did not like whiskey but he did like William Wood. When he passed by again before noon the old barn carpenter stopped him. "It's awful cold and the wind is up, Mr. McGee," he said. "Better double that order."

When William died Peter Harrison made a coffin of poplar barn siding and put the old builder in it. The McKay sisters, although fond of him, did not want him buried on their ground because no one but McKays were there. So William was taken to the village cemetery on the hill. After the maiden ladies died the land was sold and their stones moved down to the village cemetery and they are all together again. Their coffins, however, remain in the ground and corn is planted over them.

The very oldest villagers remember talk of William Wood and some point to barns they think he might have built.

In the next generation Frank Stanley, too, built barns and crawling down from finishing a roof, spit in the eye of an approaching storm. "When I build," he said, "let the windstorms come. No winds will twist my barns and I build them for a hundred years that I know of." Frank had no use for manufactured nails; he built only with oak pins his sons whittled with a draw knife. Wind twisted nails he said and he had no use for a weakness that could be avoided.

Frank was six feet four and a half inches in his socks and weighed 240 pounds. He lifted his end of a ten-inch square maple beam forty feet long—there were two men on the other end—and went to the woods with an ax and a foot adze where in two and a half hours he cut out a hickory sill 24 feet long, eight inches square. Going home in the twilight Dena Blair the grocer's daughter ran to meet him. He sat her in one hand and lifted her above his head where her laughter sounded as though it were coming from the trees or the upstairs of houses.

Frank framed Ernest Beam's barn in a six-acre field and thirty men came with teams to raise the bents. He stood on the ground, cut the gable ends and said, "Nail them away, boys." Everything fit: gable end, tenon, tie beam to corner post. For a time the countryside had: symmetry.

It is now late in the twentieth century. Many of the heavy-timbered old barns are gone, victims to: eminent domain, fire, misuse. In between the two-story white brick homes the Quaker farmers built early in the last century are modern brick ranch houses. They are everywhere, in undeniable numbers.

The older people, many of whom also live in new ranch houses, take long drives through the New Burlington countryside and look at the older buildings. Sometimes they tell each other eccentric stories about the people who once lived there. Most of these people at one time or another drive down Center Road where Elmer Lemar sits on a three-legged milk stool on the very green lawn in front of his father's house. Three large white dogs lie around him. The people blow their horns and wave but they seldom stop. Elmer Lemar is 90, the last of the old builders. He is known as both tough-minded and tight-fisted. "Elmer Lemar," says one of his friends affectionately, "is so tight he wouldn't pay five cents to see Jesus Christ ride a bicycle."

When Elmer farmed with his father, Black John, he told the old man that rain upon fresh-cut sheaves was an automatic tithe to the Lord. Black John's wife called her men from the fields by blowing through a large conch shell. Sometimes Elmer disputed the premises of the entire known world. The blueprint, he argued, was his mind's eye.

When he built the General Denver Hotel in Wilmington he said, "Pete Eveland had the contract but I built it to please myself. We were pouring concrete for the foundation and the architect said mix it one-to-three. I said, 'Pete, it won't do. If it's thicker than one-to-five, it'll crumble.' He said, 'Mix it one-to-three.' The fellow on the mixer said, 'What'll we do?' I said, 'One-to-five when he's out of sight and one-to-three when he's not.'

He came by one day with a new $7 hat on, stuck his head in the mixer to check on us and his hat fell off in there. He took it out and threw it in the gutter. I laughed and laughed. Who wanted to build a hotel that would fall down in three years? 'Boys,' I said, 'Lemar is pouring this and it's one-to-five!' Pour it his way and in three years he'd have been jacking up the floor to pour a new one. I thought to myself, 'Like hell.' I *would* have mixed it one-to-six but I thought I'd compromise a little with him . . ."

Elmer built a barn when he was 16. He built a house for a lady who put her furniture on the foundation and had him build her house around the furniture. When he was 70 he put a new roof on a chicken house. Even he cannot remember all the building that came between.

Elmer Lemar, 90

It's funny and it isn't. How I did it I don't know. I lived here with my pap and we farmed 50 acres, which was not enough for two. A man came by one day and said, 'Can I get you to help out with hauling some logs?' It wasn't harvest time so I said, 'Yes.' When we finished I said, 'That all?' He said, 'Nope. I'm gonna build a barn.' I said, 'Who's to build it, Mr. Bell?' His name was J. F. G. Bell. He said, 'We're gonna build it.' I laughed. I didn't even own a hammer. I think that to build a barn you'd need maybe a hammer. Even a saw and perhaps a square. He just hitched up a sorrel to his phaeton and soon he was back with the most complete set of carpenter tools I had ever seen. Of course, it didn't have to be but so complete to be more complete than I had ever seen. I was only 16. You hadn't seen much at 16 in those days. Well, we started in then we finished and it never fell down. I was grown then. I thought I was a man.

Next we built this house, my pap and I. It was 1901. Mom wanted a house like Dr. Murrell had. So that's what we built. After you're married your wife has a good bit to say about what's going on. The joist and studding is sugar tree with yellow pine varnished for the finish work. We built this one, then I built one in New Burlington. They thought I was too damn young to be building houses. That's the straight of it. I finished in New Burlington and someone said, 'What next?' I said, 'I can always go home and stick my feet under pap's table.'

But you couldn't step around with the girls without a little money. I worked by the month for awhile. I went to a fellow's house and he paid $17 and board. So I bought the first rubber-tired buggy in Chester Township. It cost $115. First thing everyone said was, 'He'll never amount to a thing. He's spending it faster than he's making it.' I paid $10 a month on it. That left me seven dollars. But there was only four Sundays in a month. I could take a girl out to dinner each Sunday on seven dollars. Fifty cents a meal. How's that? If I'd had seven buggies I could have had a girl in each. The rest of the time I worked until dark. This fellow said I was the best corn plower he ever saw. He said he saw me going up that bottom as straight as you please and sound asleep.

I didn't like the farm although my grandfather was a farmer. Charles Lemar. Just like my pap. Five sons, one daughter. She always looked kind of lonesome to me, playing with those five boys. Grandfather was a real farmer. He had to have something for those five boys to do. Six of

Elmer Lemar (PHOTOGRAPH BY KEN STEINHOFF)

them plowing covered a lot of earth. House on the hill. Land on the creek. Took four horses to pull a wagon of shucked corn up the hill. He really grew corn, even if he did have to hitch four horses to his wagon.

Then I went to Illinois on a bicycle. I decided to go so I got on a bike and away I went. I didn't even know anybody in Illinois. On the way I stopped at a restaurant. Someone said, 'Who the hell are you?' I turned around. It was a damned parrot. I said, 'Just to give you a short answer, birdie—it's none of your business.' He had no business talking to me that way in a restaurant.

I got five cents an hour shucking corn in Illinois. I said, by God, I'll make me some money. Good crops, but I didn't like Illinois. When it rains in the fall you need hip boots. Then Chicago had a cyclone. I went up there. They advertised for work and I wanted it. All the electric lines were down and the current was still on. It had me scared. I worked two weeks. I wanted to get back to Ohio someday, not be buried in Chicago. I had got all the bike riding I had wanted going out so I took the train back. It was during the rainy season. I brought the bicycle back and traded it for a shotgun. I came back right down the Big Four Railroad.

> *St. Joe for beauty*
> *Ossian for pride*
> *Richmond for skin*
> *and Muncie for hide*

I made that up, coming back on the train.

I didn't want to hoe corn anymore so I helped build the telephone exchange. I learned how in Chicago. I was a telephone lineman. I'll tell you how it was: it was wet that year and I had nothing to do. Farmers like to have never got their corn planted and couldn't get it plowed after they did get it planted. They had a corn crop and a weed crop and they didn't like either. So farmers had nothing to do that spring. About 10 fellows got together and decided to build a telephone exchange. The deal was, you set up 10 poles and give them $10 and they'd put the box in. I put up the wire and the boxes. Within five years there were about 300 phones in. I worked by the season. When it got dry people wanted a new roof instead of a telephone. I was a telephone man when it was wet. A carpenter when it was dry. That was quite a while ago. Maybe 1916.

I was 20 when I got married. Maybe she put one over on me. She was two years older so she had more experience in talking to the boys. I figured I should get her before someone else did. I bought her a home in lower Burlington for $350 and made our kitchen table because I had no money to buy one. Before I was married I had a new girl every time I could get one. We had dances every week. Once at a dance it was hot weather and this little short fellow was dancing with Maude Miars who was extra tall. He wiped the sweat off and looked up at her and said, 'How's the atmosphere up there where you are?' He got off a good one. We were so dumb in those days we didn't do that often.

Elmer Borton down the road said once, 'Say, what do you think of bringing some girls that's never been?' I said, 'Fine, but I don't know any.' He said, 'I do.' We went to Zora and came back with two sisters. The neighborhood girls weren't at all satisfied with these strangers. I did the calling for the dance:

> Honor your partners
> ladies bow and gentlemen pow-wow
> first lady right, second pass

All that stuff. I stood in the door and called. One of the sisters said, 'Who is that doing the calling?' Borton said, 'You ought to know, you came with him.' She wouldn't have known how to get home if she'd had to look me up. Two years later we were married. I carpentered for her. This was just an old farmhouse. I built these windows, a bath, cabinets. Whatever she wanted, she got. She appreciated it, too. God, yes. But I could never keep her in town.

I'll tell you a good one. It was Halloween. Of course, we wanted to be as mean as we could. We went behind the church where the big double outhouse was, carried it to the cross streets and set it up. Then we got Dr. Jones' sign—Dr. E. Townsend Jones, office hours 9–11 and 2–4—and nailed it up on the shithouse. Was he mad! Dr. E. Townsend Jones. That was before I was married and a long time ago.

I never cared for a man without a sense of humor. He has to smile once in awhile. Or else his own face begins to weigh him down. I went to Cincinnati once to hear an opera singer. She gave a rousing performance. There was people from all around, from Cincinnati and Dayton, and Middletown, which was in between. The people kept applauding her and she came out and said, 'I love this part of Ohio. I'd just like to stand with one foot in Dayton and one foot in Cincinnati.' And some old fellow in the back jumped up and yelled, 'O you Middletown!' How's that?

Joel Compton and my pap bought and sold hay. Pap brought it in by the ton and Compton stored it in his barn. Once pap had five cents to make change and nobody had any pennies. Three cents belonged to Compton and two to pap. 'Take it all,' said pap. Compton wouldn't. So he got in the buggy with us and rode a half mile into town to the grocery where he got the nickel changed. Then he walked back home. 'He lost out,' I said to pap. Pap said, 'Why?' I said, 'He walked home and wore three cents off his boot leather . . .'

Frank Conklin once lived at the Poague place and he raised a lot of hogs. His boy, Paul, was out in the yard one day playing with a little bit of a wagon and someone stopped and asked where Frank was. Little Paul said, 'He's out back feeding the hogs. You can tell him, he's the one with the hat on.' We'd go by and say, 'That's Frank. He's the one with the hat on.' Boy, did he get mad!

I've always been that way. I've an ear for fancy although I went through only eight grades. That's all Buck Run Schoolhouse had. I was out at 14. I went to school to play not to learn. There was a seat here, seat there, aisle in between. Next to me was a fellow name of Scroggy. He had shingles, a ring around his stomach. 'If they don't meet, I'll live,' he said. 'They're almost around me . . .'

I leaned over and said, 'Where'd you get 'em, Charlie? Off the coal house?' Well, if they're wood, they'd have to be off the coal house. The school is slate. Doesn't that sound reasonable? He hit me in the head with a spelling book. The teacher made us stand up for 30 minutes. Buck Run. It was quite a place.

> With a pocketful of rocks
> and a head full of knowledge
> I'd rather go to Buck Run
> than any other college.

I made that up myself. Nothing here anymore but me, three dogs and a cat. I have to do something.

These dogs were put out in the field. They dug ground mice to eat. Then one day they turned up on the front porch. We all became friends. Later, I heard my dogs and they sounded 'tree.' So I went out and there was a cat. I said, 'By God, come down and eat if you're going to live here.' And she did just that. I looked her over and she was poor. I said, 'You have to have a name and since you don't look like you'll ever amount to a tinker's dam I'll just call you Tink.'

Well, everything changed and I don't fit so well because I don't change so well. Although perhaps more than I thought. When I was a young man a fellow asked me if I wanted to go to Centerville. They needed four carpenters. We built seven two-story houses, pantries, cupboards, big and wide. I rode the traction car to a half mile of there then rode in with the mailman. Soon the foreman had fell out and quit. The builder came to me and said, 'Can you handle men?' I said, 'I think so. I don't know what you think.' I just had guts. It was the way I grew up. There was 16, 17 men, and we kept on building.

There were no autos then so I rode a horse to near Wilmington to build Eli Haines's house. I found me a boarding house in the edge of town. I was there six nights. The last night I found a ladies' cloth in the closet and, by God, I found there was a lady at the telephone exchange who had been using my room by day and I at night. If I had known I would have stayed later or come in earlier. I said: the lady who ran that boarding house was in business for herself. But I didn't get mad. Yoho!

I worked a gang of carpenters for 62 years. Sometimes there was as many as 36 at one time, building five houses and two grain elevators. I never jumped on a fellow and ate him up. Cuss a man and he gets as contrary as you are. When it was hot, I said, 'Boys, it's hot as hell. Take 15 minutes.' I made money out of it.

I built a house with an 8 × 8 in the corners and a 3 × 4 brace like a barn. Try that today and you'd get shot. I built a boy scout camp, a college dorm, a school, a bank, a firehouse. I built all over. Once I built 20 houses in one year. Some had only a kitchen sink. A hand pump. No plumbing. A fellow who had a bathroom and a furnace was a millionaire. We put in heavy timbers. Timber wasn't worth anything anyway, just trees hauled in. Sills were eight inches square. Today they'd be a 2 × 8 set up edgeways. Build one of today's houses back then, no one would have moved in. They'd have been afraid they'd blown down.

Hardest thing I ever built was a band shell at the Soldiers' Home in Xenia. The top was half round, open in front. How to put rafters on that? Well, I got it done. I just had to keep on figuring. The architect came down from Columbus. I said, 'What in the hell were you doing here, drawing something like this?' He said, 'Well, the ladies auxiliary wanted one so I designed them a doozy. I never thought they'd raise the money to get it built . . .'

You have to be smart in this world or you don't get there. I knew all the tricks. I was a young man. I could sleep anywhere. I'd jump in bed and be asleep before I quit bouncing. I worked hard. In the rain, in the snow. I swept snow off a house at six above zero and put a new roof on it. I could do anything.

At one time I thought no one could build a house in Peterson Place in Wilmington but me. I built the first nine houses. Good houses. They cost $15–18,000 then. Solid, wide beams. Good pine. Good stone. But the more war, the more cost. We used wood lasts but then we stopped because the government was taking it so fast. Carpenters went to sheetrock. No more wood lasts with plaster on top. Sheetrock was faster and cheaper. It was also weaker. Cut costs, cut the lifetime of a building. I ran into that in my last years. I thought: it could blow down.

If I was building for myself I'd choose the old way. The times are gone that I know about. I built a long time ago. I don't know the shortcuts. It's pick them out of a book today. Houses are thrown together. Once people had a mind about what they wanted. But things change. That's all I know. I don't belong in this generation anyway. It's hard on an old man because he didn't grow up with all this. Too much is happening. I can't keep up.

It made a difference what I built. When I was young and built that first barn it didn't mean I was a carpenter. I had pride. I fixed it well or I didn't fix it at all. I wanted no one to say: Isn't that a hell of a job and who did it? I didn't want that hung on me. I wanted them to say: He's a carpenter, not a botch. Today, though, I expect I'd turn a lot of work down. Or tell a fellow what I thought.

When the Corps of Engineers took my neighbor's house I said, 'Cheer up, Carl. Just move into the barn, by God.' I'm a simple man and always have an answer. Very often, however, it doesn't suit those who asked the question. Back several years ago, my daughter came in and I was reading the paper this way, it out in front of me. She said, 'Dad, you need glasses.' I said, 'Naw, I don't need glasses. I just need longer arms.' Well, I had to get them anyway. I was very active, then I came to a standstill. If I had a dozen neighbors and every evening one would come over and sit till bedtime, I'd be fine. I just don't like radio or television either one because it's all advertising and I don't want to buy anything. I'm not in the market.

Times have changed. Ahhey! I see it this way: in the fields, you were soon talking across the fence or perhaps in the field helping. Now tractors keep rolling because we see how many acres of corn we can get in. We butchered six hogs and hung them in the smokehouse. Our neighbors helped with that. Neighbors were no farther than across the fence. Now it seems the day isn't long enough and money comes between us.

I fill my time according to the weather. If my legs are working I walk my dogs. It isn't very satisfactory. I can't go visit a neighbor because no one's at home. They haven't the time to come see me. It's a different world. I've outlived my time. How's this: the oldest neighbor near me is 70. I'm 90. Twenty years is a lot of difference. People honk their horns as they pass, but no one stops. No time. No time.

I got along fine until I was 81. Then my wife died. She had water in her system. How to get it out? I never knew much about it. She was doctored well but she got lower and lower and so she finally died. That was all. Doctors are alright but they don't know everything. The only thing I never figured on was living by myself. I always thought she would outlive me. She took care of herself. I worked in the rain and snow. Then she was gone and I was still here. When she died I was confused. I didn't

Anderson's Fork covered bridge (PHOTOGRAPH BY DAN PATTERSON)

know where to turn. Then P. K. Peterson built a house back of the lane there. Kelsey Newman was the carpenter. He couldn't read a blueprint. They put a chair in front of the foundations and I sat in it and told them how to build and I got my dinner every night. I didn't drive any nails, though. I didn't saw any boards. But when we had built the house, I had come to myself. I knew she was gone.

The Blacksmiths

How are you, Mr. Pickering?
Well, I ain't hit my fist . . .

The blacksmith shop is in the farmland north of the village. It was not the oldest blacksmith shop in the New Burlington farming community but it survived to become the oldest. Hugh Lickliter built it behind his house in the first year of the Great Depression. One eye observed the failure in the nation, the other the rich New Burlington fields. If the shop faltered he would make it into a double corncrib: nations rose and fell, and the fortunes of men, but the fields went on forever. In the spring, plowshares piled halfway to the roof. Howard Pickering, fifth generation blacksmith, came to work and stayed.

Hugh Lickliter is not a big man but his crafty leanness implies a blacksmith's strength. Both men give generous testimony to the mythologies of hard and frequent work although younger men who worked as hard lie in the graveyard to the south. Their natures being similar, they have worked together for 35 years. The work changed slowly and the beguiling slack of time became anesthesia to the change itself. Now in their middle seventies, with the forge heated only on the sporadic days when some odd work piles up on the fire-darkened floor, both feel the change but view it mostly as spectators.

Howard Pickering perhaps feels it more because he is a fifth generation blacksmith, a man of rare continuity in any age. His grandfather, a blacksmith and wheelwright, came from Missouri in a wagon he had made. "None of my sons became a blacksmith," says Howard Pickering in a tone that combines both relief and loss. "It is a fatal work, blacksmithing. It has run out. I feel that . . ."

His grandfather recalls a neighboring wheelwright who filled an ill-matched groove with putty, which was noticed by the old wagon owner. The wheelwright explained that upon hardening the putty would be as strong as wood.

"Then why," demanded the wagon owner, "didn't you make the whole damned wagon out of putty?"

Howard likes the story because it is at once humor and fable. Neither he nor his grandfather would have considered putty, not because the substance was incorrect but rather the *idea* was. He rolls the sleeves of his work shirt to reveal terrible scars up the inside of his arms.

"It is from making wagon wheels," he says. "God, I liked it! It was hot and furious work, beside the flame and in the smoke, but what a fine and particular piece of work!"

Hugh Lickliter also has scars. His are on his stomach, from working the forge without an apron, and the hot metal flakes bouncing off his skin. The residue of Hugh's independence is a quick temper moved by a quicker tongue. Because the price is high only an independent man can entertain such character.

He chews Workman's Choice and spits upon the coal pile. Although he has lived into a modern time and made adjustments to it he is not a modern man. Both his style and substance come from the injection of an old and Calvinistic medicine: much work, no waste.

Hugh drove his old Chrysler 23 years then retired it to the barnyard like a faithful animal. Its great antiquated grill still gleams through the barnyard weeds like the mouth of a steely predator. He thinks that playing the anvil with his hammer makes a nice display but that it seems mostly a waste of energy. "It sounded pretty, though," he concedes. It is a minor concession. Hugh will never play a tune upon his anvil. His motto is: you do not appreciate a chain saw until you have swung an ax.

"I do not know if a man inherits hands," he muses. "A man is perhaps born only with a desire. My uncles couldn't thread a needle. No one in the family was a blacksmith. There are perhaps two inclinations. If your father was good you may be inclined to be as good as he was—or so disgusted you never want to hear about it again . . ."

Where work stands as expression there is no need for philosophy. Hugh Lickliter, then, handles the obvious with country humor: "The art of my work teaches me how to do something well with less work. The first thing you must remember is, you do not pick up hot iron." When Bob Collett asked him why he was late for church he replied, "Well, I expect it was because I didn't begin on time."

Over the years a subtle ritual has established itself between the community and the blacksmith shop. When the male children reach the edge of manhood they are allowed to come to the blacksmith shop when their fathers visit and listen to Hugh Lickliter and Howard Pickering fill the air with an eloquent profanity. In its quaint old-fashioned turn the words become finally not profanity but another language addressed to the work itself. The two old smiths are keeping company with each other and their work.

Hugh Lickliter, 76

I've worked at blacksmithing since I was a kid. I never took an apprenticeship but I talked a lot to the older ones. They were all my friends because I was never ashamed to acknowledge that I didn't know everything. They took a real pride then in their work although now it seems that the sloppier a damn fool can be the more he's respected. We now put out work anyway to get it done. We are sloppy and automatic and we end by scrapping half of it. We don't do anything right down to the scratch and we don't have real mechanics anymore, we have parts men. They take off one part and put another on. Now there are machines that determine what is the matter with other machines and I just don't know about it. There used to be a type of work that a man took pride in his ability to see it through but now one man does this, another man that, and when it's finished, no one knows what he's done nor has any authority about it. A man has no interest but in pay day and quitting time.

My father came here from Virginia and we've always lived within 20 miles of here. My grandfather was a cabinet maker and an undertaker. When someone died he would measure the old fellow up and make a casket that very night. He worked with walnut which would be worth a fortune today. He had the lumber planed and ready and I remember once that someone asked him for a casket made of cheap lumber and grandfather refused the work.

My dad was a good man but he didn't stay put too long. When he was broke he came right back but when he got on top he couldn't stay there. I think he wasn't a good businessman and made mistakes but who among us haven't? He liked race horses and that was no poor man's hobby unless he had money set aside. When I was 11 he harnessed a team for me and I plowed in the fields, out there on the hillsides. I had to do it and so I took it for granted although I was young to be handling a team. Some say it is a lie but I know because I was there. It was a gentle team and they did what I wanted done. Of course, when I got to the end of the row I couldn't lift the plow out to swing it around. I had some of the awfulest looking ends. Once I plowed in under a root and I was so small I couldn't do anything but unhitch the team.

When I was 13, we had a little blacksmith shop on the place that wasn't used a great deal and I made some shoes one day and shod the pony. When Dad got home, Mom said, 'Hugh has shod old Joe,' and Dad jumped right up. He thought I had drove the nails too high. I didn't drive them very good, I admit, but they were still on the next day. I liked that, and I've worked at it all my life.

I worked on A. E. Beam's farm from 1921 until 1929, then I bought this little place and set my shop back here where I could throw it into a double corncrib if I didn't make it. When the depression happened I was like all the rest: I had no money in it and the stocks went first and men killed themselves I heard but what was stocks to me? It was later, in 1930 and 1931 and 1932, when men were unemployed but this kind of business thrives in bad times because no one has money for new things and so they repair the old. We got enough in to keep going and we put the rest on the books and when they got it they paid me, with the exception of two that I remember. I had always wanted a little shop and now I had it and 11 acres and we survived the depression although we had very little money, but we lived, and as time went on, things got better.

One spring, I don't remember which, the ground turned dry and we had 283 plowshares on the floor at one time to be sharpened. There is nothing like a hard ground to wear them down. We usually did fifteen or twenty a day and we shod a lot of horses and did a lot of wagon work. If a man is lucky he can sharpen a plowshare in three heats. It was an awful job to hammer a plowshare out by hand but I've done it, although soon I paid $325 and got a jig hammer. Now it would cost $2,400 and there's an art to it either way. The walking plowshares had to be just right or they wouldn't run. If they were not right they'd kill a man. It would pull, go too deep, Lordamighty. A tractor, now, it just rams a share in the ground and no one knows right or wrong, but the man after a walking plow knows.

All walking plows were left-handed and when the tractor came they turned to right-handed and did the blacksmiths cuss at that. A left-handed share, you see, threw the ground left so your lead horse was in the clean furrow and the others on the unturned ground. It put your team on the land. I'll be damned if I know why they changed as they did. When the blacksmith sharpened the left-handed ones they could lay it up and hammer it from underneath with no trouble. But when it changed over it was the other way around and awkward. It was the change of it. It was hard to work with smoothly because it was all backward, and the older ones took a pride that no hammer marks showed on a share. With the machine it made no difference, but by hand it make a big difference. Now it makes none at all because they've done away with the sharpening. We do a few but most buy shares which last five times as long and they're cheaper. The old ones cost $6, the new ones $2.85 and I don't miss it.

I'd rather shoe a horse, though, than anything. To do what another man can't is my consolation and can't everybody shoe a horse, not by a long shot. There's even an art in picking up a horses's foot and if you don't believe it, you should see some of them around here trying it. Some horses will bear down pretty well on you, great Godamighty. Once I got the hell kicked out of me. I went down to pick him up and he found me off balance and they say he whirled me three times. It stove me up a bit but I was younger then so I beat the hell out of him and shod him right away. What you have to do is let him know you are there, go down his side to his leg, pick it up and get your leg under his so he can't kick. That doesn't mean he can't jerk, don't think it doesn't.

Sometimes we've shod two feet at a time, one at the back and one at the front on the other side. The horse has to be decent, of course, so it's not often practical but we've done it. Many a day we've shod two teams in the morning and three more in the afternoon. Sometimes we quit at three and sometimes it was after five. It all depended on how the damned old horses stood. Some would kick and some would jerk and others would lay down on you. I have been around horses a long time but I've never seen anything to admire about a horse. I didn't like them although I liked the shoeing. A lot of men make a great to-do about the affection of a horse but I found it like an old man once said: all whiskey's good but some is better than others.

I never did any fancy shoeing because all our trade was work horses and that never took great brains. There's more of an art to shoeing a race horse and as much difference as night and day. You have to balance his feet and trim his hooves just so or he'll hit his knees or his back feet will overreach and hit his hocks. It's quite a job to know that and we never went into it here. Most horses, however, I can look at the feet on the ground and work it right out on the forge. O maybe I have to hit it a crack, then she's right in there. Of course, I haven't done it now in some time because the best part of me is over the fence. Today I might have to stick their feet in a bowl of plaster to fit them.

No one makes big money here. It would be hard to average $4 an hour and in a factory you're getting paid whether you're working or not. I've just been content with a living because what is a million dollars laid up in a bank? I think a lot of people work that are not adapted to it. They do it and they don't like it. You have to like it. I've never taken a job I didn't like and I'm no different from any other man. If I didn't care for it, why, I'd be mad when anybody came to me.

You have to start back to know why. People began saying 'I don't want my boy to be like me. I want him to have a good job and not have to work like me.' Then he's married and has to have a new home and an auto and he goes to the bank and it's all done and there isn't a great deal of satisfaction in it somehow. There are no sacrifices except the bank has you tightened up and to my way of thinking there are no values to it. We start at the top rather than at the bottom and the attitudes are all different.

I started pretty moderate when I was married and what we got we sacrificed for it and we knew what it was. We began with $11 and a table and it never bothered me what my neighbor had. I've been satisfied with my lot. If my neighbor had something better, why, then, I'm glad he's my neighbor and I can go look at it. I never envied no man or wished I could do what he did because I did what I wanted. I have admired those who accomplished more than I.

At one time it seemed that nearly everybody bought a new automobile. I admired them but mine got me where I wanted to go. Autos are all made to run and transportation is all you get from any of them. I never fell in love with any material thing too much because anything you can replace doesn't have such a value to me.

I had a Desoto I bought in 1948 and I drove it for 23 years. I ground the valves on the little fellow and at 100,000 miles I overhauled the engine and bored it out and drove it another 60,000 and then I retired it to the barnyard. I have neighbors that trade cars every two years and it costs them about $1,800. I go just as far as they, and it doesn't bother me. I spend money because that's all it's fit for, that's my attitude, but I won't spend it so that charity will have to bury me.

I was 75 this past Ocotber and I've been very well satisfied. I've had aches and pains but I'm not completely broken down and the work has helped. When I close the shop door whatever it is remains behind until the morning. I don't think about it and that's God's truth. My wife, she worries, but I've never seen it do her any good. It makes her cross sometimes. If I'm responsible for error, that bothers me. But nothing else. Why, I've a neighbor who worries about the weather! He frets and stews and fumes, jiminy good God!

My work has been a small service in this world, to my neighbors and friends, and they're glad I'm here when they break down. I've made a living from it and I've liked the work. I've tried to be reasonable in my prices and I've caught hell from my competition but I've always charged what I think it's worth and what I would pay for the same job myself. I've not accumulated anything but I've lived and enjoyed it. All that counts in this life is to be satisfied in work.

Howard Pickering, 77

I am the fifth generation of Pickering blacksmiths but it is an antique trade now. The wheels and wagons and horses are gone now and so is the work. We do a few plowshares still but that is all. Today, most plowshares are throwaways although there are those who bring us a few of them to sharpen and occasionally we get some of the old ones. They are from old two and three bottom plows for those that don't farm real heavy. The shares just get so dull it takes gasoline as much again to pull them in the ground. They're hard to sharpen also. Too much heat and they warp and you begin again but like everything else there's a knack to it. I give them all a little suck to make them run right. Right on the point, just make it bend down a bit for a little clearance under the landside holds the plow in the ground.

I'd rather shoe horses than anything I've done because it fascinates me. I like to smell the hoof burn against hot iron although most hold their noses and run from the shop. And I love the sound of an anvil. My dad could drink more water than any man I've ever seen and when he wanted a drink he would hammer on the heel of his anvil and you could hear it a mile. He wanted a drink and we knew we had better be there for people made their children mind in those days and so I grew up to the sound of the anvil. When I was eight or nine I stood on a box and pumped the bellows for my dad, using a buggy shaft for a handle.

I was always about the shop. I was clinching when I was 12. It is done with a clinch-cutter which cuts the horseshoe nail off square, then it is rasped smooth. A lot of horses have a spur on the inside of the hoof and that, too, has to be rasped down. Dad would drive the nail in and leave the clinching to me. At 15 I could do it all. It came a fierce sleet around Christmas the year I was 18 and I shod over a hundred horses during January. What work that was! They never invented anything to make it easier although some of it is gifted to a man. A good blacksmith can watch a horse travel then shoe him right. I've seen two do that. Stanley Dancer the race horse man had a German fellow, paid him $30,000 a year and called it cheap at that.

My grandfather made wagons in Missouri then be came to New Burlington. If a thing was to break, a blacksmith shop was where it came because you just didn't go out and buy things new every day. Hooks, singletrees, tongues, open rings, chain, all these things were made by a blacksmith, not bought off a shelf. Grandfather Joseph could make any-

Howard Pickering (PHOTOGRAPH BY KEN STEINHOFF)

thing. I have hammers and tongs now made by his hand. He sharpened plowshares for fifteen cents and shod a horse for thirty cents a shoe and I have his ledger to prove it so.

I began working regular with him and my father in 1910, when I was 12 and our work was mostly wheels and horseshoes. We made everything but the hub. Grandfather made the spokes of hickory with a draw knife and a wood rasp, with a tenant-cutter for the ends. It was a very particular job, hot work and fast, but it was work I liked. We heated the metal rim in a fire in the yard, packing wood around it with bark on the outside to hold the heat and let it burn clean down, although my dad was always pecking at the metal to see if it was ready. It makes a dead sound when it's hot, you see. The metal tire is always made from one-half to three-fourths of an inch smaller than the actual measure because it expands in the heating.

After it is heated, it is put on the wooden feller, then the whole thing is put into the water and you can hear the spokes just crack in the hub. It would damn near smoke you to death, but the tire was on to stay and there were no bolts used in those days. It would be so tight that some-times it would be hard to budge with an eight-pound sledge when we began to center it. It was a simple matter to get the tire too tight and dish the spokes, especially with the back wheels of a buggy which usually had three-fourths inch tenants when a wagon wheel had them seven-eighs or one inch. To keep the wheel tight, it helped to keep it painted, or boiled in linseed oil. That was my grandfather's work and he died in 1913 and I do not believe he ever saw an automobile.

My father was a very particular man and I was glad of it because he taught me that anything worth doing is worth doing right. He would sharpen a plow and it would run clean across a field and no one had to hold the handle. When I was six he made me a sled out of a pair of buggy shafts and it was never beat down a hill. When he bought buggy shafts he always bought three. When you put one in, you'd do three. No one knows why but that seemed to be the case. He never worked on an automobile. He was the afraidest man of gasoline. But all of the younger ones wanted an automobile. It was something to get hold of.

I drove a huckster wagon when I was 16. I got in there and just gripped the wheel as hard as I could. I ran it a mile and it got away from me and into a ditch and back the other way, by golly! My father finally bought one but he was very afraid of it. He had some age on him then and when you have that, there is such a difference in the speed of things. When we were young, why, none of us ever thought of what the automobile would do. Today, having the choice, I'd do away with it. The horse and buggy days were the best of my life.

In my day everybody had a driving horse. Dad had a grey mare never beat on the road. It was 10 miles to Xenia and Dad could drive there in an hour and it took a good horse to do it. In those days you meet anybody on the road and him with any speed at all, why, a race was on. Then I had the smartest horse I ever drove. I'd be asleep and she would ride into the yard, go to the trough for a drink, then back up and turn left so she wouldn't catch the buggy wheel on the trough and go to the barn. Dad raced her one night and she struck her knee and the next morning when mother went out, she stuck her leg straight out the door to show mother where it hurt. I always liked horses because I was raised with them. I did all my running around with a high-life horse and a good buggy and they were pleasant times because everybody knew everybody else and you left your doors open and people didn't steal everything you had.

We never turned away any horses to shoe and that was saying a lot for those days but my dad died at 57 because he had shod too many mean horses. They claimed that every time a horse jerked you it enlarged your heart. I missed part of my first year in high school when a mule kicked my father and broke his leg and I went into the shop. I was kicked some and I've caught a few nails but when they kicked I always went into the horse and not backward and I wore a thick leather apron which cracked like a board when I was kicked. Once a big horse caught a nail under my ring and fairly led me around on my knees. I never wore one again, I'll tell you.

I remember my dad resetting a mule's front shoe and getting his cap kicked off with the back one. He just threw the mule down in the lot and someone sat on the mule's head while dad finished with the work. He charged fifty cents to reset two shoes instead of the usual thirty-five and the fellow really hollered about it. However he wasn't there when the work was being done. Old Amos Faulkner had a team and like most teams there was a good horse and a bad one. The bad one, I could have killed her twelve times and so could have my dad because she would just piss all over you. To keep her still we would roll both her ears with a rasp and put a twitch on her nose but the piss was something else, yellow like an egg and gallons of it. Well, you have experiences with anything you do in life and that was one of them.

The driving horses had to be shod every four weeks because of the gravel roads. A macadam road would eat a horseshoe in two trips to Xenia. I had a pacing horse which would twist his hind feet to the outside and use three pairs of hind shoes to one front pair. I tipped—some say 'teed' or 'corked'—many shoes, just hammered out the tip so it sets against the hoof and the shoe cannot slip. Once I tipped the shoes on John Brannon's horse and he was an old Irishman who would rather cuss than eat and he took a look and said, 'Goddamn you, you've pounded half my shoe away on the tip!' He was just that way—I believe he would cuss his wife—and I took no offense but I never tipped his shoes any more, nor any Irishman's.

I had six brothers and a sister and seven of my own children but no one learned smithing but me. It was getting away when I was small and I would have been better off doing another job. I worked for Hugh Lickliter for 35 years just for a living and I made Hugh his money and although he didn't raise his prices nor my wages he was the best man I ever worked for. I was offered a job welding in Dayton once but my family didn't want to move and I didn't want to change and with that against a man, he can't do much. I worked in the factory at Frigidaire only briefly but I am hell on those kind of people. I cannot get along with them. After ten months I was laid off and although I could have gone back later I never did. The foreman didn't like me from the first. He would say, 'Come on, blacksmith, get the lead out of your ass.' And when I left I said to him, 'If I ever meet you someplace out you'll have to be a better man than I . . .' O there are a lot of bad jobs in the world. Once I was offered a job with the state and the man said, 'You'll have to divvy up at election time,' and I looked at him and told him where he could lay his job. I guess I just headed that way when I was young.

There was always too much temper about me. I liked the blacksmith shop although with seven children I never had the money to own my own shop. We got by and part of it was hard getting by and I don't know how we did it. I worked thirty years and not two weeks' vacation. I just took the money instead. That was how hard up I was. To work for myself, now, that means keeping book and with Gilligan wanting three cents of every dollar I just think better of it. Blacksmithing has run out. I feel it. It's quit off and I am 77 years old and when you get old you hate to begin anything new. But my grandfather used to say this: only two blacksmiths ever went to hell. One didn't charge enough and the other hammered cold iron.

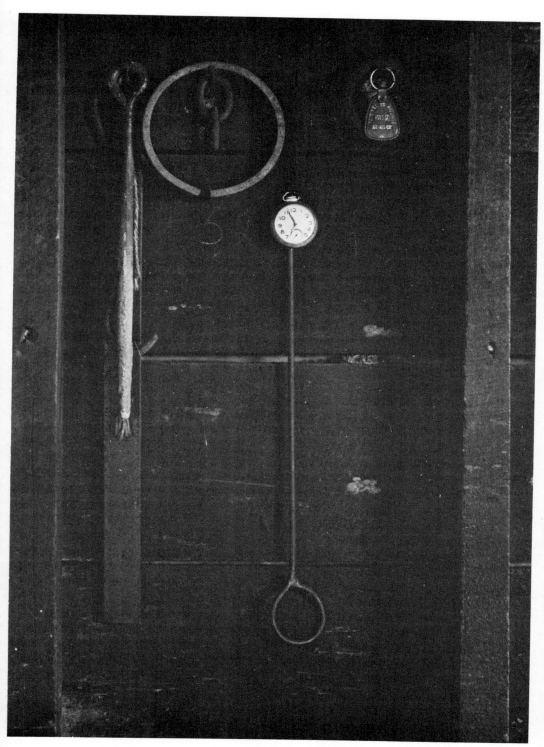

Pickering's watch, beside the forge (PHOTOGRAPH BY KEN STEINHOFF)

Letters

They believed in Indiana because some of them had seen it. Kansas, however, was suspect. Who of them had seen Kansas? But now there was a letter. William was in Kansas and writing home. They read and re-read his
letters, then passed them along in other letters.

William was the restless one. Ohio, Indiana, Kansas. As though
enough distance improved the odds for a man's profit. And back home, in-
fected by those dreamy fevers transmitted by mail, even the old man, John,
pondered horizons he had never seen. Could there be enough feet in Kansas, enough traveling feet hard on bootleather and bonus to a good cobbler? John writes to nearby Poast Town and asks the relatives: how's the
shoe business?

And in between the unsettling letters, the family goes on: William's
brother Ed learns to cobble in the village, the relatives marry, sicken, die.
They trade horses and their dogs go into heat. Cousin Sallie drinks sugar
maple beer with Kittie. And William? God knows. William has discovered
Arkansas. "The best place for a poor man," he writes home to New Burlington, "is Arkansas . . ."

April 18, 1867

Dear Ed,
I will tell you I have broke your colt to ride. Now I will ride it a-spark-
ing to see your girl if I can find her. Who is she? Wills is a-trading
horses yet. He traded five times the other day. There was a man told
him the mare was 25 years old and had fits. George is on the place and
a-trying to read. He can talk rite smart. Ma says you have had the
measles onst so you needn't be afraid.

Joseph Purdy

76

March 5, 1870
Allegheny City, Pa.

Dear brother and sister,

Mother Brown sent your letter to me and you might think it strange me
here and them thaire but so it is. I got tired thaire and to doe nothing
all winter I thought it best to come back here and make something.
Now it may be that I will goe back this spring if I thought I could mak
eneything in the shoe bisness.

James Brown

April 12, 1870
Poast Town

Mr. Edward Brown:

Your father told me Ed that you wanted to go to Xenia to work and I
have thot a good deal about it. My advice is for you to stay with John
and Malindy awhile yet. The man that you are with is very much of a
gentleman and you do not find them every day and you know that practice makes perfect workmen. The chances of getting a good plaise with
good men are very rare and you will be deceived nine times of ten.
Besides you take a great risk in getting into bad company which is very
demoralizing. I don't want you to think hard of me for this advice for I
giv it to you sincerely as a friend.

W. B. Poast

July 12, 1870
Poast Town

Mr. Edward Brown:

By the way, I hope that you did not take eney offence from the leter
that I rote to you last spring. I ment no harm when I gave you advice. I
thot that as I was older than you I should advise you as such and so I
did as I would a brother but I hope you ar not offended.

W. B. Poast

October 3, 1871
Kirks Crossroads, Ind.

Dear father,

Shoemaking is good at this time. I would like for you to come out this
fall if you can. There is plenty of apples. Harriet has dride two bushels.
Tell Edward I have got plenty of hickory nuts to crack this winter.

William Brown

November 11, 1871
Kirks Crossroads, Ind.

Dear father,
I want to come out here at Christmas. I will meet you at the railroad. I
would like for you to come out and see my babys.

William Brown

February 12, 1872
Kirks Crossroads, Ind.

Dear father,
You wanted to know if it would pay you to move out here. I don't think
it would for there is not much shoemaking here in the summer. I
would like for you to come out if it would pay you. I am not going to
work at shoemaking this summer. I am going to farm.

William Brown

March 30, 1872
Kirks Crossroads, Ind.

Dear father,
Our house is empty for you.

William Brown

January 10, 1874
Poast Town

Mr. Ed Brown,
The snow is growing verey fast. It is about 10 inches deap. The excitement here now is fox driving. They get about five hundred men and
surround a scope of four or five miles squaire and blow hornes and
hamer old pans and everey noisey thing and drive them all in to the
center and hollow and yell until they are scaired to death.

W. B. Poast

January 30, 1874
Kirks Crossroads, Ind.

Dear father,
Shoe making is getting dull out here and money is scarce. Eva has got
to be a big girl. She carries all the wood in and goes to the store.

William Brown

August 7, 1876
Wilmington

Uncle John,

We want you to come down tomorrow for our baby is dead.

Eva Lewis

Kirks Crossroads, Ind.
February 7, 1877

Dear father,

I have got a big boy and I am elated.

William Brown

November 19, 1877
Poast Town

Mr. John Brown,

If you have not got eny thing to do you and aunt might as well come down here and stay a few weakes as not and then you can see for your selfe what you think of the chances. Thaire might be considerable repairing don here on shoes and harness but for new work I cannot say for thaire is so much eastern make sold. You can try and that would test the matter.

W. B. Poast

Augusta, Kansas
December 17, 1877

Dear father and mother,

You think that I have forgotten you but we have not. We left Indiana on the 26th day of September and it took us five weeks and four days to come through. I came out here to get a chance but there isn't any to get and I don't think that I will stay here very long for I don't like the coun- try. It is not what I expected to see before I came. There is no work out here. Shoemaking is dull. I have been shucking corn. I get three bushels a day for 15 cents a bushel. We live 60 miles from Indian terri- tory.

William Brown

Augusta, Kansas
March 18, 1878

Dear father,

I rote in my last letter that I was coming back but I think now I will stay here. I like it better than I did. I am going to commence working in the shop in the morning but I don't know how long that will last. I live about four miles from town but I can stand in the door and see the town. I have bought me a good cow and a lot of chickens. The weather is warm and the peach trees are in bloom and everything looks nice.

Willian Brown

Allegheny City, Pa.
March 20, 1879

My dear brother and sister,
I am at home now. My health is tolerable good only I am blind.

James Brown

Poast Town
January 29, 1880

Mr. John Brown,
I am requested to say to you that Mrs. Sallie Long, widow of George Long, is still on the land and among the living.

W. B. Poast

Poast Town
April 13, 1880

Dear Uncle John,
Aunt Eliza Marsh's house is a sad one tonight. Daniel died at a quarter of eight this evening. He was taken sick last Sunday morning. He had pneumonia and it seemed he got worse from the very moment he took sick. There has been no arrangements as yet. Aunt Eliza is broken up for he was her dependence.

Sallie

Augusta, Kansas
January 18, 1881

Dear father,
It has been a long time since I rote you but I have not forgotten you. I always think of home and my dear ones that I have left behind. I would like to see you all again and if we live I think that I will next fall for I don't like this country and I think I will come back home. I have not worked at shoemaking for a year. I have rented a good bottom farm on the white water river about a mile west of town and I am going to farm for myself. We have had a nice winter, the roads are dry and dusty, and the railroad is going through this place.

William Brown

Poast Town
March 23, 1881

Dear cousin,

Kittie and I are not married yet. We still remain two. I have been up twice to eat wax with her. I am invited up again to drink sugar maple beer. That is splendid, you know? Pa has been having terrible luck with his chickens this spring. Nearly all of them have died. They had the croupe. Grandma sprained her thimble finger last Sunday night, ma has been complaining all week, and I have a slight touch of spring fever although it spit snow today.

Sallie

Poast Town
February 7, 1882

Mr. Edward Brown,

I am tiered of the mud and the roads never was worse than they are now. All I have to say about it that it is good for ducks and cisterns. Several of the young men have gon to Dayton to work in the factorys and some of them who can't find eney thing els to do have got married. Eneything for a change.

W. B. Poast

Poast Town
October 3, 1885

Mr. Edward Brown,

Will you inquire of eneyone who you may think would be likely to know whaire I can find a blue fox hound to breed Bell to. She is in heat.

W. B. Poast

Augusta, Kansas
February 5, 1889

Dear father and mother,

Things are good here. I had fifty acres in corn last year and gathered it all myself except what Eva helped me. This fall if I want I can go to the Indian territory. A man can do a good deal better there than he can do here.

William Brown

Augusta, Kansas
March 26, 1889

Dear father,

I have got most of my plowing done and am going to plant corn next week. I want to come home this fall if I have a good crop. Tell Edward he better not go to Indiana for he will not like it out there. Tell him that if he wants to go any place to come out here and we will go to Arkansas for that is the best place for a poor man. I know of aplace down there of eight thousand inhabitants and no shoemaker within fifty miles. Get Peter to come to and then you and mother come and all come.

William Brown

Mrs. Brown,
You will please allow Anna to attend a birthday party in honor of Ida Blair at her home in South Burlington on September 18, 1891, between 5:30 and 7 p.m.

Mr. and Mrs. Blair

Dear Jannie,
I can't stand it eney longer without hearing from you. This is the first weak, Jannie, that I have past for a long time without seeing you and it is the longest. Jannie you must not get mad at me for not coming down. Jannie dear, I haven't been well, indeed, if I felt well enough to walk I would have been down before this time. Jannie, I don't suppose you done eney good with Dave as you would have been up if you did. I feel sorry for you, Jannie, it is to bad for you to be fooled this way. Jannie, please rite and let me know wether you done eney good with him or not. You must be shure and let me know all about it, Jannie, for I am anxious . . .

Ed Brown

Mr. Ed. Brown,
I will be down home this evening after supper.

Jannie Noggle

Village Ladies

Sweet Marie, come to me,
come to me, sweet Marie,
not because your face is fair
but your stocking's full of feet
and I'll swear you're hard to beat
sweet Marie . . .

—village song

Marie Lemar Heller, 81

My mother was born in 1852 and when she was very small her mother didn't want her to run the streets of New Burlington. I don't know what she was afraid of. A Quaker couple by the name of Mills wanted my mother and her mother thought it was a good idea for her to be in the country and so she went. They paid her a penny a day for doing chores and sent her to school. She was one of 14 children and likely they needed to put children out.

When I was born my mother was 43. In that time women took Lydia Pinkham's Tonic for the menopause and then I came along so she would say, 'You were in my Lydia Pinkham's bottle . . .' There was 17 years between my brother and me. Because of my mother's age when I was born he was terribly embarrassed and so he left home. Just moved to the country and lived with my sister. He wasn't a bit happy because to him the whole affair was a disgrace. He never liked me until I was nearly 12.

I was born at home and soon I loved to go fishing. It was born in our family and there was some seriousness to it because we put them on the table. We called them goggle-eyes but they were perch. I caught a bass with a soft crayfish and it weighed two and a half pounds at Joe Blair's store. Once I went barefooted behind the blacksmith shop and got an awful bite. It was a turtle. I was so excited I pulled it into the shop. We fished all the way up to the cemetery except late of an evening when the boys went swimming near the covered bridge. The hole was good to fish when they didn't swim. The girls didn't swim. I never went in my life.

Marie Heller fishing in Anderson's Fork with Sarah Haydock (standing) and Joshua Inwood (center)

But if they did it was later in life and then up on the other creek. They wore black hose and maybe black bloomers. No nakedness and nothing tight fitting. The boys wore nothing at all.

The manner of play was entirely different in that day. We fished. We played in the sawdust at the lumbermill. In the winter we rode sleds to gather the sugar water and had chicken roasts on the coals. We gathered beechnuts when they fell and grandmother DeHaven roasted them in salt and butter. We skated on the creeks nearly all winter because the winters were severe and we had oranges once a year at Christmas when they would smell throughout the house. We had nothing like television and radio so I read in bed, eating popcorn.

In warm weather I ran off every day and got a licking with a little willow whip. I went to play with Bessie Martin. There was a fence no wider than that and I'd up over that fence to Bessie's. I'd get a whipping and go again the next day because the whipping didn't hurt bad enough. The fence was picket and I skinned it real well. I was a ringer. I came late in life and my father was pretty elated over me. Because I came so late I was a spoilt little egg. I'd go uptown and the boys would sing 'Sweet

Marie.' That was my name, Marie. I'd just stomp. The more I was angry the more they would sing. Once I was sent home from school for dragging my shoe. You see, kids weren't perfect at any age . . .

And I drove a fractious horse to Spring Valley for music lessons. When I drove by Thomas Haydock's cobbler shop to fetch Sarah, Thomas would predict we'd never be seen again. Going to Xenia with dad our horse knew nothing of an automobile. When we saw one coming dad pulled off the road and mother and I stood in the ditch while the horse leaped up and down. They would let me drive to the outskirts of Xenia but I had to leave the horse and buggy on a farm there and take the traction car into town. I was an adventuresome girl!

In 1913 we had a bad flood. Water met in the cross streets. Water was all around us and we watched it late. It was a frightening time. People took the tacks out of their carpets and put their furniture upon trestles. We put our piano on a trestle. The men would go house to house and do this. One of the boys decided to stay in a house on the other side of the creek. The water got so high they handed him a plank through an upstairs window, he put it to a tree and they got him out of the tree. Some people went to friends in upper Burlington. We went to the Martin Rooming House for my dad did not wish to impose. It generally lasted one night. You saw lanterns everywhere. There was no fun about it. It was a glare of mud everywhere, and sadness. Then it was clean up and repaper.

I met my husband when he came to see the high water. I came out to go to the store. He was hitching his horse to a telephone pole. It was a Tuesday or a Wednesday. He said to my nephew, 'I want to meet her.' That was June. We were married in December. I was 19.

When my father bought the grocery I went in with him. He never paid me wages but I had a new outfit for spring and fall. Our little store was nothing to a supermarket today. We had groceries on one side and general goods on the other, a pot-bellied stove in the back for the men to gather around. We had salt fish in round barrels and dill pickles in the brine with a long fork. Bread was delivered fresh every morning by horse from the bakery in Spring Valley. We had oranges and cranberries in the winter but no celery. Vegetables were grown in gardens for Burlington had fine gardens.

People bought only that which they couldn't grow. After I was married two dollars any week would buy my groceries. Wheat was exchanged at the mill for flour. Cabbage was grown then buried in hills. You pulled them up, turned them upside down and piled dirt on them. In the late fall we made our kraut, then the cabbages froze for the winter. You just went and dug them out. A person could live on a few hundred dollars a year. My husband carried newspapers for which he made $60. He trapped along the branches for $60 more. And the mailman put his horse up in our barn and ate dinner with us at $8 a month. We lived through the winter on that.

'What will I get for dinner?' my daughter says. Well, in green bean season we had green beans. On Monday we washed on the board. We ironed on Tuesday. Wednesday was for baking and there was pie on the table three times a day because dad liked it even for breakfast. Thursday was nothing special but we cleaned on Friday, baked again on Saturday and Sunday was church day.

In the winter before I was married Weldon and I drove into Wilmington and I had an oyster sandwich. He had ham. After we were married I asked him why he didn't like oyster sandwiches. 'I like them,' he said. 'But I couldn't afford two.' When we were married we were rather poor. But those were different times. You hitched a horse to a hitching post and that was that. But Good Earth! I'm not the same person I was no more than anything. I'm so scared of things. I'd no more handle a horse than I'd fly to Guinea . . .

Rose Devoe, 85

My father was Harrison P. Moss, named after President William Henry Harrison, who was granddad's general in the Civil War. He was one of the first electricians and was so full of electricity he could lay a piece of paper on the wall, run his hand over it and make it stay there. He wired Richmond, Indiana, and tended the footlights at the Bradley Theater which was around the corner from our house. The town was changing over to streetlights then although many were still carbon, and dad repaired them.

Two deaf and dumb brothers lived across the street and operated a pop factory. Whenever they spotted a streetlight out they would come to the house and pound on the door no matter where or what time of night because they knew dad fixed them. He would yell down the stairs at them but of course they were deaf and pounded until he went down. Finally he learned to talk sign language.

Next door was a seven-year-old boy who played the violin. People often came to the window and serenaded the house and dad gave them beer. People just did that in those days. Once dad went away on business and a whole crowd went to the train station to see him off. He was only going overnight to Cincinnati but that was the way things were.

At the Bradley Theater I saw Sophie Tucker in person and Wheeler and Wilson and the Van Dyke and Eaton Company. I was eight and my mother made me pretty clothes and since the traveling actors did not often have children about I was in the plays when they needed a child. Once I skipped across the stage and said, 'Come, poppa, I'm ready,' and this perfect stranger picked me up! They never rehearsed me and I just acted natural. I was there whenever they needed me and they gave me expensive candy.

We had electric lights and gas and went everywhere and in 1898 my father left us and my mother and I moved to New Burlington to live with my grandmother. My father was too handsome, that was the matter. When people separate they do not know what they do to their children. At first there was nothing. We lived in a house on the lower end of town, my mother and I, my grandmother and my aunt, who was the village dressmaker and a maiden lady. It was very dark and no sounds in the night. And once we had had electric lights and gas! Now we had to go to the millyard for wood to keep warm.

I didn't see my father again until I was 12. He didn't know me. He

Rose Moss Devoe (left) and cousin, 1913

called on the telephone and said, 'Do you know who this is?' I said, 'It sounds like Mr. Moss.' I was a little girl in Mother Hubbards when he left and then I had become a big girl in shirt waists and skirts. He later ran hotels in Springfield and Cleveland and after I was grown he came to see me right often. People said, 'Rose, how can you treat him so nicely?' And I told them I did because I loved him and was glad to see him. He saw his mistake and so did his wife who was only nine years older than me, and my mother loved him until the last.

We lived first in lower Burlington then we moved to upper Burlington, right on the county line. We cooked in Greene County and ate in Clinton. My aunt was the village dressmaker and she was awfully good to my mother and grandmother. She seemed to feel obligated. She got $1 or $1.50 for a dress, big full skirts with French binding on the bottom so it wouldn't wear out. She had a little low-armed sewing machine she treadled with her feet. Mostly she made ladies' dresses and shirt waists and shimmies—we call them slips now. Women were *this* big around. The corsets were laced so tight they'd often faint, squeezed in so tight they could hardly get their breath. Everybody in those days kept whiskey for medicine and one old lady always had a fainting spell. It was every time she came. Aunt Emma finally told her she was out of whiskey.

Emma Jane White. She would go in people's homes and sew and fit, 50 cents a day. When she wasn't doing that she'd get her garden work done early and go fishing. It was a happy house. We had a summer kitchen—everybody did then—and when the rain barrel went dry we used the well water for washing. It was not as good, however, because the water on the lower end of town was salty and hard. My grandmother poured water on wood ashes to make lye, dipped it off with a gourd and poured it in the water for the washing. She knew just how much to use and soon it would make the lime rise to the top to be skimmed off. The lye would cut it loose, make it 'break the water,' as they said. And the water would be softened. I do that today. Some make fun of me but I don't care. I don't *feel* old-fashioned.

I helped Emma rip seams, baste things. When I wanted a dress I had to make it. She was busy with others. She was afraid I'd break the sewing machine which was her livelihood so I learned from Josephine Blair. After I learned, I could use the machine. If you had a Sunday dress, a second best and a couple of everyday ones, you had quite a wardrobe.

We made everything: readymade sheets, everyday shirts and some Sunday ones. I made my son a hat, sport coats for boys six foot six who ducked in my door, a school jacket out of a bathrobe, awnings of canvas, rugs of rag, curtains for the old Ford, lampshades and baskets. I refinished my grandmother's old rocker and recaned the bottom. I get scolded now at my age but I enjoy it. Old people who sit around and whine make me angry. 'Go down and fold bandages if nothing else,' I say.

Well, there are many lost arts. I've lived when there's been so many inventions. Trains were once new to me, and the streetcar. And how does television work? I remember when we didn't have rubber erasers on lead pencils. Sometimes the intelligence in the world makes me feel dumb.

We had fun as children but we never destroyed property. O we got out on Halloween and took people's gates off. I never dressed in costumes like the others, however. People would say, 'That's Rose. She has small feet.' My father was a big man and wore five's. He traded with mother once. She had some manly oxfords and they looked comfortable.

Jim Peterson lived above us, below Jack and Julie Martin's boarding-house. Once he came in real late, 11:30 or so, and Jack and Julie saw his light and thought he was up feeding his horse so they got up and ate breakfast. Jide Dakin ran the hotel and he ran strings through holes in the walls, creeping upstairs in the night to yank pillows from under sleeping heads. Once Jide went to Indiana to sell buggies and ran out of spending money. So he began preaching. He made such an impression that an Indiana pulpit committee came to New Burlington to see if Jide would accept the call to be their minister.

"We are looking for the Reverend Dakin," they said at the grocery store.

"The Reverend Dakin?" someone said. "I suppose you mean Jide."

The committee found the minister Dakin presiding over a buggy shaft from the pulpit of a buggy seat. O there were many characters in the village. Once Jessie Hill came into Trevor Haydock's store and began pointing all about the store. When he left the drummer, Frank Carroll, said, "I didn't know you had anybody like that in New Burlington." And Trevor said, "We don't."

During an eclipse someone gave old Jake Scammahorn a smoked glass to watch it through. "Do you see it, Jake?" they asked. And Jake replied, "Only the edge, only the edge."

There was no noise in those days and everything was as still as a mouse. The only things you heard were the rooster crowing and a horse going up and down. I'm glad I grew up when I did. It was before automobiles and I could hear the town clock strike the hour in Xenia. Once lately, though, I visited in the country and it was so quiet I could not sleep. All I could hear was crickets.

As for school I didn't get a diploma because they didn't give one. I always made 98 in mathematics. When I learned something young, it always stayed with me. A young man of the village wrote a letter to his sweetheart and some of us saw it. We memorized it and said it real fast to each other. It went like this: 'I seat myself down to write right square dab at you the old cow died last Tuesday be up to see you next Sunday if it suits you seat yourself down and write right square dab back at me.' How we laughed!

In school I sat by the window so I could see my boyfriend, Bill Devoe, come down the street. He was four years older than I and helping to build a barn. I met him at a medicine show. The place was fairly crowded. There was one seat way up high and he picked me up and sat me in it. I didn't sit with him, though. I was only 14. He was my first and only boyfriend. Three years later we were married. Bill was a railroad man, a car-whacker. He inspected cars underneath. Later he worked at the creamery in Xenia and was both a buttermaker and a plumber. They called him 'Whispering Willy' because he had a great booming voice to call dances. He was a jolly man who had many friends and when he died they filled even the balcony at the Methodist church.

By the time I was 22 I had three girls and they were like small dolls. I never put them back in a room during the day. Being with them keeps them well and right. Now one is dead, two are still alive and soon to be old ladies like I am. I had five children and only two are left. In 1921 my first boy was stillborn. In 1922 my oldest daughter was hit by a car. It is strange the things you remember. I went to the school to help one day and one kid cried because we washed him. His mother had sewed his underwear on. He later killed my daughter. They took me there and I saw blood this thick and something on the road with a duster over it. It was my Ruth, to be 14 the next month. I couldn't hold my purse. It was in the fall of the year and I had put an old sheet blanket on the bed and when they put me to bed I remembered being ashamed of that patch on it for everyone to see. I had just made Ruth a new knicker suit. She had that on, that suit, when it happened in front of the graveyard.

My husband, Will, died in 1932 of an infection of the toe because there was no penicillin. After he died there were five generations in that house for the winter. I had to hold in to keep peace everywhere. I was between the devil and the deep blue sea.

Harry Devoe was my second husband. He was Will's younger brother. I didn't like him much when Will and I were dating because he never had a horse and buggy. I thought he was always butting in. His wife, Mary, died in January before Will died in September. I grieved after her like a sister. We got together and laughed about the Devoes. They didn't go to square dances at all because she didn't want his arms around another woman. I wasn't jealous of Will. I wouldn't want a man no one else wanted.

Harry came a long time to the house. I thought he was coming to see the kids. He was like a brother to me. I treated him well but I didn't know. I said I'd never put two sets of kids together and I didn't for Harry and Mary had none. The children were glad to see us get married but they said it knocked them out of another aunt.

Will and Harry were as different as day and night. Harry had the first fifty cents he ever made. Will had a good time and spent it. I called Harry 'Will' and he called me 'Mary.' We just laughed about it. I enjoyed it on the farm but Harry was skeptical. 'Are you sure you'll like it?' he asked. 'It's my home now,' I said. When I was a girl you didn't marry with the idea you could give it up if it didn't work. We listened to the vows and that was the idea: you worked at it.

I had a dining room big enough for two tables and it was like Grand Central Station. Harry put water inside for a bath and a window over the kitchen sink so I could watch the garden grow. He had a green thumb. He could raise anything but lima beans and I taught him that. 'You're putting them so far apart all the moisture is leaving them,' I said. 'Try planting them thicker.'

We grew dewberries, blackberries, raspberries, currants and gooseberries in my garden. We cured our own meat and made our own soap and it floated. I raised two lambs the mother didn't want and when one got sick I gave it a dose of James' Vermafuge, used for children with the worms, and the lamb got alright. We did not rely on doctors but had our own remedies. We believed there was such a thing as too much medication. And I myself want to know what I'm doing when I die. When you're older you think of such things.

I helped bring a dozen babies into this world and only one died. I delivered the hired hand's children and, once, the father fainted and I had to work with him awhile. It is such a miracle, a life coming into the world. I've heard it said, however, that if the man had the second there would never be a third.

Harry died in 1958. He had cancer and I knew he wouldn't get well. I never dreamed he would go before I. He was so healthy. I'll admit I used to think a farmer wasn't too smart but I knew a lot of town people who couldn't hold a candle to Harry. Because I knew he would not get well I took care of him at home. I had time to think. Afterward I stayed alone all winter in our eight-room house. I wonder how I did it. I didn't know what I was going to do but I figured it all out and decided to get rid of the farm. I guess I never got attached to a place, really, because I was so bumped around as a kid. Everytime we settled into a place they would either raise the rent or sell it.

I've had a lot of trouble but I did not look back. I have had several cycles in my life. I was married to Will for 24 years, a widow for eight, married to Harry for 17 and now I've been a widow for 14. I have now been single as long as I was married.

Harry used to say I smelled things that weren't there. I can taste, also, and I'm thankful I can hear. I am thankful for what is left me. Some days I answer the telephone and I don't recognize my own voice. Being alone, I haven't heard it that day and I am surprised.

When I was a child I dreamed the telephone poles would all be underground. When I learned to drive an automobile I pulled back on the wheel when I went to stop. And so I never learned. With a horse you didn't have to watch the road. When we got automobiles it didn't really help because we just went farther and it took us the same amount of time as before. I fly now to see my daughters and people say, 'Aren't you afraid?' and I say, 'Why, no. One way or another, I'm going home . . .'

The Chicken Thief

If this is July Douse will sit inside the covered bridge over Anderson's Fork and eat his lunch from the pail which is still bent from the time Ed Brown's jersey kicked it when Douse tried to fill it with milk before returning her home. Douse is the village herdsman. He takes the cows out in the mornings and grazes them along the roads leading in and out of the village. Late in the afternoons he brings them back to the pump in the cross streets and after they drink they each turn away and walk by rote to the stables and small pastures behind the houses filling the air with great gusts of their sweet breath. And little moons in irregular orbits up the street in front of the cobbler's shop for Thomas Haydock's customers to dodge with their new boots. And if not to dodge then to curse Douse.

Herdsman is Douse's job but not his art. When someone new in the village asks about Douse the villagers say, "O, that's Douse. He's a Civil War veteran and a chicken thief." They say this matter of factly, as though they are describing a man's business. Some of them might mention as an afterthought that Douse is also a herdsman.

It is now after midnight and Douse is in Jessie Compton's chicken-house. He is just inside the door where he has stopped to look over the tiny room which is filled with the dusty acid smell of chicken manure. The smell is pervasive. It affects gravity, bleaches the hair of the nose, warps weatherboarding. Perhaps the chickenhouse will at any moment explode and hurl Douse to an eccentric death. To be found near Jessie Compton's barn covered with feathers. Douse's eyes widen. They suck in the insignificant light until he can see as well inside the chickenhouse as if he were downtown at Trevor Haydock's store choosing confections from a glass case.

The chickens are roosting on several tiers of horizontal poles which have been worn glass smooth by generations of chickenfeet. But the white leghorns stand out and obscure the poles. They are luminescent. They seem to float before his eyes as if they are buoyed by the darkness. He admires them all. He will take this one here. The plump young pullet there. He moves so expertly that the chickens are not disturbed. In the village they say Douse knows each chicken on a first-name basis.

He does not hear the outside bolt as it drops into place. He does not notice anything but the chickens until Jessie Compton's voice says: "Tell me who thee is and I'll let thee out." A chicken clucks drowsily under Douse's arm. For a moment he is frozen into place, a statue of a man holding a chicken, rising from a pedestal of chicken manure. Then he moves. "Jake Scammahorn!" he shouts. And dashes past Jessie even as the old Quaker farmer is still holding the lifted bolt.

Afterward, Douse is undisturbed. Someone is always locking him away in one tiny place or another. One Sunday, Emma Blair comes home early from church and finds Douse in her cellar taking stock of her freshly made peach preserves. She locks him in then goes upstairs to carefully put her Sunday bonnet away. Then finds the broom and stands by the cellar door and whacks Douse with it as he runs up the steps and into the yard.

There are even rare times when events occur in village chickenhouses which Douse does not promote. One night George Hosier hears a noise and he sneaks outside in his night shirt where he peers over his shotgun into the chickenhouse door. And his collie places her nose on George's bare backside whereupon he fires both barrels through the doorway. And half his chickens are gone.

Once in William Mills's chickenhouse Douse frightens the chickens and the racket awakens William who pokes his shotgun out of the upstairs window and fires at the chickenhouse as Douse is leaving. The next morning William finds the shot has sprayed the little house and also the man who was leaving; a man in flight is outlined by the pellets. William takes visitors to the chickenhouse where he points this out. He refers to it as the "Portrait on the Chickenhouse Door."

Douse does not come after the village cows until very late in the morning. He has walked to Spring Valley to have a doctor pick the pellets out of him. This is the same doctor who attended Babe Grimes when Jesse Hill fired into his chickenhouse one night and caught Babe bending over a sack of chickens.

Several days after Jessie Compton locks Douse in his chickenhouse, Douse is sitting in the back of Trevor Haydock's store with several of the village men when Jessie comes in. Everyone recognizes Jessie even at a great distance because he always wears felt boots and a corduroy coat. He sits down with the men. "The other night," he says, "I heard someone in my chickenhouse and I went out to see and when I got there I decided to bolt the door. 'Tell me who thee is and I'll let thee out,' I said. The fellow said he was Jake Scammahorn but when he ran past he looked very much like Douse."

Jessie laughs but he does not look at Douse. The other men are laughing, too. Douse does not move. He pretends that he does not hear anything at all. He is unmoved, stoic, serene. He is still sitting there when they have all gone. It is as though he is exalted by failure. He wears it like a decoration.

When Ruby Smith returns to the village to teach school, each morning she plays a game with the children. "This morning," she says, "we will play Show-and-Tell." One of the children waves his hand in the air. "Do you have something to tell, Jack?" she asks. "Yes'm," he says. "Yesterday I went home and I couldn't find my mother anywhere and finally I went upstairs to her room and she was playing Hide-and-Seek. She was hiding under Douse."

When the villagers hear what the child has said in Ruby Smith's classroom they shake their heads knowingly. "Ah, Douse," they say, "Caught in the henhouse again . . ."

Two Teachers

Irma Evans, 73

I began school in 1907. After six years, I was ready for high school. We were farm people and the nearest high school was in New Burlington. So I boarded with my aunt and uncle who lived in part of Trevor Haydock's grocery. My sister, who was older, came with me, to teach at Cornstalk School which was just outside the village. I was rather excited. Such freedom, and no cows to milk! At grammar school, we had one room. Now there were three. It seemed so big!

Afterward, dad began running behind on the farm. 'Irma,' my mother said, 'we are faced with losing the farm. The only thing I can see is for you to become a teacher.' I lived on five dollars a week and had two dresses. 'Don't think,' I said to her, 'that I'll spend my life in a school room.' But soon a feeling grew on me. I felt I was doing something. So I kept on. I never looked too far into the future.

My schoolroom was a typical society. There were those who cared and those who did not. I taught 35 years and watched my students grow into men and ladies. In my time, children learned by working things out. Today, learning seems passive. We were closer to our materials. One child studied one word all day and went home happy because he knew it and returned sad in the morning because he had forgotten. He became so angry when he forgot. Often he was teased, you see. But he lived on a farm and explained machinery to me. Years later he pulled up beside me at the barber shop and said, 'You thought I knew nothing and I didn't.

But today I have a baling machine and I can look in the fields and tell how many bales there will be.'

The schoolyard was adapted to the needs of the children. A lot of space, you see. Little folks here. Baseball there. Space is very essential. At the larger schools there are organizations but sometimes they take over further than they can or should. I believe in the individual character, the will. Although sometimes I think such a thing is inborn. I have seen whole families that way. Some pull up and go ahead. Others do not. Once we made quilts for a lady and in the spring when they were dirty she burned them.

At Christmas the children were so anxious to tell what they had received. All but one little boy. 'What did you get?' I asked. 'Switches!' he said. Such hatred in his eyes. His mother put switches in his stocking. 'Anything,' he said. 'An apple. An orange. But she thinks I am bad.' Later, she died, and there was no one. Martha Beam and I put on a bucket of water in the morning and washed them when they got to school. They laid out in the ditches. The little girl was four and chewed tobacco and spit at everything. There is much pathos, if you care. I had girls who never had a boughten coat. They were the children I loved most. The troubled ones. The hurt ones.

Farmers were often considered hayseeds. A successful farmer said, 'That's the first time he spoke to me as an individual . . .' Or a lady might say, 'She had never spoken to me before because she was of the elite . . .' At PTA, some ladies were talking and one said, 'I don't know as I have ever *seen* a bedbug.' And a little fellow nearby piped up and said, 'Lady, I'll run home and bring you back a cupful.' He was just being helpful. Of course, these things caused class distinctions. One of my favorite pupils was a girl from a troubled home. She later wrote me from nursing school and signed it, 'your girl from across the tracks.' She was aware, you see. She did not have the things other girls had. To a point, her perceptions were correct because her parents lived a life others did not accept. These things brought about distinctions.

Only a few did not attend church. The church and the school held the community together. If such a life was sometimes dull, it was also safer. A teacher knew the community and all the families and how to meet the different children. When I was in school at nearby Richland, we had no generation gap. Everyone gathered, from babies to grandmothers. Ladies in their sixties went sledding. There was popped corn and singing. Imagination could not conceive the difficulties of today. We have become so large. So many. Then, our children married and stayed to farm. They did not need the broader education. They studied the fields for themselves. College educations were rare because men remained on the farms.

Village school, 1891

The farms required a different intellect. The farms required patience, and an active, working knowledge. The farmers built and improved and were smart to do it. The finest read man I ever knew was Uncle Adolphus Foland. He read the Bible and much history. I was surprised at his broadness as he spoke. That was true of the Hills and the Haineses. And Uncle Adolphus had a library. Where did he get his books? I do not know.

I had eight boys in my seventh and eighth grades. The year before they threw the teacher across the recitation bench. The first week my brother who was a farmer walked by every noon to check on me. He did this for weeks. The first week one boy asked me, 'What would you do if someone threw you over the recitation bench?' I said, 'I'd go to the proper authorities.' They didn't always obey me, but they were good boys growing up.

They told a story on me, that I once threw a young rowdy down and sat on him. I weighed over 200 pounds, you see. It was an unpleasant picture to most. The boys took me sled riding and upset me at the door but I was surprised to get that far. Once the kids sat on the fence and threw their lunch scraps over. The man there got angry because he said the boys were calling his chickens away. So the boys went home and tied string to corn and threw it over and the chickens ate it and found themselves tied to the fence. O, I liked the devilish ones. I could not help it. They said, 'You're scolding us with your mouth but your eyes are a merry jig.'

Whenever there was a flood, the school was let out. Then the state school law came in and said every child absent must bring an excuse. I had two little fellows who missed because of the high water. But I had to have a note because of the law. So the father wrote: 'The water was out of its banks so Peanuts and his brother had to remain at home to herd the frogs away from the well.' The superintendent was angry and so was the janitor. It was *his* well. He shared it with them. They were so angry they wanted something done with the law. I told them I was the teacher and if it went any further they would have to take it there. They had no sense of humor but I myself have laughed ever since.

Well, there have been many good people and some of the other kind. I have been told I was strict and they said to me, 'We didn't get by with much,' and I said to them, 'But more than you thought I knew about.' They said to me, 'You were fair,' and I was glad. I always wanted to know. What did they think of me? What did they feel? I always felt inferior. I was too heavy and didn't look good in my clothes. People said to me, 'You haven't a family. You don't know anything.' I accept that. It is true to an extent. I knew the bell rang and they left me and were not back until it rang again in the morning. But their cares were on my mind always and I was trusted with private things. And so I cared for more children than most. Others raised one or two or four and cared for no one else. I cared for many. What does *she* know? they asked. I did not know. But I watched, and I cared.

A little child in my fourth grade had tuberculosis and was sent away for treatment. When he returned home, he ran to the barn and said to his father, 'Father, father, I'm back!' and the father said, 'And where are you back to?' and the little one said, 'Why, Miss Evan's room . . .'

In my time, there was not much science in the world. We had only observation. Today, we have much science and great wealth but a different kind of poverty. I think of a busy life, and of what value, and I am uncertain. I took care of my father and my retarded sister. I made less than $800 a year and milked cows for my board. I did not consider it duty. I had typhoid fever and was covered up for death. We worked but it was not slavery. If it was a sacrifice I made it. I valued life and have always had great faith. We need fewer rules and more good living. Rules do not make a country great. It is the spirit of living well. People think I have had a dull, poor life. But I have been rich.

Carl Smith, 86

In Xenia there was a Smith Manufacturing Company and when I was young I thought they manufactured Smiths. When people ask I say all Smiths are related. We're all first neighbors-in-law. And I'm the early settler. I settled for cash.

I was supposed to have been a doctor. Dad was a teacher before he was a doctor and he thought I should do as he did. His way was what I did, you see. So I taught. Unfortunately I was too successful. If I had failed at teaching I suppose I would have gone to medical school. I was not big and strong, however, and the life of a country doctor was not attractive to me and I never got around to being one.

I thought once of going to Michigan and staking a claim. I considered that. In 1911 I went west and met a group of girls from Montana, handsome girls, who were homesteaders. They'd go out and live on a claim in the wintertime when there wasn't much else to do. They had supplies, a dog and a horse, and four claims that cornered together. There were 160 acres in a claim, 640 in a square mile. They built a house with a room on each corner and lived together. We used to sing: *Uncle Sam is rich enough to give us all a farm* . . .

But then I became a teacher. Before I taught in New Burlington I taught in Ross Township. I stayed with Marshall Rogers, a fruit farmer. It was the wealthiest township in the county. No waste land, flat as a floor. No hill higher than your head. It was a little country school but I was rich. I got $45 a month and $1.50 for being my own janitor. It isn't what you get but what you can buy with what you get. I got the very best of country room and board. Country plumbing, too. I got my ironing done and lunches put up. All for two dollars a week. And before I boarded with Marshall Rogers my landlady loaned me a stout farm horse to go see my girl. The horse needed to be stout because of the mud roads.

Jamestown was nearby and it was a little dance-mad then. The Ross Township people didn't want their children to get town ideas so I taught the Rogers' daughter her first year of high school. Then they let Gwen drive into Jamestown for the last month. She just woke them up. Three years later she finished as valedictorian.

My first month at Ross Township, before the boys came in off the farms, I had five pupils on a two-acre school lot. Put one in each corner, another in the middle, and they could barely shout to each other.

When I came to New Burlington I had the front room, seventh and

Carl Smith

eighth grades. The other two teachers had three grades each. I was 21 and in my class was Claire Ewing who was 19. The room was overcrowded and the desk was in the back of the room so that I looked into the light from three directions. Before the year was up I was almost blind. I boarded free at my grandfather Mann's and drove old Harry, a tall Hamiltonian, one of the main trotter lines. Great wind, old Harry.

Lizzie Reeves was in the middle room and Nannie Shambaugh in the other. Nannie was quiet, precise, and easily embarrassed. She had the first, second and third grades. When you taught by the word method you tried to bring back the word in another manner, without repeating it. The word was 'leg,' you see, and Nannie said, 'Think now. A cow has four and I have two.' Such an answer she got. I thought the room would burst. The merriment last all day.

My uncle, E. Dawson Smith, had a similar problem. The line was 'the frog sits on a log.' So uncle Dawson said, 'Where does the frog sit?' And a little fellow replied, 'O, he sits most anywhere, long as he's comfortable.' Well, they're all gone now. Uncle Dawson, poor Nannie and Lizzie, and many of my pupils.

In those days the teacher was boss or the students put him out. The early challenge was: let's see if we can whip out the teacher. I once put a young man in the aisle and choked him. I had to. I was small and at a disadvantage. But at Ohio University I took boxing lessons from John Corbett, a cousin of Gentleman Jim Corbett. He put you in a corner and made you fight your way out.

Before OU I went to Antioch where I was known as Horace Mann's nephew. I was, of course, but it was different Horace Mann. There was a place in town said to have had the same bedbugs that bit Horace Mann. I took German with the hardest man on the faculty. His name was Dawson. He expected you to speak German from the first day. He was also a minister. He couldn't make enough money just teaching German at Antioch. Dr. Fess got a thousand dollars for being president and spent part of his salary buying coal to keep the girls' dormitory warm.

I had a dozen great teachers and I feel like I'm walking on their shoulders. Those who go to only one school talk as if there is no place like Old Paregoric. I picked my work with outstanding men. Anyone can read from a text and still know no more than a hog knows about holy water. There has never been a time when people just naturally got smart. We can see this in English literature. Dr. Samuel Johnson, for instance, dominated his age with bombastic poetry:

Let observation, with extensive view,
survey mankind, from China to Peru

Boohoohoo. What he didn't approve went to oblivion. All his little fishes talked like whales, they said. His man Friday, Boswell, followed the great man around to make him immortal. Johnson stuffed himself with over-ripe chicken and rolled when he walked. Today no one reads him.

And after him was Browning, an arrogant fellow. A woman once asked him what he meant with such-and-such a passage. He said he didn't re-ally remember himself but told her to keep on reading and it would give her a thought or two. Sir Walter Scott turned to prose because he recog-nized in Bryan 'a fire he could not equal.' What he recognized was a contemporary popularity. The only time Bryan got away from self-con-sciousness was when he wrote a tombstone epithet for his dog. I wouldn't trade one canto of Scott for all of Bryan. Things of the moment, you see. When Thoreau wrote *A Week on the Concord and Merrimack Rivers* he had a thousand copies printed and sold only a few. With his typical dry wit he said, 'I have a library of nearly a thousand volumes, most of which I wrote myself.' Well, he described the taste of strawberries so that he ac-tually improved upon them. They sounded better than they tasted.

Today we do not have an aversion to very much. We are a bit dulled to events and it seems that we see none too clearly. We are like Missus Mulrooney and the elephant. She had never seen an elephant and one escaped from the circus and the dark was dark and so was the elephant and at daylight it was standing in her cabbage patch eating cabbage. It was putting away a nice breakfast. She looked out and almost fainted. She dialed the police and said, 'Sergeant, send the whole squad!'

'What is it lady?' asked the sergeant.

'It's a great big animal pulling up cabbages with his tail,' she said.

'And what would he be doing with the cabbages lady?' asked the sergeant.

'O sergeant,' said Missus Mulrooney, 'you wouldn't believe me if I told you . . .'

Myopia is a kind of eternal condition, it appears. It helps explain why we do things for the wrong reasons. The Puritans, you know, weren't against bear-baiting because it hurt the bear. They were afraid it gave pleasure to the spectators. And sometimes we don't even have any rea-sons. As the old Irishman said as he was being ridden out of town on a rail, 'Boys, it's not much of an argument but I reckon it's the best you've got.'

We are very fond of looking backward and glorifying the past. We are very sentimental about the countryside these days, forgetting that the farm once gave us overworked hearts, little profit, and an early grave. Looking backward, we see the high spots. The low places are obscured. Candor is lacking. Why *is* the past glorified? The crawfish swims backward because he isn't going anyplace and he likes to see where he's been. We old-timers are like that. We are inherently a conservative creature and more so as we get older.

Perhaps I am too old-fashioned. I don't have any halos but I do try to hit a kind of balance. I deplore the dropping of standards everywhere. I once said to a principal, 'Students do not learn the parts of speech and not only that, they do not know a simile from a smile, a metaphor from metaphysics, and probably think an asyndeton is one of the cardinal sins.' I like to say: our schools are dying by degrees.

We have many teachers, some of whom are not recognized at the time. Once an old farmer, William Babb, came to our house and while waiting to see my father he said to me, 'Young man, I guess you think you know most everything there is to know.' I tried to modestly disclaim any such omniscience. And he said, 'When I was your age I could tell my father a good many things about his business. But when I got older I found myself driving a good many miles to listen to his advice.' I found that to be true although I was rather skeptical at the time.

And no one knew anything about our greatest teacher from the time he was 12 until he was in his late twenties. Nothing but these words: 'He went around doing good.' How fine!

Perspective: Ruby Higgins

Even her birth was unforeseen and therefore startling. Robert was born first. Afterward, Doc Finley asked Wayne to bring more hot water. When he returned from the kitchen the doctor handed Wayne a daughter. A *girl-child, by God.* He might not be able to contain himself. He wanted to take this child, raw and red-faced from the grief of labor and run through the streets. To the hardware store and up on the feed scales a prize for display. *My jewel!* he thought. And named her: *Ruby.*

It is a name she has always disliked. It is, she thinks, a coarse name of no particular beauty. Yet not without some accuracy. Ruby: a variety of corundum which is, next to the diamond, the hardest mineral known. An excellent abrasive. A color for all the passions. The Smiths were, after all, a passionate family. Ruby's great-grandfather, James Smith, came to New Burlington from Virginia, preaching and shouting. James was first a blacksmith yet a man with a taste of metaphor could perhaps see both callings in the fanatical heat of the forge.

James stayed wherever there was a roof, finding New Burlington among the accidents of wandering. He stayed, returned to the forge, married. The Smiths were men inclined to spirits, both real and imagined. James's son, Lewis, said he was marked; his mother drank when he was embryonic. They had dreams and visions, following them to distant cities where there were lights, energy, companionable noise. Harley Smith carved the hanging beef of family history with a sharp censor's eye, laying it out as he wished it to be. If others drank unwisely, then old Harley sank himself in an airless chronicle. And when Wayne died, 2,000 people came to his funeral, enough honor for any family narrative of that time.

Ruby grew up holding outrageous opinions. She parked in the graveyard in an automobile after the Epworth League. saying: "If I wanted to
get into the back seat with somebody I figured it was my business." And
smoked cigarettes and, upon occasion, tasted whiskey. The old Quakers
in open meeting prayed for the delivery of her gypsy soul. Her family,
however, knowledgeable to eccentricity through the generations, remained as it always had been. She was Wayne Smith's daughter and the
child of a new time.

Years later, she considers the family: "Dad was a great man because he
did not judge a great deal and because he laughed a lot. He embarrassed
me on vacations because he was always getting into conversations. 'Why
do you talk to these people?' I asked. 'You don't know them.' He would
look at me kindly, as from a distance, as if there were things I would
know later, then he would say, 'People, Ruby, people.'

In her sixties, nearing retirement as a teacher, Ruby Smith Higgins
thinks herself sentimental. *But I knew the truth. Even as a child I knew
it. Even then I did not belong to New Burlington. I could not* . . .

Ruby Smith Higgins, 64

If the village had something to decide, then my father decided it. That
wasn't often, however. There was never much to decide in New Burlington. It was Wayne Smith who decided because he belonged to the Masonic Lodge, the Methodist Church and the Republican party. Two out
of three was alright but three out of three granted you entrance into
heaven. He would never lie except in a horse trade and that was the way
it was in a horse trade.

It didn't hurt to like baseball either and he did. Once he took the train
down to see the Cincinnati Reds play and was most impressed by the
number of foul balls that ended up in the stands. He came back and said,
'I bet they wasted a whole manure spreader full of baseballs.'

It was his money that ran the village and when he died none came in
and then the village died. He covered three territories, bringing people in
from all over. It was always Wayne Smith when they ran short to pay the
preacher. How many funerals he paid for! When I closed out his estate
more than $10,000 was owed him and only he knew who the people
were. I didn't go to church for eight years. I could not understand why
anyone as good as Wayne Smith had to die so painfully. I resented it. He
lived a good life yet died a horrible death.

One day, Tom, my older boy, who was four, and I were driving by a church and he said, 'Who do you have to know to get in there?' He was asking a serious question. I began to think that perhaps I was depriving my boys for my personal reasons. So I went back. I still think, however, that the Methodists build bigger churches only to impress the Presbyterians.

In New Burlington the weight of sin was so enormous. So out of perspective. You sinned and spent the rest of your life paying. At revival meetings they came and got the little kids. I was in the second grade and they got me so worked up. I'd shout and carry on. I was converted every night. I was converted so many times that year I never had to bother the rest of my life. We went up every night and they would say they had so many conversions. They listed them. Fifty. Sixty. More than half were very young schoolchildren who didn't know any better. I confessed and yet I didn't know what I was confessing to. In Sunday school we were taught about the world. China was filled with heathens. Everyone there was a heathen. Later the Methodist minister went crazy, running down the street with no clothes on. It was a very hush-hush thing. Perhaps the spirit of the Lord moved him, I thought.

All social life revolved around the church. And in church the poor souls Douse Wood and Roy Harvey were saved. They drank. They got saved in April. In May they were drunk again. The church needed them perhaps more than they needed the church. They gave the church a mission. The same souls were saved over and over. There weren't a lot of souls in New Burlington.

Horace and Lucy Compton prayed for me in open meeting. 'O God give us back the young people who are becoming so wild.' I was not a bad child. I went to the Epworth League on Sunday nights only to get a date. Then we went up to the graveyard and parked. I was only necking. The old ones enjoyed no aspect of life. Sex, like everything else, was a duty. The dresses were down to *there*, up to *here*. Such primness and propriety. Some young thing gets married. What a *shock.* suddenly everything is revealed. There is suddenly an elbow. The shoulders. An entire leg, perhaps. Such a traumatic experience. No wonder sex was considered a wifely duty. A *chore.* It wasn't my idea of it. If some of the people of New Burlington had lived together before they were married perhaps they wouldn't have *been* married. Some of them were married for fifty years and didn't speak to each other for thirty. I sat and thought: my God they even *look* alike.

We were not allowed to say the word 'whiskey,' yet the family was full of drunks. Uncle Les died a drunkard. Aunt Ren was 90 and died pickled. She was a schoolteacher in New Burlington. Aunt Hattie drank, and

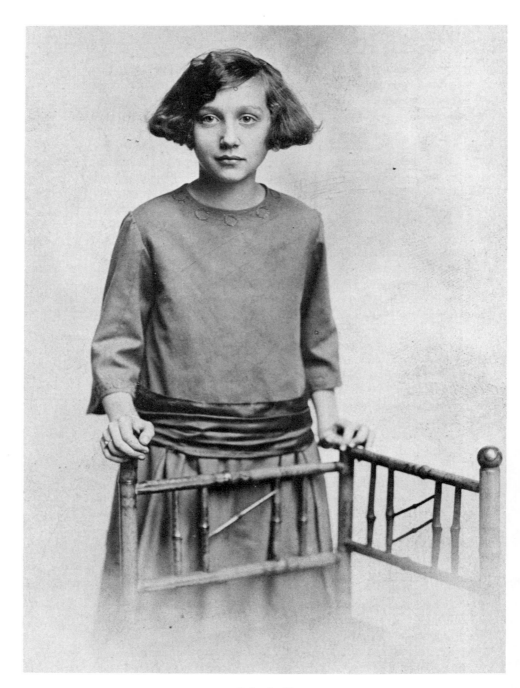

Ruby Smith

Wayne Smith

Uncle Will, and grandmother was head of the WCTU. Aunt Nancy had an illegitimate child and the Smiths said, 'Well, she isn't quite *right*. She didn't know any better.' Of course, she knew better. She was doing what she wanted to do. She got caught. It was a disgrace to the name and so they excused it by saying she was like a child and she didn't know what she was doing. She knew, and she probably did it plenty of times afterward, too. As a child I knew there was something that was never mentioned about Aunt Nancy. She just sat on the porch and rocked. She was enormous. She never said anything. Then when I got older, I knew that one of the Blair boys was her son.

Neither could Uncle Harley contain all the urges. He was the great mind. The intellect. He was marvelous in front of a class, teaching Elizabethan literature. But I found him a vile old man. He considered himself religious, and every time we got a new minister, he was right up in the Smith pew for about six weeks. That was about as long as he could take it, then you did not see him again until we got another minister.

We always had Smith reunions and with nine brothers and sisters in Dad's family, it was quite a gathering. We had it every summer. One year Uncle Harley tried to branch out and bring in all the cousins and he wrote to a cousin down around Clay, Ky., and invited him to be a house guest. Cousin Smith of Kentucky wrote back that he was honored and would love to come but he must tell him one thing: he was a colored man. Uncle Harley's research came to an abrupt end. I suspect Cousin Smith was a legitimate Smith, but we heard no more. We laughed at Harley so much he never came to the reunion again. So the Smiths had colored blood. My grandfather, I knew, was a blacksmith, but I had never thought of it that way!

When Harley got into the Smiths, he found many things he didn't want to face. He could never put down in the family history that his two brothers were drunks. My dad always said: say good about others, or nothing. And he did. I never say anything good about Uncle Harley, however, and I said this to him. You shouldn't do this, he said, or that. And all the time I knew he would love to be doing it himself. I didn't like him and I didn't go to his funeral. I said if I didn't go see him when he was living. I certainly wasn't going to see him when he was dead. He is secure in the community, and I imagine I am, too, in their eyes. But my life has been full, and I carry no burden of guilt.

In 1932, I was in summer school at Wilmington College and dad had just bought me a new car, a new Ford with wire wheels—my, it was good looking!—and I drove fast and up over the hill past Uncle Harley's house and I hit an old hen. I thought it went off the road someplace because I didn't see it anywhere. Two or three days later the car began boiling over and I stopped in the garage and the mechanic found the old chicken flattened against the radiator. I had just sucked it right up, and Uncle Harley was standing there. He said I was a hellion. Such a strict, narrow world of judgments and hypocrisy! I could not live in this world.

The Smiths made conscious choices to get away from New Burlington because of its provincialism. Roy, Will, Les. They went to the cities. To the life they wanted. Those who stayed settled into such a life. Great boys. Fine boys, But *dull* boys. They were frightened to go out. Always pushing the wheelbarrow of responsibility. In Burlington, everyone had a place. Everyone was accepted. Outside, there was no place. Outside were things they didn't know about. But there were no mysterious corners in New Burlington. Even going into Xenia, or Wilmington, scared them. There was an aroma of sin about these places. Move to Dayton, and you were lost to the legions of Hell. We sometimes visited Uncle Will on Saturday night, and there were parties. I think perhaps dad sneaked into the kitchen and had a drink with Uncle Will. My mother would die.

We were put to bed early but I remember the laughter and lights up and down the streets. When we returned home, I felt that coming back was so terrible. I had seen how you *could* live. I saw people laughing and having fun. Even as a child, I wanted to live this way. In no time, however, we were back and into Epworth League and the church and the old Chatauqua plays on a drab little stage in the Methodist church. I thought: *if I have to live this way the rest of my life* . . .

I remember rebelling when I was 11 or 12. I knew who ran to Dayton on Saturday night to the whore-houses. I knew who had a huckster route and who spent the morning with whom. Could they have been drinking coffee all that time? There were cock fights under the pool hall but the children were not supposed to know of such a thing. We never thought to ask how Banty Blair got his name. We were never to go there. If we went for ice cream Jumbo handed it out the window. So you were who you were. Comptons, Haydocks, Hawkinses, Joneses. All so deeply imbedded in their religion. Yet I looked back and wondered: how *really* religious? I had no inhibitions and I was resented for this. If I wanted to do something, I did it. Perhaps it was because I was not disciplined like the others.

Of four children, I was the only girl, you see. Dad always wanted a girl. My childhood was beautiful. I was a child of privilege. Our front stairs were winding and we had the first bathroom inside. I never remember not having a bathroom. We had the first radio and people used to come to our house to look at it. It was an old Atwater-Kent wireless and all we got on it was static and once in a while the weather.

My mother had a washwoman, a nursewoman and a lady in to iron.

They were hired help, however, not servants. That was an important distinction. Dad never drove so he had a driver but not a chauffeur. He could have had a limousine with a liveried chauffeur. But that would have been living above the people of New Burlington. He would not do that. He was one of them and he stayed one of them until he died. Mother made dad dress up to meet one of the bank presidents. 'Now, Wayne,' she said, 'you have to put on a shirt and a tie.' He said, 'No, I don't have to do anything.' He went to Xenia once with his pants held up with a piece of twine. Dad knew the president of the Xenia National Bank was the biggest woman chaser in the county. Why should he put forth any impression for him? He didn't care if he made an impression on anyone. He was largely what he was. He dressed on Sunday, however. This was tradition. Some things he was very traditional about.

Bob and I were educated during the depression but we always had automobiles. My dad never wanted anyone to know we had money and when we bought a new car he'd apologize. We had to apologize for anything we owned which was new. This was the Quaker influence on the village, you see. You never made a display of worldly goods. Dad would be embarrassed for several weeks after buying a new car. We had to say Albert Chenoweth got him a good deal on it. I had to say this to my friends, and I resented it. It made me rebellious.

We went east in a new Buick with isinglass windows and curtains for the rain. We went up into the Adirondacks, into Washington and Philadelphia. Dad displayed farm implements at the county fair and as soon as that was over we went on vacation. I think the people in the village resented this. We did things no one else did, you see. They *could* have, some of them, but they wouldn't. They never wanted to get out. They were secure and so they stayed forever. It was good for the community but it was narrowing.

After the first six weeks at Ohio Wesleyan, I was on probation for drinking elderberry wine. My brother, Forrest, was on probation, too. I'll tell you what for. He and Norman Vincent Peale made a still in the basement of their fraternity.

Two summers, I drove for dad to earn my allowance. He told Bob Collett one afternoon that he was going out and collect from someone who had owed him for a long time. So I drove like a bat out of hell and we got there and dad stayed and stayed. Finally we got back to the village and Bob came out and said, 'Well, how'd you do? Did you collect?'

And dad 'No, by God, I didn't. But I sold the sonofabitch a manure spreader . . .'

I was very lucky. I had marvelous parents. Of course, everyone likes to think he has good stock, a fine heritage. I want to know where I came from, and that it's good. In the back of my mind always is the Smith name. *Never do anything to desecrate the image. Don't hurt the name.* This is so inbred it will come out. Yet I go ahead and do what I want as long as no one knows about it. A contradiction in myself. The contradictions, too, come down. It is inherent in me. I cannot completely get away. When my husband, Eddie, and I became parents, we went back to the old instinct. *We mustn't drink in front of the boys. We mustn't swear in front of the boys. The family must stay together.* It sounded as though our ancestors were talking. We sat down one night and said, 'Look. We don't *believe* this.'

The name, the name. I was always Wayne Smith's daughter. But he was one of a kind and there was no hypocrisy between us. He knew exactly who I was. He knew I wasn't bad, too, but he knew I was strong enough that if I wanted to do something, I would. He never tried force, and my respect for him came from the tolerance. I worshiped him. One night, I had a date and Dallas Marshall and I were in the living room until 2 o'clock. At 2 o'clock he started pounding on the floor. 'When he gets to pounding, Dallas,' I said, 'better get out.' Dad never said anything the next day. Mother and I had crosscurrents. Why did you do this? Why did you stay out late? What did you do? Where did you go? Of course, I never told her. I didn't think she should ask. I never asked my boys. I don't think dad cared if I was up until 2 o'clock. It just didn't look good for Wayne Smith's daughter to have a boy in the house until 2 o'clock.

When I was young, I was engaged to this boy and we eloped. We get as far as Alpina, Michigan, and when we got there it was after five o'clock and the courthouse was closed. So I said, 'I don't really want to marry you. I want to go home.' So I made him bring me home, and we got there at 2 o'clock in the morning and the sheriff was waiting for my fiancé for forgery. And of course I had been missing. The boy's father was cashier of the bank dad was president of. He bought my wedding ring with checks he signed my dad's name to. We got back and on the fourth of July he shot himself. That made headlines in the Xenia *Gazette*. I felt terrible at the time but it didn't last long. He lived, although he had a hole in his lung. After I had him, you see, I didn't want him. I did that three different times before I got married. Whatever I could have, I didn't want. The thing I couldn't have was most desirable. But when I did get married, it was as near perfect as possible.

Eddie was like I was. We were wilder than March hares. If we decided to take off at 4 o'clock in the morning, we put the kids in the back seat and took off. Even through such a thing as the elopement, however, dad was sympathetic. Never once did he reprimand me. I had been gone for two days. This caused the greatest commotion in New Burlington. It was a long time before I went back to church. I knew they would say, 'Well, she had certainly better be in church.' I looked out across the pews and thought: *where were all of you last night . . . ?*

After school, I thought I would never return to New Burlington but I did because my dad wanted me. I taught school in the village for five years. He said that if I would come home he would pay me the same salary as I got teaching. Just to have me at home. The first year I taught, I bought a mink coat and a Buick. My salary as a teacher was $78 a month. I was there not because dad paid me but because he wanted me. After Christmas of 1939 I took them both to Florida and stayed with them until March. The day he came back he went to bed and never got up. He told mother not to tell me: he had cancer. But she had to tell me or I wouldn't have stopped teaching. She stayed with him during the day, and I sat with him at night. I never slept at night. He didn't want me out of his sight the last few months, and I never left the house. It was the first death I had to experience. It was very difficult for me to accept. I never fully got over it. Belle Haydock wrote his obituary and read it at his funeral. She read from a poem: He lived in a house by the side of the road, and was a friend to man. *Yes,* I thought.

After his death, I left. Bob, who had gone in with dad in 1936, took over the business. But Bob couldn't stand it, either. He wouldn't even live in New Burlington. He lived in Xenia, played golf on Wednesday afternoons, wore knickers and drove a LaSalle town car. You do not call on New Burlington farmers in a LaSalle town car, wearing a coat and tie. So the business began going down. When I closed out after dad died, the business was in debt about $21,000, which in those days was a lot of money. I would have loved to have stayed there, but I could not. I wanted it to change and when it did change it changed to a different class of people who were in no way connected to the deeply ingrained religiously narrow-minded people of New Burlington. It was a change for the worse. New Burlington died then, during the war years, with the influx of new people, the factory workers. I wanted change but not this. The community broke down and the land got away to outsiders.

I truly loved the village but not its lifestyle. So staid, so provincial, those old Quakers. Their huge sense of sin. No one must be happy because to to be happy one is suspect. We are on the earth to make a living and live for God. But I was what I was and if I wanted a drink, why, I had one.

In school, I have tried to teach my children basics. We will not be perfect. We will have idiosyncracies. We will perhaps seek that which is exciting or different. So we establish guidelines. Consider others in proximity to yourself. Be loving, and do not cause injury. The human principles, you see. Mine are: live a peaceful life, and have a drink if you want to.

They can say New Burlington was different from other communities but it was not. The villagers had their shames and disgraces. I hold no resentment, however, just a great sadness. Something has gone that will never be again. In spite of the hypocrisy, we were all very close. The good things override the marginal things. I still had an intimate relationship with all parts of it. I was just as much a hypocrite as anyone while I was there. I did the way they did. But they knew I was not that way. At any moment I might fly off and there was no telling what I might do. New Burlington was a lifestyle that was typical of its time. But it could not perpetuate itself. The ones who stayed there were ones who couldn't stay anyplace else. But it is gone and so is our sense of community. We seek community today and we do not find it. I was too outspoken, they said. I did not understand. But later, I did understand: no one wants to hear the truth . . .

The Doctor

A woman is having a baby. 'Doctor
Whitaker,' she says, 'what position
should I be in?' Doctor Whitaker says,
'The same as when you got this way.'
And the woman says, 'My God! You
mean I have to have my feet sticking
out of the buggy?'

—village story

Watching the farmers regard the moon for statement, Dr. Smith perhaps feels himself an impostor. Should a man consider signs? In his bag are Belladonna and pepsin. No more than incantations. And where is science in the face of: obscure poultices, cobwebs for bleeding, a slab of salt fat on a nail wound, chewing tobacco for toothache, a bag of heated salt on an ear ache? He once considered being a carpenter. He thought he built well. Like the Dutchman's duck, he said. Not much for looks but hell for stout. But neither carpenters nor moon-watchers are so frail as physicians.

Dr. Smith spreads himself over the countryside like a palliative. He is physician, dentist, obstetrician, dietician, health inspector, veterinarian (less than fifty years before there were only 46 veterinarians in the United States), apothecary, farm manager, lodge keeper, confidant, husband, father. After making his rounds, dozing in the buggy while ancient but great-winded Harry finds the way home, he thinks that he too would like the delicious isolation of a restful disease.

Sometimes he envies the rowdy disposition of his friend, Dr. Turnbull of the nearby village, who prescribes with impartiality medicine, advice, or blasphemy. Dressing for one of the few social events he ever had occasion to attend he was called to look at the injured limb of an old lady whose prior treatment was a cow dung poultice. When his freshly starched cuffs ended up in the poultice he yelled at the rafters. "Goddamn such a heathenish practice! I'll send for the veterinarian!"

Above the village was the summer home of a wealthy family from Day-

Dr. Smith and family

ton. The daughter rode a bicycle, wore bloomers, and kept a pet monkey, all of which contributed to her reputation as overbold. The monkey developed a skin condition and its hair began to fall off. The bloomered daughter on a Sunday rode her bicycle into the village and up to the doctor's fence where she found him in his porch swing.

"Doc, I want your advice," she shouted over the gate. "I don't know what's the matter. But all the hair is coming off my monkey."

"Stay off the damned bicycle," Dr. Turnbull answered, "and it'll grow back."

We may silently admire such anarchy but we may not all participate. Dr. Smith has not the temperament. He is regarded as a pious man, a bit stately, remote. He was born in a log cabin. In winter mornings the snow drifted through the attic clapboards and piled on the outside of his coverlets. He broke ice in the bucket for a morning wash. He was bound out to a wealthy relative for low pay and high work. Afterward, he became a teacher in the hill country south. The schoolhouse, he said, was in the only place it could have been. Part of the way the creek was in the road and the rest of the way the road was in the creek. Some of the girls chewed tobacco. He worked his way through medical school and came north where he considered himself a self-made man. He tried to maintain perspective, however. When he pronounced himself self-made he quoted Horace Greeley who said about such a man: it relieves the Almighty of a terrible responsibility.

The country practice is consuming, debilitating. When the telephone comes he thinks it may alleviate distance. Instead, it *creates* distance. He may be summoned. The bells ring in the night and an unfamiliar voice, disconnected from a familiar person, calls him out into the valley where he drives old Harry through the countryside past dim yellow lights flickering occasionally in farmhouses behind endless lanes under the full weight of the stars. Before the night air clears his mind of sleep he sometimes feels the whole valley is malevolent, that unutterable substances wait for him. He uses a disinfectant on the metal receiver of the telephone box and in his mind he sees the disinfectant spreading throught the lines, dripping silently into farmhouses.

Because there are three telephone systems in the nearby country he must have three telephones. Days and nights often blur. Each telephone is one of several on a party line. Each family has its own ring and each telephone a slightly different tone. Sometimes two telephones ring at once. People use the doctor's telephones to transfer messages from one system to another. During threshing season entire evenings are given to the passing of messages. He is called from the dinner table three times before he is able to say grace. He returns wearily to sit, heads bow, he says in his firm professional voice, "Hello!"

The country people pay with what they have. Often it is not money. While he is inside the farmhouse, trying to catch fever in the sieve of a tenuous knowledge, they slip butter and jugs of milk into his buggy. "Coal to corn, labor to lumber, meat to masonry," says his son who becomes instead a teacher.

When the automobile comes he buys that, too. And after a wild ride down a gravel road with the Maxwell salesman chooses instead a 1912 four-cylinder Buick touring car which will spend the winter jacked up on blocks in the buggy shed, secured with the white cover that once went on his wife's phaeton. He sits on the right side as he sat in the buggy. In a sharp curve he slides out into a field and into a pig. One of his best friends is enticed into an automobile on only one occasion: his own funeral.

A farmer stops the doctor and forbids him to drive past his farm because the machine sends his stock into fits of madness. The lights, attached to a magneto, dim to nearly nothing when going up a hill. Magnificent old Harry, now at 30, pulls the doctor's sister to Xenia but spends more and more time in the pasture. The automobile like the telephone creates more work. He is to be faster, go farther. He has both, yet life expectancy is still 40 years. In his bag are still asafoetida, laudanum, castor oil, and calomel. *Men and green things, all mend or they rot. We have science and cylinders but also diphtheria.*

While treating a smallpox victim under quarantine the doctor keeps a long white robe in the upstairs wardrobe near the front window. To keep away from everyone else as much as possible he dresses in the white robe, climbs out the window and down over the porch to pick up his bag. He returns the same way, removes the robe near the window, standing in his underwear while he sprays it and himself with disinfectant. Children, considering germs as invisible leeches sucking health, pinch their noses while walking past his house. His son is ostracized at school until the doctor keeps him home.

The daughter of one of his backwoods patients returns home unwed to have her child. Presiding at the delivery the doctor sterilizes the water bucket while the girl's mother chastizes her daughter. "Do you suppose," says the daughter painfully, "it could have happened to me in my sleep?"

"Indeed not!" shouts the mother. "That's the most wakenest thing that is!"

Survival yields minimally to craft. It retains mystery and unpredictability, like sunbaked clay holds to itself. He finds the mind largely curious.

His friend, Dr. Whitaker, who organized New Burlington's telephone company, keeps the switchboard in his house and performs lineman's duties, persuades him to take time off to go coon hunting. Dr. Whitaker wears his lineman's pole climbers into the woods. They allow him to climb a tree after the racoon. They laugh through the midnight woods but Dr. Smith hears the triple bells of telephones in his inner ear. He feels guilty because he is not in his office. To monitor pain.

Dr. Turnbull is taken to the Xenia Hospital where his friends come to wish him well. "We hope to see you again soon," they say. "You will," he replies calmly. "In a box." He tells Dr. Smith that he is worn out, that he is dying. *Diagnosis correct to the last*, thinks Dr. Smith at his funeral. *Peace to his ashes and rest his good soul.* When Dr. Smith himself dies, it is in a peculiar accident: he falls off the running board of an automobile and fractures his skull. If there had been time and consciousness, he might have been surprised.

He is buried near the church he helped build. Although held in the feverish heat of August the doctor's funeral is attended by a crowd larger than the one at the church's anniversary. This too might have surprised him. The doctor's son, a scholar, quotes a German proverb: Der brave Mann denkt an sich selbst, zuletzt. *The brave man thinks of himself last.*

Patients

A catalogue of incidence in which the people in and around the village of New Burlington are born, suffer, heal, and die.

✵ Herman Jones's suicide.

Herman Jones, because of the mumps, is in severe and perpetual pain. After several weeks he kills himself.

✵ The amputation of Sam Ellis's leg.

Sam Ellis is cutting wood when a tree falls on his leg. The leg is amputated by a Catholic doctor with a pocketknife who pauses first to offer a sentence of prayer. Mrs. Ellis has the leg embalmed, places it in a baby's casket and buries it. There is a short ceremony over Sam's leg at the Methodist church. Sam lives on for another twenty years. When he dies he is buried beside his leg.

✵ Warren Shidaker goes through the manure spreader, as told by Sarah Shidaker.

"Eddie and the boys were cleaning out the chickenhouse. They went across the road with a load of manure, Morris on Eddie's lap and Warren standing in the back. He was holding onto the spikes which shred the manure. It was July of 1921 and Warren was six. As they were returning, the spreader ran over a stone and went into gear. For a moment, Warren was the manure. He went in so far he locked the wheels with his little body. Eddie had the awfullest time. The spikes were digging into him, you see. I had dinner ready and Eddie came in holding Warren up, by his waist. 'The little boy is hurt awfully bad,' he said. He was calm as a summer sky. We got in the automobile and went to Dr. Randall at Harveysburg. 'My God, Ed,' he said. 'This is no case for me. I'll call ahead to Hale's Hospital.' We went to Wilmington and Dr. Hale laid him on a table. He said to my brother, Jim, 'You better leave because I can only care for one patient at a time.' Jim said, 'I can take it.' When Dr. Hale began, Jim fainted and fell on his face. Afterward Dr. Hale said, 'Here's your boy and I wouldn't give you a dime for him.' That was Kelly Hale. Straightforward and a bit crude. 'Thank God his guts weren't punctured,' he said. Warren was in the hospital three weeks. Cut? My lands. Hipbone to hipbone. They took straw out of his side. You could feel the knots of catgut in his groin."

❋ Entry from Ralph Baker's diary, December 3, 1936.

"Today Doctor Johnson filled one tooth with gold, one with silver amalgam, and extracted $4.50 from my pocketbook."

❋ Ray Taylor's tonsillectomy.

"Life is the last thing we want to give up. We are constructed that way. Even if it is painful. Old Doc Vandiman treated me when I had unguent fever. I said, 'Doc, I feel like I'd be better off gone.' He said, 'Hell, no, Ray. You don't know what's waiting for you over yonder.' When I was seven I had my tonsils out. Doc Murrell and dad took me on the train to Washington Courthouse to Doc Huey. He had a chair like a barber's chair. Dr. Murrell sat in the chair and put me in his lap, wrapped his legs around mine and held me. I remember that Doc Huey had a beard. It was murder in the first degree. No way to cut flesh without pain. Afterward, I walked to the depot, back to the train. I'm still here. It is just one thing that happens to you."

❋ Shirley Wilson's comment on hearing his wife has triplets.

"If I'd have known you were going to have a litter I'd have taken you to the barn."

❋ Sarah Shidaker discusses cures.

"For pneumonia there was turpentine and lard, put on the chest. A mush poultice for quinsy. Onion tea for coughs and colds and catnip tea for squalling babies with the colic. Mouldy bread poultices for a wound of some kind and perhaps a piece of side meat wrapped around the neck for a sore throat. And sheep tea—brew the little dumplings, you know— for milk fever perhaps. Those who had a degree of superstition burned onion leaves every Monday to head off evil spirits. When I was just a small girl I had the measles and knew I would die. They heated corn in sacks and pressed them around me to make me break out. Lib Hawkins brought me an orange and I put it under my pillow. I thought: how they will grieve for me after I've gone and they find this orange under my pillow. Comforts were hung on the windows to keep the light away from my eyes. They said you would go blind. It was only the measles but I knew people who never saw a well day after the measles."

* Howard Leaming has the flu.

"I am thinking that the second hitch of influenza came the following spring, in 1919. I got sick on a Sunday evening, sitting in a rocker. I got up and fell on the floor like the rocker had been upset. I was delirious for ten days and was reported dead. The only thing I can remember is a great big nigger trying to get in bed with me. I fought him and kicked him until I couldn't wiggle my toes and he came back for more. I lost fifty pounds. My hair came out, it felt like great handfulls of straw. Water tasted just like cistern water and everybody knows how cistern water tastes. . ."

* Rose Devoe's mother has the milk leg.

"I couldn't nurse because of the milk leg so they took me down to Josephine Blair's and Dena and I nursed at the same time. That saved my life. When we were older and they told us about that, we decided we were sisters. She was my very best friend and she died when she was 10 of the scarlet fever. She had five brothers and they were quarantined out of the house so the Colvins propped her coffin up in the window so the boys could see their little sister. They were heartbroken and could not be consoled.

* Newspaper item from the New Burlington correspondent.

"Last night while crossing the viaduct on his way home from the service in the Methodist church, Reverend Henry Witham was stricken down with apoplexy."

* A recording of Samuel Compton's final illness.

"During the first three weeks of his illness he suffered but little, often remarking that he felt easy in body and mind. On the 16th of February, 1861, he observed he had felt doubts from the first as to how his illness would terminate and said he never before had such a foretaste of heaven and heavenly things, and this favor had been continued to him almost continuously from the commencement of his illness. He felt he had nothing to do but arrange his temporal business. On the evening of the 18th after the scriptures were read, he entreated those around him to prepare for the final charge, saying, 'The fields look as green to harvest as I have ever seen them . . .' He prayed for the whole human family particularly the slaves under oppression. To a friend he remarked, 'I want thee to take notice that I die in full faith. I have followed no cunningly devised fable, but the pure and living substance.' He loved plainness and a few days before his death, he gave directions for his funeral, desiring that the coffin might be entirely plain. He often said: 'There is not even a shadow of a cloud in my way.' He said, 'We deliver all to thee, O Lord,' and he ceased to breathe."

* Charles and Ladonna Stanley comment on hardship within the family.

"My mother has died," says Ladonna, "my aunt was found dead, Uncle Lawrence just died, Charles's brother was badly hurt in a wreck, and our daughter's father-in-law seriously injured his hand in an industrial accident."

"And," says Charles, "we got an old cat over home that don't look too good either . . ."

* Carl Smith considers living to be 86.

"I do not know why I have lived so long and healthy. Possibly restraint and awkwardness. Good luck and narrow escapes. My medical history is outrageous. Once I fell 27 feet off a balcony. When I came to, my classmates were seated around me like an Irish wake.

'Keep still,' they said.

'Why?' I asked. 'Will I fall apart?'

I got up and walked down to breakfast.

In 1916 I had an appendectomy. It was done by Dr. Ben McClellan. He prayed before all his operations so I say I was opened with prayer.

A long life is partly care, more mystery. Providence watches over fools and children. And I'm no kid."

The Farmers

*Roy Conklin was driving his wagon
into the village when he came upon
Nellie McKinney who was walking.*
"Give you a ride, Nellie?" he asked.
*"No, thanks, Roy," said Nellie. "I'm
in a hurry."*

—village story

Albert McKay is a grown man when he first hears of the forty-hour week. He thinks it must be a joke. He tells his neighbors across the fence that people are beginning to take half the week off. He and Walter Lackey are running the threshing machine when their wives call them to dinner but they are not ready to quit. "Women made the forenoon," says Walter while he watches Albert across a plate of fried chicken, "but God Almighty will make the afternoon." They return to the fields where they remain until it is dark. Coming home they tunnel through the dusk like miners. They are tired but a little arrogant. "A day," says Albert to Walter, "is as long as the Lord makes it."

This is the way the McKays begin. Into the fields at first light when the shadows are grotesque. And ripple across the ground where they are painfully thin. Albert is ten years old. He is afraid but not of the shadows. Sixty years later, watching his grandsons drive huge tractors in fields he plowed with horses, he remembers that day. It seems clearer to him than any of the days in the last week.

* *My father wanted to see how game I was, how stout. He left me to put out two acres of corn with a two-horse plow in an alfalfa field. The field had been in alfalfa for years. The roots were as big as your thumb and the plow fairly vibrated. Shook me this way. If you didn't get out of the furrow the roots would fly back and crack you across the shin. They snapped around me like a dry brush fire. I ran the plow under a root, finding it very hard to bear down on the handles to raise the tip. There I was, yelling*

'Get up there! Get up there!' in my tiny soprano voice. I had to come home for the ax and cut my way through. It was new ground and I turned it. I was itching to get hold of those handles. There wasn't a very thick stand but it was awful good-eared. I got 70 bushels to the acre. That was my working acquaintance with horses . . .

* He never wishes to farm any other way. He courts his horses as if they were handsome women whom he admires. At one time there are nine horses and mules. They are strong-minded and idiosyncratic, reminding him of his sons. The black mule will crowd over when plowing near ditches. The brown one pulls the gate pins with his teeth. The sorrel and the blind Percheron will run away with the manure spreader. Maude brays at noon in the fields.

In the spring Albert keeps Maude in the barn near her harness. This is because the road gets soft in the spring and the machines get stuck often. Albert charges the motorists but after two times he does it for nothing. "Once there was a fellow drove into my cornfield at 1 a.m. He said he was going to see a girl down the road. He was going to pay me next time. I guess he never got back to see her. So I stopped charging because it felt bad to have people dodging me."

He feels it is his duty to help people out of the spring mud because his grandfather built the two miles of road from above his house into New Burlington. His grandfather and Jack Mitchner who plowed up the road-bed with a six-horse team. And walked beside his horses talking softly into their velvet ears.

Albert's neighbor to the west, Frank Lundy, shares his affinity for horses, and good corn in straight rows. The road that passes the farms of Frank and Albert runs east and west but Frank's corn rows run north and south. This is not without design: Frank thinks he can plow as straight a corn row as anybody in the country. "It showed well running north and south," he says, "gave a different look to the field and made a very nice picture. They would say at the bank, 'I saw your corn rows . . .' "

The Anderson's Fork bottomlands are famous for good corn. Albert remembers hearing a story about them which was passed along from a time just after the Civil War. Thomas Haydock is making a pair of boots in his shop while the barn carpenter, William Hood, stands in the back door looking across the creek. It is early summer and between the syca-mores on the creek bank the tiny green shoots of corn are already pressing upward where they will soon obscure the horizon.

"You have traveled," says Thomas Haydock to the barn carpenter, "and where in the country do the best lands lie?"

Ada and Albert McKay

The barn carpenter does not turn from his view. "Anderson's Fork bottoms, sir," he says.

When Frank Lundy was much younger, before he began plowing the bottomlands, he was uncertain about the work he would do. He watched his brothers and waited for a sign. There were five boys and two girls in Calvin J. Lundy's house and whenever someone asked Calvin how many boys he had he said, "Thirty feet, six inches." One son became a carpenter. Another became a teacher. One went to town where he was watched by Frank who said finally, "I didn't like the way he had to do." He then said to his father, "Farming is all there is." Once this vow of country asceticism was taken, Frank rented some ground for wheat, worked it with three horses, and kept close records. "You're not supposed to keep records," snorted old Calvin. "Take what you can and forget about the rest."

By the time Frank begins to farm the bottomlands he is no longer an apprentice. He brings the horses in from the fields at six o'clock and eats his supper sitting afterward on a fence and watching the livestock eat. At such times it seems that all sounds flow together into a stately music that he has never heard anyplace else. He is surrounded by a thousand living things. The barn expands with the heat from the horses' bodies. The hogs crowd together while eating and in the growing dark become a single vast low beast spreading across the yards. The cicadas scream in the grass. He thinks that he can hear the corn pushing its way through the earth. He thinks he can look to the ends of his fields and over the curvature of the earth.

In late summer the cornfields surround New Burlington with a density which visitors find startling. They are not prepared for this forest of stalks, plume and ear. In august the stalks climb until the roads into the village become canopied. Farmhouses disappear. Green shingles, green stalks, green thoughts. By September the silken plume has darkened. The earth tilts under harvest weight.

Albert, too, contemplates his fields. He is putting an edge on his corn knife with the grinding stone. At dark in the waiting breath between full ear and harvest, Albert walks through his fields. Sometimes there are tides in the deep cornfields which give them a surface life. Under the moon the leaves move when no wind is felt. Albert stands in the fields where he feels his feet root into the dark soil. He can feel the blood pulse in the veins of his arms and his weariness lifts and he thinks that he and his horses will go on forever.

The McKay genealogy runs through the farmhouse and over the countryside, filled with living McKays, and into the graveyard between Albert's house and Frank's, filled with the legendary McKays. And into the fields where Albert's maiden great-aunts lie buried under the corn.

The McKays, like Albert and his father, Clarence, are modest, unassuming. Neighbors sometimes talk about "the McKay money" as if it were a solid and precious lump buried someplace nearby but no one sees evidence of McKay wealth except in the fields during a good season. When Clarence buys a new suit he orders it to be made exactly like the one which he has just worn out. It is only in the fields that the McKays are immodest. Here they are bold, unabashed, almost fierce.

Albert's great-great-grandfather, Moses, came in 1818 from Virginia. Albert says Moses was following rumor. "They heard people brag on Ohio land," he says. Moses McKay brought 11 sons, enough to buy 1,600 acres of land, and horses to plow it. Albert's great-grandfather, Francis, 16 years old, drove the horses through while Moses and his other sons came on a flatboat with the gold. Albert tells his grandsons that the reason no one stole it was because Moses' boys sat on it.

"They were so lazy they just sat there. And they were so heavy no one could lift them off. Three of them weighed a thousand pounds. Francis was a big man, too. But he married a little bitty Frenchwoman and some of the kids didn't seem up to snuff."

The land begins at the New Burlington Road where Albert now farms and stretches into the next county south. Moses paid three dollars an acre. Most of the land was still forest and had to be cleared. Such a family as this is watched carefully for signs of sloth, neglect, and insufficiency. These are qualities which would make the McKays vulnerable and therefore more equal.

The family has always been a landowning people, which is possibly why they are considered wealthy. They can trace their history back to the early 13th century in Scotland where there, too, the McKays raised livestock and grain. This was even before the Norsemen were expelled. In Scotland the McKays were blunt, intractable. Their name itself is the English equivalent of the Gaelic which means "son of the impetuous one." Theirs was the longest highland feud in Scottish history. For four centuries they fought almost continuously to protect their ancestral lands from invasion and claims of feudal superiority. Such perseverance is not lost over obscure centuries. Character is transformed but not diluted. It is others, however, who speak most of McKay history. And only McKays refer to other McKays as "lazy," in that manner in which only intimate friends can carelessly profane each other.

When Albert's sixth child, Rosalie, is born he is threshing wheat and does not know that Ada has been taken to Jamestown. She goes at 2 p.m. and Albert learns of this when he leaves the fields at 6 with the horses. Before he goes to see Ada, however, he plows the potato patch. He is pleased to learn that Ada has given birth to a daughter. "That evened them up," he says, explaining his pleasure. "Three fellows. Three girls. I had my boys to follow me around for company and by that time I had three following me and I'd just as lief she was a girl because I couldn't herd many more . . ."

Albert's conception of time remains old-fashioned; he watches the light instead of a clock. He tells a story about a fellow from Xenia driving into the country where he sees a New Burlington farmer holding a pig so that it can eat apples off a tree beside the road.

> *What you doing with that pig? asks the man.*
> *Feeding him, says the farmer.*
> *Don't that take a lot of time? asks the man.*
> *What's time to a damn old hog? says the farmer.*

He teaches his sons to work as he works. If he has not finished by dusk he works on until he cannot see. He says, "I'll do that at any cost." Although tractors are beginning to be seen in the neighborhood Albert plows with a two-bottom gang plow pulled by five horses. He has liked a walking plow since the day he was ten and plowed the alfalfa field by himself. He likes the way the dark ground peels off the moldboard in the spring when the sweet smell of the earth rises from the furrows to overwhelm him. He stays in his fields until dark and plows five acres. Later he will tell his grandsons about this work. "I thought I had it made," he says. "I put out a hundred acres of corn and thought I had a dickens of a crop. Yah! Woah! Hey! Get in that furrow! Gee-up! That old plow threw the dirt. I could let my team go halfway down a 40-shock field and stand and talk over the fence. A shock was twelve steps and you measured that way because when you paid help you paid by the shock and sometimes if you weren't careful there was more shocks than supposed to be because some of the fellows tended to get a little short-legged late in the day. I have cut fourteen shocks of wheat next to the branch, helped fill two silos, plowed the potato patch and milked twice. By the time I got the second milking done I was awfully sorry I only got in twenty hours. I didn't know what to do with the rest of the day so I just went to bed . . ."

Albert thinks to himself: *a man still likes to keep up.* He remembers racing Jim Grimes with a corn knife. When he sets up a shock Jim is already one step ahead. Jim is hanging his knife on a leather strap from his wrist. When Albert does his knife the same way he manages to keep up. He cuts himself on a corn stub and bleeds in the field until he feels himself turn white. George Hosier spits tobacco in a dirty handkerchief and presses it to Albert's leg and the next day the cut is not sore. Jim works all day for a load of hay. "Get a sweat up," he says to Albert. "Get a sweat up. It's twice as easy with the sweat running."

Albert remembers Jim's wife, too. He was always a little bit afraid of Babe. But so was Jim. Babe wore a man's coat, work shoes, a bonnet. The brow of the bonnet threw a deep shadow over her face and Albert found it made him uneasy to look back into the darkness under the bonnet to meet her spiny gaze. It was like she was holding him on the ground until she decided what to do with him. People said Babe stole from gardens and had money buried in the ground. At the auction after she died people bought anything with upholstery on it and afterward they ripped the upholstery apart looking for the money they had heard about . People said she died on a pile of rags. When she was alive, Jim was afraid to use her side of the hay mow. When they argued, Jim went to the barn and slept. On his side.

At this time there are yet eccentrics in the countryside. Adam Ellis lives to the north of Albert, on Graveyard Road and through the covered bridge. He is very wealthy yet uses twine to hold up his pants. When someone asks Adam why he does not marry, Adam replies, "Why, it would cost me a hundred dollars a year to keep a woman." When he kills chickens he leaves the feet on because this makes it easier to turn them in the frying pan. He hides money in his seed bins and when he dies it is the finest funeral the Colvins will ever have. Velvet rope across the coffin and gold tassels as if to match the flowering corn in the bottomlands he worried about on his deathbed.

One day in the fall when the weather has turned cold Albert steps off a hundred yards and races his sons in the wheat field to keep warm. He tells them about running every May Day in high school, running home from Kingman beside the horse which is six miles and undoing the buggy shaft in the yard and jumping over it and falling down where his legs feel like glass and he thinks they have shattered.

In college at Ohio Wesleyan he makes the track team. "I got acquainted with a bunch of fellows who liked to run," he tells his sons. "Then I beat everybody in the first two classes. Everytime I heard someone puffing behind me I laid it on. The coach came over afterward and said, 'What do you do in the summertime?' I said, 'Drive cows for my dad.' He said, 'Couldn't be a better job.' I came back in the fall, he handed me a track suit. Once I asked a fellow name of Lowderback, a good two-miler and a football player too, which was harder. 'Why, don't you know?' he said. And I said, 'I don't know as I do.' He said, 'Well, in football you can call a *timeout*.' I once ran a four-mile race at Ohio State but I wore out before the finish. My legs just stopped working. A colored man name of Ferguson came along driving a nice machine and said, 'Get in, boy, and don't feel bad. I been picked up a few times myself.' He was a record holder there. Five men from every college in Ohio were running that day. Some got medals. I got hauled in but it was also free."

For a time, while he is in college, he thinks he may become a school-teacher. But when he comes home on holidays he goes straight to the barn to see the horses and throwing down hay from the loft the pitchfork in his hands feels strong and familiar.

One day much later in his life he and his son, Robert, mark off a quarter mile in the pasture but when they run Albert cannot begin to keep up. He thinks that Robert may become the best farmer of all his boys but Robert becomes a minister instead. Albert is disappointed although he knows that he must not be. "It takes a lot of faith to be a farmer, too," he says.

* *There is new hope in the promise of this clumsy century. In nearby Dayton, even as the Bishop Milton Wright thunders from his pulpit blasphemy to such dreamers his own blood betrays him: his sons conquer gravity in a dusty bicycle shop. And promise the moon to men in their time. The agent of such thaumaturgy will be machinery a steel-ribbed hunk of a word which rattles across the tongue a heavy blunt instrument of a sharp-edged word to bludgeon a reluctant age into manageable proportions. In New Burlington, Ohio, in the difficult fields, the farmer looks at the ill-conceived shapes of the new technology and turns reassuringly to his horses. He will not yet turn away from the muscle and blood pulling him through the furrows. If he is stubborn then it is a lesson learned well in the fields.*

* Albert's son, Wilbur, begins to farm nearby. Albert can see Wilbur's barns from his kitchen door. It seems that most of the horses are gone from the neighborhood and in their place is machinery which he sees everwhere. Albert can remember when there was none. This memory startles him because it tells him he must be very old to have seen such a change. He can remember his grandfather saying that in his time the worth of rail fences in Ohio exceeded the state indebtedness.

The machinery has crept into the fields, over the roads, and into the houses. Irving Blair has a refrigerator. It is sitting in the living room for everyone to see. Irving's mother is angry. She proclaims it unnecessary. "We have a cellar, Irving," she says. "Cold, fat stone." Young men learn to drive Model T Fords in their barnyards and when they learn to steer they drive out in the roads where they terrify the horses.

Jack Skimmings heads from New Burlington to Wilmington in a phaeton buggy pulled by his mare. On the graveyard hill below Albert's house they meet a man driving a motorbike. The mare takes the bit in her mouth, turns around and runs Mr. Skimmings back into his own barn. Mrs. Skimmings is watching from the porch.

"Why, Jack," she says, "I thought you were headed to Wilmington."

"Well, yes," Jack says, "I was headed to Wilmington but I met a fellow on one of those farting bicycles and the old mare brought me home . . ."

Howard Pickering the blacksmith drives his father in a Model T while the elder Mr. Pickering holds the door open, riding with one foot on the running board ready to leap into the fields. Rose Moss, the seamstress's daughter, cannot remember to use the brake. She pulls back on the steering wheel and yells for the motor to stop. Sarah Haydock learns to drive forward but she cannot learn to back because in reverse the driver must turn the wheel the opposite way. This seems inaccurate to her so she does not use reverse. Albert's cousin, Bernard McKay, buys an automobile which he drives to the the grange meeting. When he pulls in at the grange hall, the chickens are still roosting on the rear bumper.

At first the farmers do not like the machinery. The automobiles frighten the livestock and the farmers think the iron-tired tractors compact the soil. Noah Watson of Spring Valley does not speak to anyone who drives an automobile. Some of the farmers join the Farmers' Anti-Automobile Society which insists: "All motorists must carry sugar to make friends with the horse. When a horse approaches the motorist must drive into the nearest meadow or forest and camouflage his vehicle." The society demands that automobiles be painted each season so they will blend into the scenery. In Port William Oscar Pidgeon is arrested for driving through town at six miles an hour.

In the bottomlands across Anderson's Fork from Frank Lundy, Everett Mendenhall is among the first to buy a tractor. His brother-in-law refers to him as "one of those tractor farmers." This makes Everett feel apart from his neighbors as though he had a diseased herd or left his corn rows to the crabgrass. When the tiny Farmall digs into the earth on the hillside overlooking the bottomlands he feels high above the ground, exposed. He can look past the covered bridge and see Roy Reeves plowing with his horses and he wishes the tractor were quieter.

But soon most of the farmers have tractors. Volcah Hackney buys a new tractor and gives himself a hernia trying to crank it. His neighbor, Everett Early, also has a hernia which he got the same way. On rare occasions when they meet in the village they are aware of their gingerly steps and smile sheepishly in passing. To take care of the new machinery the blacksmiths must become mechanics. Pappy McClure opens a garage in the village. His son takes Pappy's old forge to his backyard where he converts it into a barbecue grill.

Even Albert buys a tractor but he leaves it largely to his sons. "What you can't do with horses," he tells them, "isn't worth doing. I scorn the darned thing." Going to the fields, Henry Carter explains to Albert the difference between a tractor and a mule: "A mule be good to you all year to kick you on Christmas . . ."

His friend Billy Hazard who is retired still keeps his horses, making just enough fodder to feed them. When somebody asks Billy why he doesn't get rid of his horses he says, "Why, I wouldn't have anything to haul my fodder with . . ." Albert laughs with Billy and they are sharing both laughter and sentiment.

When Albert is 70 his grandsons throw him out of the hay mow where he is pacing himself with them in the liquid heat under the barn roof. On his way to the house he sees in his mind Uncle Frank Beam hoeing in his garden. Uncle Frank is sitting in a high chair holding his hoe and chopping the earth around him. Then he moves the chair and sits down again. Albert also remembers Neri Moon who shocked eighty shocks of wheat on his eightieth birthday.

Albert can still look into the fields which surround him and see McKays working. His son Wilbur has become large and successful. He is farming with his sons 1,600 acres which is the number of acres Moses bought for three dollars an acre in 1818. Within sight are four Ada McKays who are separated only by the fields. Albert's wife is Ada Albert and his son's wife is Ada Wilbur. Across his cornfields to the south he can see where his cousin, Ronald, farms. When the setting sun splashes the vacant farmhouse across from where the bachelor Ronald lives with his mother who is also a McKay Albert thinks for a moment that the old house has been painted. "Look out!" he shouts. "Ronald has painted the old farm and is getting married!"

Sometimes when Wilbur cannot find his young son, Tom, he knows to look up the road in Albert's barn where the old man is telling his grandson about the Civil War. Tom's older brother, David, keeps horses and has a full beard which reminds Albert of the old photographs of older McKays staring out of albums and picture frames with their indomitable presences. Sitting in the kitchen with Ada, he says, "They stay, Wilbur's boys. They have plenty of ground and good equipment, too."

Albert acknowledges the work going on around him but he is no longer a part of it. It is not that he is 75 years old but that the changes have been so severe. He likes to walk to the barn and feed the hogs and see his grandsons passing by with the machinery which he finds extravagant, intricate, somehow fierce.

❋ *The earth does not seem to change under them,* he thinks. *The McKays have been here a long time and I am glad they stay . . .*

When it is late in July and Frank Lundy's cornfields are shining richly under a full moon Charlie McIntire races Skeeter Reeves's new car the quarter of a mile from New Burlington up the gentle hill to the graveyard while Skeeter stands on the running board and sends a mighty stream of urine into the corn rows. These are farmer's sons who will soon work for distant corporations. And the automobile will carry them there over roads built through grainfields.

Clive Lundy, 89

I am the oldest Lundy. I was born in 1887. James is the youngest and Frank is in between. English on one side of the family, Dutch on the Hurley side. What they call slop-bucket Dutch. I had a friend, an Irishman, married a Dutch woman and when he wanted to make her mad he would say, 'Well, Irishman and a Nigger don't amount to much but anything beats the dirty Dutch.' I don't know why they said that. Only that they did.

When I was young I went off to college in Wilmington. Then I broke my leg. I was home for the weekend and asked dad if there was anything to exercise on. He pointed to a tree that was down. I cut all the limbs out from under it and still it didn't fall and I tugged on it and it came down on my leg. I heard it crack. After the tree quit bouncing around I sat down on a log and held my leg. A fellow came running over the hill and said, 'Somebody get hurt?' I said, 'Not bad. Just broke my leg.' He took a look and said, 'Excuse me, I have to lie down awhile,'

Then my older brother, Ernest, came and two neighbor ladies and they had a cot and I sat down and said, 'You'll have to put my other leg up.' And my mother was there, too, and she said, 'Don't put that up there, you'll get the cot all bloody,' and I looked down and the bone had broken through the skin and it had bled my shoe full and made that man sick. I was not sure which of us was getting the cot. But I never went back to college after that or perhaps I would have been smart. O I went back for two weeks but I couldn't catch up so I came back home and said to dad, 'You thinking about hiring a hand this summer?' He said, 'Yes,' and I said, 'I'm the boy.' Then he said, 'You can't work in that shape,' and I said, 'You just get the horses out of the barn.' So he got them out and I never went back to college. I had as much fun as Ernest did even though he was a graduate.

Cut corn in the fall, harvest the wheat and let the grass come along.

Life was in that order when I got old enough to notice it. By the time I got into the fields we were so civilized we had a binder for the wheat. It would cut three or four sheaves and the man running the binder would tip them off and we would come along with a couple more sheaves under our arms if we knew how and set them up and they'd lean together. A shock was about ten sheaves with one on top broke over for a hood to sort of run the water off. You let that sit and dry until the straw cured pretty well and then the horses pulled the threshing machine into the field. Dad threshed for thirty-five years so by the time I was grown I found that I was a thresher, too.

Threshing was this way: dad paid off the machine just as he had to buy another one. I remember one he bought, a Huber made up in Marion. They shipped it down on the train. It was a huge machine, good Lord, a man could stand up in the back wheels. It was all metal, a firebox full length of the engine and took a field to turn around in. It was steam-powered and fired with coal. You got in trouble with wood because the sparks would fly and set the field on fire. You wanted good coal, though. Bad coal looked like sorgham molasses running down into the grates. Good coal, good fireman. I liked to fire. It came natural to me. I used to make the kids open their eyes. I'd take my glove off and jerk some coals out of the firebox with my hand and light my pipe. Go into dinner and somebody pass you a dish from the oven and say, 'Watch this because it's hot,' and you pay them no attention and fill your plate while they stare at you. My hands, you see, were toughened from firing that engine. Tough as whalebone.

A threshing machine was the first engine a farmer had ever seen. You drove it out in the field where a man wanted his straw pile and fed it by hand. There was a platform on front and one on either side of that and a man stood in the middle and done the feeding while a boy or man stood on either side of him and threw the sheaves to him, cutting the bands with a good knife. A fellow who knew how to feed would take that sheaf and shake it so it went in gradual. A good feeder made the machine just hum but if a man didn't know his stuff and didn't shake the sheaf enough the machine would go 'Huffffff.' That made the engineer mad.

First year dad ran an engine he got paid for ninety days of threshing. Imagine that! He said, 'Son, don't let the farmer wait on you or he'll raise the devil.' We got ten cents a bushel and furnished all the help. We had a water hauler, a separator man, an engineer, two feeders and when they got an oscillating blower for the separator we hired a fellow we called 'Charley Blower' to run that and build a nice stack. He could top it up pretty good, Charley Blower could. They used that straw for bedding.

Farmers who couldn't get a thresher when they wanted one they

Threshing crew, noon at the cook shack, 1913

Clive Lundy running a threshing machine

hauled their wheat to the barn and waited on us. It was rye first then the wheat and then oats. That's the way they ripened. We could thresh around 500 bushels a day although one day we ran 1,180. In those times, however, a day wasn't eight hours. It was a day. We had 600 bushels of wheat out in the barn once and some company came out from Xenia and the kids were playing out there and they came back and said, 'Mom, uncle Cal's got a big barn full of *rice* down there.' Rice!

I liked that steam engine. I thought I could eat as much dust as the next fellow and I did. Once I went blind eating dinner. We were having some trouble and we got to the table as they were passing the pie. Well, they put the stuff to us, you know, whatever we wanted and we sat down and went out with the rest of them and I didn't miss my pie. But I was sitting there by the old kitchen range and the more I ate the hotter I got and when I finished my pie the sweat was pouring off me and I went outside and tried to get up on the engine. 'Darned if I can find the step to the engine,' I said. And somebody said, 'You're trying to get up on the *tank*.' I said, 'I'm blind. I can't see where I am.' Somebody said, 'You're too hot.' So I sat down awhile until I could see again. Only twice the heat ever bothered me. One day I was shocking wheat. It was past ninety in the shade and I fell. The old man came over and said, 'What's the matter?' I said, 'Nothing, only I fell.' He said, 'Yes, there is and go there and rest in the shade and afterward just shock what you can shock.'

It wasn't long before those engines pulled themselves. I drove one home from Jamestown once. I left at six o'clock and it took me near all night to get back. All I had was a coal oil lantern I used for coon hunting and I hung that on the front end and the way I stayed on the road was to stand on the right hand side and watch the light from the lantern and keep the right wheel as close to the ditch as I could without sliding off and let the other side take care of itself. A coal oil lamp, yes boy! That's just the way you had to do it. Sometimes you didn't have that. I stopped along the way and refueled with some of the rails off Pappy McMillan's fence.

Just before the threshing season began one year, I took my girl to be X-rayed and I was standing there smoking and coughing and the doctor says, 'Let's have a look at *you*.' Then he said, 'Come look at your old man.' He said this to Mrs. Lundy whom I always called Carrie and she came and looked and the doctor said, 'Look at that darn thing.' He said my windpipe was as black as a rubber hose and that I had eaten too much dirt in my time. 'Now listen, Doc,' I said. 'I got on a separator the first day of July, got off that onto a cob roller, got off that onto a corn shredder and got off that in March or sometime in April and then I was ready to begin all over. I been at it fifteen-twenty years and I'm glad to know what's been wrong with me because my neighbor has been telling me that from my cough I wouldn't be here next spring and I had begun to believe him but it won't kill me anymore. I'm going to quit.' Uncle Jim Hurley came over the next week and said, 'We'll start threshing Monday,' and I said, 'You're starting without the old man this time.'

I never farmed much after the machinery began to come in. I don't know if I could have farmed that way. You had to get big, real big, more money in the machinery than the farm was worth. I took an old grey mare and two mules, hitched them to a breaking plow and cut 45 acres. People thought I'd done a day's work. Now they turn six, seven furrows at once. I was turning fourteen inches of ground. Round and round, don't you think I wasn't going round some. Ride awhile, get tired of riding, get off and walk. Grassland, getting it ready for corn, see.

There was good land and bad land and I've known both. I worked fields so poor a killdeer would have to carry a knapsack to get the other side without starving to death. But most was good earth. My oldest boy followed me to the fields when he was nine. I got so cold I got off the plow and walked beside it. There was an old fence row there so I couldn't turn too good and the kid said, 'If I couldn't do a better job than that, I'd quit.' I said, 'here's the lines. Help yourself.' I watched for a few rounds and, by God, he *was* doing a better job so I said, 'Well, I'm turning you loose.'

He was plowing three behind the sulky plow and after a bit I heard a commotion in the fields. Carrie was ringing the dinner bell and the old mare heard it and when she got to the turn she started for the gate and he couldn't stop her. Boy, was he mad. The old mare was going to dinner and he was going along for the ride.

Dad said, 'Whip a horse if he needs it but there's a difference between him needing it and you overloading him.' He said, 'When you trade a horse, tell the good qualities, they'll find the bad ones quick enough. Don't lie to a man but don't tell anything but that they ask for.' And he always said don't believe what you hear and only half of what you say yourself.

After the machinery came, I did a little carpentry work. Once I fell off a stepladder and was out eleven months. I went back to the same place and walked in and said to the office girl, 'Now where's that lock you wanted fixed?' I worked with my brother-in-law, Elmer Lemar. We married sisters. I told him, 'I took my choice and you got what was left.' Carrie and I had eight children and we raised six. Two died young and one fell in an airplane. We heard it on the radio. People could have easier lives today but they don't. Always going somewhere but they don't know where they're going nor why. Why drive that way when they don't have anyplace to go and don't expect to get there? I have worn fifty-cents overalls and dollar shoes and I gave Hugh Lickliter his first chew of tobacco. Clive Enoch Lundy. I'm what's left of him. I'm no boy. It was a circus. You should have been there.

*   *   *

The indenture papers of George Cooke

This indenture witnesseth that I, Jacob Cooke, gunsmith, do put and bind out my son, George Cooke, aged three years and 24 days, as an apprentice to Seth Wilson to learn the art, trade, or mystery of a farmer, the said George Cooke after the manner of an apprentice to dwell with and serve the said Seth Wilson from the day of the date hereof until the 31st day of the eighth month which will be in the year of our Lord one thousand eight hundred and thirty-nine at which time the said apprentice, if he should be living, will be 21 years of age. During all which time the said apprentice his master shall faithfully serve, his secrets keep, his lawful commands everywhere and at all times readily obey; he shall do no damage to his said master, or wilfully suffer it to be done by others; and if any to his knowledge be intended, he shall give his master reasonable notice thereof; he shall not waste the goods of his said master, nor lend them unlawfully to any, at cards, dice or any unlawful game he shall not play; he shall not commit fornication, nor contract matrimony during said term; taverns, alehouses, or places of gaming he shall not frequent, from the service of his said master he shall not absent himself day or night; but in all things, and at all times he shall carry and behave himself as a good and faithful apprentice ought, during the whole time or term aforesaid.

And the said Seth Wilson on his part doth hereby promise, covenant and agree to teach and instruct the said apprentice, or cause him to be taught and instructed in the art, trade, or calling of a farmer by the best way or means he can; and also to teach and instruct the said apprentice, or cause him to be instructed to read and write and cypher or to have three and a half years of schooling, one-third after he is 16 years of age, and shall well and faithfully find and provide for the said apprentice good and sufficient meat, drink, clothing, both woolen and linen, fit and convenient for such apprentice during the term aforesaid and medical aid if necessary, and two suits, one of which shall be new.

24th of September, 1820

John Cooke
Thomas W. Cooke

Jacob Cooke
Rebecca Cooke
Seth Wilson

In case the urchin named George Cooke inclines to learn a trade when he comes to be 16 years of age, he is at liberty to choose one, not be bound by me, on my being paid what three judicious friends shall say I am entitled to have for bringing him up to that age.

Seth Wilson

* * *

Jacob Spicer Leaming sees the corn on a boat docked along the Ohio River. The yellow ears are striking. Large and sound. He fills his saddle-bags with them and brings them home for seed. He plants them in the spring of 1856. With this handsome seed corn, Jacob Spicer thinks he can influence the indifferent fields.

Such consideration, in the middle of the 19th century, may be heresy. Farmers plant by the phases of the moon, debate the advantages of hornless cattle, and ring church bells to deflect lightning. The concept of agriculture as a business is not yet universally recognized. The farmer is a man described as "keeping himself aloof from the specious novelty."

But Jacob Spicer will make his considerations. He is, as one biographer states, "acquiring inspiration for his future work through the medium of a hoe handle in the Langdon bottoms." He recognizes most corn as non-descript. He will change this. From the time he plants his healthy new corn in 1856 and for 25 years afterward on his Clinton County farm, he experiments. An image is growing in the fecundity of his mind. He will make the fields match his imagination.

By selection he influences the ear itself. In the fields with a hoe he stud-ies the ear, stalk, the seasons, the ground underfoot. Unlike other farmers he does not plant corn in hills, but one grain in a place, 14 inches apart. He plants shallow and hoes so frequently his seven sons grumble in concert and ponder mutiny in the deeps of green fields. He rotates corn, wheat and clover. He believes in red clover as a manure crop.

Jacob Spicer has no agricultural college, no textbooks, no advice. He is following the formulas of his own discipline and invention. Before his death in 1885 the "Improved Leaming" seed corn is grown all over the world. His sons and grandsons continue his work. His grandson, Howard, does not remember his grandfather but he remembers the fields, hoeing corn until it was cut.

*"Hard, hard," he says. "Some died trying to make their interest money.
But we had grandfather's work. A man named Addison Russell took some
to the Paris Exposition. It went through all their tests and beat the world's
corn. The medals are still in the family. We sent thousands of orders everywhere. The experimental station at Wooster wrote me and said his corn
was two crosses away from hybrid. They say practically all the yellow corn
grown in the country has been developed from his variety. He began when
people planted anything. Golden something or another and so on . . ."*

*Howard Leaming is an old man now although his memory accurately
covers most of his century. He spends his time sitting in the sunlight which
streams through a picture window. Children who pass by on their way to
school wave to him from the road. The window is a prism, refracting age.
In the kitchen cabinet, wrapped in cellophane, are three ears of Jacob
Spicer Leaming's seed corn.*

Howard Leaming, 83

I was born in a log house near Wilmington and had pneumonia when I
was two. Luke Norris, an old Irishman, sat up nights with my father. It is
one of the earliest things I remember. Luke Norris was short and heavy-
set and made his home with the family of Henry Crouse. He helped on
the farm and got what he ate and the clothes he wore. That's the way it
went. A lot of people who weren't sound of mind lived like that, not to
say that Luke Norris wasn't sound of mind because he was. Once in a
while he'd go to Wilmington on an old sorrel mare, get drunk and walk
back, leading the mare. But he sat up with me when I had pneumonia
and you don't hear tell of anything like that today.

In 1904 we moved to a farm on Cornstalk Road. It had once been
owned by Noah Whitson, an old-time Quaker. The land was heavy with
timber and we cleared it the hardest way, by a hand on the ax. We didn't
have tools to work with then. There was some of the biggest poplar I ever
saw, both red and white oak and a few black oaks which were no good for
nothing because the grain was interlocked and couldn't be split up for
wood.

In the winter, Noah Whitson put up ice. He lived on the Xenia Road,
just outside of town, with a pond on either side of the road and an ice
cutter pulled by horse. He cut a streak in the ice, took a spud bar to
knock it loose, and buried it in the sawdust house. I was there many a
time. We would get tongs and a shovel for the sawdust, then wrap the ice

in a piece of old homemade carpet and it would take the both of us to get it to the buggy. I'd say, 'How much?' and he'd say, 'Oh, a dime. It cost me nothing to make.' He had ice fourteen inches thick there till the next fall.

He would hitch his mare to a spring wagon and during the season bring eight or ten crates of strawberries into town but he sold no more than three quarts at a time. 'But come to my patch,' he'd say, 'and I'll sell you a crate.' He did it that way because he thought if he sold more than that in town, everybody might not get some.

Noah was quite a horse man. He cut his colts every spring and someone said, 'Noah, do you follow the signs?' and Noah said, 'Yes, I always cut when my knife is sharp.' He had an Arabian horse for breeding and he always told people to come back if the colt didn't have spots because his stud had spots. 'They have to have spots to be from my Arabian,' he would say although of course the colts didn't but there were times he insisted on refunding money. Those kind of men are dead and gone now.

The village was laid out in 1832 by John Grant who was the town's main man. The way I get it, people immediately wanted to come and he organized a 'smelling' committee. No outlaws were wanted, just honest and upright people. Grant built a general store on the corner and a mill up the creek and a tanyard. He was in sympathy with the abolitionists and built a chute in the attic of his store so that at night slaves could slide into the backyard and leave by the creek.

My great-grandfather owned a hundred acres between the two streams. He bought it from Aaron Jenkins and sold it to a man named Jay. It was where all of the village was built. It was a fine place and had all a man needed and I remember how it was. On one corner was first a hotel with a bell on it made of bell metal, a real good piece. It was not just cast iron and you could hear it a long way when dinner was ready. Wayne Smith owned the hardware and a lot of farmers thought that if they had to buy a plowshare, then it had to be from Wayne Smith. He had a big business and trusted a lot of people who owed him when he died and, of course, he had nothing then, but he had lived high and gone everywhere and had four men working for him. Up the street was Tom Haydock's cobbler shop where the old Civil War soldiers hung about and fought the battle through again. Once Pat Murphy, an old Irishman, got to fighting a battle in there and remembered having seven horses shot out from under him during the war. Later, he continued the fighting down at the general store and recalled that he rode a mule throughout the service. He was some old Irishman.

For the longest time, I was a cow trader. I met some good people and some I don't care to see again. Most were friendly and I never had my check refused. My customers came to me from New England and many of them were Jews. They would insult you before they got out of the car and you had to talk to them like they talked to you. They'd drive up and say 'You got any baloney cows?' and I'd look at them sharp and say, 'Well, now, there they are, and I didn't send for you.' You had to talk that way because that was the way it was. But they were always ready to buy. I would say, 'That one is awful bad to kick,' and they would say, 'It is no matter. The other fellow can wrestle with her,' meaning the poor devil who bought her, without a sharp eye to see what no one was saying.

A cow, you know, is the queerest animal on God's good earth. She has many deceits and holds them from you until you have been with her awhile. Something the way of a woman. A mule is that way also. Gentle for a month and one clear chance to kick you into the wall. The orneriest cow I ever knew was raised by an ornery woman. I've known it to be that way. If the woman was ornery, why, so was the cow.

I have had some experiences with cows. I have been kicked and tramped sure enough. Once I had a cow with very mean horns. She was a Guernsey and Brown Swiss, a sound, good-looking cow. I was loading her in a trailer, trying to put a halter on her and as I got her nose into the halter she rammed me into the corner, a horn on either side of me. I broke my finger gouging her in the eye and she finally backed off.

I had a little Jersey who was the fightingest cow I've known. I owned her twice. She had no horns but she would put them all on the run. She was quiet to handle but a fright among the others. She would take on every strange cow and try her out. Once she got in with a bunch of cows who all had horns. She took them all on and when she came back it looked like she had Chinese writing all over her. I had one who wouldn't come to the trough until the others were done drinking then she would lap the water like a dog and leave foam over the trough. Kickers, suckers, fighters, I've had them all and been attached to many of them. I can tell by looking at a cow's mouth how old she is. Two teeth when born, and each year two more and six makes a full mouth, all lower. When they get older, the teeth get broader unless they've been in short pasture.

I've bought them two years old in Kentucky and the corner teeth wore down like with a file from eating Hickory sprouts because that's all the green there was in the pasture. They'll eat the leaves off a wilted cherry tree until it kills them and alfalfa with a wet dew or clover after a rain until they're bloated and you couldn't beat them away with a stick. But if you give them salt before grazing wet they're not as apt to bloat. I have stuck a good many who were bloated. Just stuck a hole in the hide with my pocketknife. It is done on the left side in front of the hipbone where there's a place as wide as your hand. Punch right in there. Then keep away because the gas will just whistle by. A cow is a fine and strange animal, one of the most regular creatures in God's universe.

I have known different men and strange times, and I have made strange habits. I froze my right ear in Texas riding for groceries and I once had a pig that tracked my horse. I had an aunt in Kansas who remembered when it was all open territory. The first batch of bread she made after she was married she buried because she was afraid the dogs might eat it. I knew a barber at Port William and when I asked him why he never raised his prices, he said, 'I'll tell you the facts of the case: I've been too busy.' And he kept on charging thirty cents and that wasn't but so long ago. I knew an old Civil War soldier who ran a grocery in Wilmington and sometimes I sold rabbits to him and he hung them up. His name was Samuel Stiff. A woman came along one day and picked one out, the head off but the feet on and the guts in and Samuel Stiff wrapped him up and directly she was back saying, 'Why, Mr. Stiff, I can't take this, it's all shot.' He patted her on the back and said, 'That's alright, lady. You know, we have to shoot the little fellows to catch them.' He was some old man and married three times that I know of. When nigger ladies came in to use his grocery scales to weigh themselves he would usually feel them up a little before they left.

As for habits, I'm foolish about my winter shirts. I want them wool and I want them Pendleton. They'll wear right on. And I want a Stetson hat. I knew fellows in the southwest who would sweat a ring of grease around one and send it to the plant in Philadelphia and it came back as new. No one ever wore a hole in a Stetson. Things that do not last, I call them 'the Jew's shoes.' That's because you use it awhile and it doesn't last. I always wanted quality and I wanted it to last. I had two saddles made to my order in my time, one at Cheyenne and one at Pueblo, Colorado. They quilted the seat to my measure like clothes at a tailor's and I had a pair of shop-made boots where they measure your ankle, calf and heel, everything of a kind, and you don't find them anymore without hard looking. There were once good cobblers everywhere who made boots of good quality, then they got smaller and fewer and the automobile began to take people to store-bought things.

My name is English, originally spelled 'Leamying.' Two brothers came to this country. One died on the boat and was buried at sea. The other landed at Cape May, N.J., and scattered from there on. He brought with him a leather-covered Bible with the family history. I have seen it years ago. It was to be handed down to the Christopher in each generation, one generation to the next with its Christopher and it did so through the eleventh one and now my great-grandson is Christopher and by rights the Bible is his but a fellow in Detroit has got it and I wrote him and he answered me this way: 'My mother was a Leaming before she married and she left it with me and made me custodian.' Well, now, she was related, but his name isn't even Leaming and I don't understand it.

But I grew up at a different time. I have know a good woman and grew two sons to manhood. I have seen some of the country and read about the rest. I have lived largely a farming life and I don't know the why of things in the world anymore. Today the young ones make a habit of going around and disturbing the ground. It is not just here but all over the world because I have read about it being so in England. They are wanting to destroy things. Parents do not teach in the homes and there are no manners. Manners go a great deal when you're away from home and among strangers. People once passed their land on to their children and now the worst thing is that the children do not want it. They want to go to the city because all they hear is about big money and they know it is not on the farm. When I talk of all these things people say, 'I could not of stood that,' and I say to them: 'You don't know what you can stand until you're put up against it.'

*   *   *

Mr. Taylor's letter

The fragrance of new-mown hay is floating in at country doors and freighting country air. It steals upon the senses, and upon the heart, and brings again memories long forgotten. Don't you wish you could be as happy as you once were, among the hay-cocks? That you could follow as delightedly as ever the wake of the mowers? That you could feel like begging for a bed on the new hay in the mow?

But you never can and the only provision is that you can live it over in thought; that you can go back through the years as easily as one can thread a field of corn, and be somebody younger and happier and better. You are lying under the maple again. The Bob-o'links are swinging on the meadow rushes, and the great sun is shining over all. The cattle are grouped where the creek runs deepest. The sheep are panting under the bank. The roof of the house dances with heat. Through the meadow, the mowers advance. The swath-note comes to your ear on the air.

You will be a man by and by, you think. And wield the scythe and lead the field. You will have meadows of your own and a stream through it. You will marry Ellen Loveland, whose father lives just over the hill, if she will only keep as beautiful as she is now. And you will live in a house of your own, a very fine house. With ever so many rooms in the house and ever so many things in the rooms. Children will stand in rows and make their obeisance as you pass the school house at noon. As you and your comrades do now in homage to the Squire. You will be a Squire, too, and always have a pocket full of new pennies to give them. You will be very grand with your gifts, and carry a cane, and a watch, and an immense seal depending therefrom. You will be a richer man than Joseph Sykes, who calls you names. He shall mow for you, and eat in the kitchen, while you sit in the parlor and read.

Human nature is packed away very closely in the smallest of bodies sometimes, and so there is a world of it in the bosoms of children. But the little boy who divided his dinner with you, because you had fed your own away to the fishes and fancied you would never be hungry—he shall ride in your carriage: if you should be very rich, perhaps you may give him a farm.

It is then you will be able to pluck the fruit without climbing, and wind up a clock without mounting a chair. And so you dream on, until a yellow butterfly flutters along, you in pursuit. You are on your knees in the grass. No farm and no Ellen Loveland. Just a butterfly under a hat. Very splendid were our morning dreams long ago in the meadow, but like the grass the mowers cut, they are faded and gone.

B. F. Taylor,
The Ohio Cultivator,
August 15, 1855

❋ ❋ ❋

Thurmond Mitchener, 78

I have always known farming. It is what I began with and I'm still at it. I went to school for a while then I was working one summer on the farm of Frank McIntire and I just didn't stop. I began for myself in 1927 on 115 acres on Cemetery Road. It belonged to my aunt. I had some dairy cows then, sheep, hogs and I raised corn and soybeans and wheat. The work was done by hand and horse and walking plow. I don't like to talk of it because it makes me seem old. I used to like horses an awful lot then it got so it seemed they wanted to tramp all the fences down to get on the other side when there was plenty where they was. They were like many people I know.

I have always been near here and haven't moved around much. The fartherest I've been away was for two years to Ludlow Schoolhouse on the other side of Xenia, and I was taken away during the War. I was sent to Florida and after Armistice was signed they loaded up about a dozen of us and kept us around for a while. I have no idea about the why of it. When I got back to Burlington, I heard I had been in the guardhouse, but that is not on my discharge. They asked me there to sign up again, but I thought it was to go to Paris to bury dead bodies and I didn't go in for that. Then they said they would give us land on the St. James River if we would homestead it and I didn't want none of it. I wanted to come back to Ohio where I knew people. Florida wasn't much of a looking place. It seemed to be all swamp and razorback hogs and wild cattle. If you were out somewhere and saw a razorback hog, you just didn't know whether you would make it back or not.

When I came to this farm, I had eighty head of hogs ready to sell. Prices were $12.50 a hundred weight and there was a ceiling on. They didn't look like they would do any better so I sold them and then the ceiling was taken away and the price went to $30 a hundred weight. I wasn't too happy about it, but I lived through it all right. Now I have the orneriest bunch I've ever seen. They don't seem to be satisfied anyplace. They just root out if you don't keep them rung, so I'm putting them on the ringing tree and sending them out with so many rings they'll stand on their heads. But I won't brag because it's only been done a week.

I sometimes think I ought to have been a veterinarian because I've done so much of it, ringing and castrating pigs and such. Farming is not sentimental because you're up against all things here. You're in mud or hog dust seven days a week. It never says a pig knows anything about Sunday. I don't make a business of it but things go on. I like it because it was how I was raised. I think it is where a man is born. My father stayed with it until he was 85. I have never known anything else and I'm not sorry for it. I paid $12,500 for this place when I came here and some say my 145 acres are worth $70,000. That's a right smart more than I paid for it, but it's not for sale because I want to die here.

I have no thought of retirement because I can't sit around. I'd go crazy. The fact is, I'm that way now, but sitting around would finish me. Some of the younger ones I know complain something awful about the hard work, but it doesn't harm you. I can't tell you when I took a dose of medicine. Of course, I don't believe much in it. Once I had double pneumonia and Dr. Smith came and said, 'You'll not last until the morning.' I think that was a help to me. I decided I wouldn't die. Afterward he said, 'Thurmond, you'll never have anything again.' The measles came, and whooping cough, and all my brothers and sisters were sick, and I tried to catch it to get out of school but I never did.

I've just never been much for doctoring. Disease is from the head, I

Thurmond Mitchener (PHOTOGRAPH BY KEN STEINHOFF)

think. Usually, I just had the feeling I didn't *need* medicine. I was given pain pills for a broken shoulder but I never took them. I figured if I waited until I got to the place where I *really* needed them, why, they would help just that much more. I was opening up that field one day and I stopped to cut a limb out of the way when it hit me in the head and knocked me out and cut me. I didn't tell my son because when anything happens he wants to take me to the doctor. One day I was getting a haircut and the barber said, 'Thurmond, what happened to your head?' and I told him and pretty soon, my son was over wanting to take me to the doctor. I said to him, 'I'll outgrow a little thing like that.' And I did.

I've always thought medicine took your senses away. My wife took so much she just stayed mixed up all the time. I talked to her but it did no good. She died of a heart attack when she was 56. She dropped dead while I was looking at the fire. I had already lost my son, so it was a shock. He died of a heart attack at 32. I always thought he overdid himself. He did some boxing when he was a boy and boxers take an awful pounding. Then he went to work in the factory and he would come home at midnight and come over and say, 'What a night for some coon hunting!' And maybe I had already been out three or four hours but I always got up and went with him for it was what he liked.

Coming up, I had four brothers and four sisters. My worst deal was that I was in between and I took off those that were older and I took off those that were younger. Except for Lawrence, who is too contrary to get along with even though he is my brother, the rest of us boys were great for coon hunting. It began with me when my uncle died. I went to look after my aunt and she had chickens roosting in the woods. I took her old beetlehound and went to fetch them for her and this old dog brought back two possums instead of chickens, and I got twenty-five cents apiece for them. I say a beetlehound although he was too big for a beetlehound. He was part coon dog and he was also a rabbit dog. I was about 12. Horace hunted with me more than Walter and we started in with one or two dogs, then we had eight. They would fill up the woods with music. My boy always had some about, and I did, too, but when it came time to buy their tags, it seemed as though he never had any dogs.

Farming now is easier than it used to be. With a tractor you can do in a day what once took a week. But I do think there's more horses in the country today. I don't know what they do, but I see them in all the pastures. We got by on very little when I was young. Now there is fertilizer and seed corn and machinery. All that is high and sometimes the things you sell are not so high, but it used to be that 40 bushels of corn to the acre was good and now we get 100 bushels. I've used fertilizer for twenty years and it has not hurt the water or anything that I know of. What I think is that much pollution comes from airplanes. I see them come over here and there is more smoke than from a hundred cars. But I don't know about these things. When I was young, we butchered all our beef and pork and never worried about such things.

Once when I was a boy, we were hoeing corn for Frank Conklin and when it was time for pay the men didn't like it that I was getting the same as they. 'He's but a boy,' they said to Frank, 'and we should have more.' And Frank said back, 'But when you got to the end, he was there with you,' and that was the end of that. We all got a dollar a day.

It doesn't bother me that my son doesn't farm. I never told either of my sons what to do. I don't know what he does in the factory and I figure that if he wants me to know, he'll tell me. I myself never had a desire to go into a factory, although there are those who are used to it. My notion is that there's more nature here, but of course it depends on the person. I wouldn't want to be tied up in town and at my age I don't think I could get used to it. I never liked elevators and those stairs that turn and the traffic. When the bridge was out on 68, they detoured through here and they drove like they had to be there right now. I don't know where they were going. When I drive I know all the curves and where all the children live, and I know where I'm going.

It is lonely here but I read and watch the television some, but I don't let it get in on me. One good thing about television is that you can turn it off when it offends you. You can't always do that with people. There are a lot of programs that don't interest me but if others get enjoyment out of them it's none of my affair. I read the papers and magazines and when I can't sit anymore I take a ride to see what others are doing. I know that we are in Vietnam, but I see no sense in it. Where are England and France, I wonder? I can't say I'm a religious man, but I understand the Bible well enough. There are strange deals in the world today. It's never changed too much around here, but I don't know how much longer things will stand as they are.

Howard Hackney, 65

My great-great-grandfather, Aaron Hackney, came here after losing all he had in Virginia, having gone security for a friend. He even lost the family silver. He got to Wilmington with fifty cents in spending change and the family has been looking for that ever since. He ended up out here on some of Moses McKay's land which upgraded the McKay family since

Hollis Peterson and cow. 1912

my great-grandfather married one of Moses' daughters. This farm was once McKay land and my grandfather and father worked it together. They lived only a hundred yards apart. My grandmother had a very keen sense of how my grandfather liked his food. She knew, for instance, that he disliked the crust of warm bread. She also knew one who had a desire to eat the crust of warm bread, especially if it was well fixed with butter and cherry preserves. I was a well fed youngster and between my grandfather and me we lent an interesting order to the universe.

My grandfather, Albert, was killed by a threshing dinner. Lena Early brought down something special for him and he had as sharp a consideration for her and therefore tried to eat all of it and he ate well and went into a diabetic coma.

When my ancestors came to the land here, the Manns, McKays, and Hackneys, there was absolutely no end to anything. There was no need for conservation. One man felt he could not dent this magnificent nature. But he had to clear the land. If you were going to push into this country, brutality was a prerequisite. The meek did *not* inherit the earth. There had to be a few robust souls. The Bennett family cleared two farms before they got to their land. In those days there weren't quite as many billboards marking the way and Bennett ended up on the wrong farm. He knew it was the wrong land but the season was pressing so he put in a crop so he would have something to eat. Then he came east to Caesar's Creek and cleared some more land on the fringes of the prairie and found he didn't own that one either. Finally he got to his own land. It was a magnificent community gesture.

The neighborhood as I knew it was closely knit. People had to work together. One man alone could not build such barns and houses as were on the homeplace. In the evening they found a little time to make some ice cream. This was a spillover from the closeness in the work. The matter of *in kind* was a rather complex social situation. My parent's generation was getting away from this. In my time it has become total. The machines created a division in the neighborhood, no matter what their virtues were.

My great-grandfather was the first farmer here to try the mechanical reaper. It was in that field at the top of the hill which is now in bluegrass. People came from all over. It was a new way of doing things. People were using the *cradle*. So my grandfather became proficient in binding the sheaves, and my father was one of the families in the McKay Company, which bought a thresher. They threshed for each other, then they worked for outsiders. I was the young upstart using rubber tires and I bought the first small combine sold in the county. That act was possibly the beginning of the breakup of the McKay Company.

In the mid-thirties it seemed that a man might be independent. I bought a tractor, cultivator, breaking plow and combine for $2,000. In 1936 I did custom work for $2 an acre and paid for the combine. I wanted to be independent, and to avoid the extra work. If a rain storm came before the threshing machine reached your farm, you had to tear down the shocks and dry them and begin again. In 1931 the wheat was a heavy crop and my father traded for a larger grain binder and hitched the horses to it. It was an extremely hot summer and horses were dying in the fields. So he said, 'We'll put the tractor on it.' On those old tractors, you never suffered from the cold even on the coldest day. You sat down in there, the fenders up around you like cliffs and the longer it ran the hotter it got and if you touched anything around you it would burn. Some fields of wheat burned, set afire by the tractor's exhaust. This is how we cut the wheat.

But the threshing ring started on the other end of the neighborhood and by the time they got to us it was September and the rainy season had begun. We tore down shocks and set them up until they were past salvage and they went to the hogs. It was wet and hot and grain sprouted in the sheaves. I went back to college and my father improvised every place he could to dry the grain after it was threshed. Of course there were no big grain bins with dryers then. My father was the dryer. He scooped hundreds of bushels of wheat every morning, every night. After everyone had called it a day, he was out there turning the wheat and he finally sold some for the extreme sum of twenty-five cents a bushel. I watched my father do the best he could with what he had and it was impossible. It speeded up his death considerably. It wore him out. He was fifty when he died. Men howled at the farm programs in 1934. They said the farmers were being regimented. I never saw a man more regimented than my father, scooping wheat at night to make ends meet.

We were still planting corn with horses after World War II. My father was never without horses. He was a horseman and had an aversion to the machinery. He enjoyed the steam engine but he thought field work was for horses. My grandfather said one of my father's greatest satisfactions as a child was getting pieces of string and harnessing the kitchen chairs together. The height of his glory came when grandfather allowed him to hitch the chairs together with real harness. In the early hours of the morning once, grandfather heard my father crying. He wanted grandfather to go to the barn and bring in a set of harness to make him feel better.

You went to the field with horses, and brought them back. With a well-trained team, you had more time to yourself. There was more quiet, the pace was slower. The horse did not always have good days as the driver sometimes didn't. My father could spot these characteristics and he kept an extra horse and on those days he took another one to the field. His judgment of men came from how they treated their horses. Upon this one area he based many of his opinions. He thought that a man who would kick a horse would likely raise his foot in other places which is quite possibly not a bad sentiment. When the horse was gone from the farm so were many values.

I recognized this rather abstractly, however. I had an aversion to horses. I never owned one, never expected to own one. But I've been pestered by them. I did not like the touch of the sweaty animal. I found the odor repulsive. The horse was a nuisance around the pig which I did like. I never got away from the pig. My college education said I was a chemist. But even while going to college I was feeding pigs almost every day. The twig was bent early and never straightened.

It took World War II to completely seal the doom of such things as threshing rings and field horses. The factory system during the war began the migration to the towns. The wars brought us the hour, you see. Factories ran on the hour. They offered more reward for less time. So labor became a problem on the farm but the machines were available. The threshing company fails, the machines rise. Life in the cities was enticing to the rural children, no matter how firm their foundations. City life was said to be a better life. There was a stigma attached to farm boys. Farm boys were simple. Their traits were not honored in our worldly system. The army liked the farm boys, however. They wanted as many of them as they could get. Farm boys took a little wire and a bent nail and patched things up. Later on they became pretty good welders and machinists. They could take hold of something they didn't know much about and make it go. This was their nature. To survive the changes on the farm they had to change themselves. The migration began during the First World War. World War II almost finished it. The depression came in between. We were just trying to live. No one is immune to that.

Luther Haines, 79

My great-great grandfather Isaac Haines was the first of the Haineses here. He came out and began to clear land. Later he found it was not his and he had to move and begin again. It was quite a bit of land, too. I was raised here and my father before me and my son and his sons. I can tell you everyone who has owned this land. Except for seven years it has

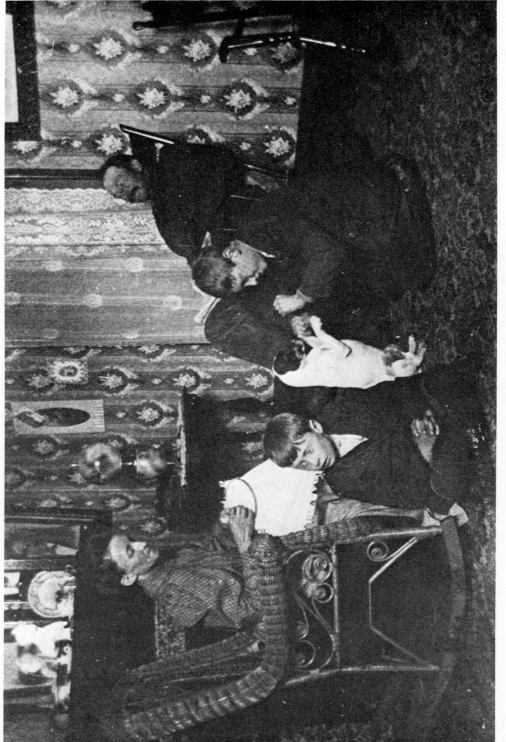

Luther Haines (foreground) with brother, Everett, and parents

remained in two families for over 175 years. The land did not change. Nothing changed. My father told me: you only need three store-bought things. They are salt, sugar and a little kerosene. When company came we went to the cellar, not the grocery.

I began with one mule and a walking plow. He turned and went down the right row. Later on, we thought the tractor was wonderful but the horses were sacred. The teams thought for a man in the fields and he cared for them. The tractor gave us nothing. But the machinery was coming on, you know. You had to compete. My dad and I bought a Fordson in 1919 and a three bottom plow. They cost us $900. Gasoline was fifteen cents. We used the horses to save gas. We tried to keep the money at home. When we got behind, we used the tractor. But we were independent with the horse. I wonder how it would have been to have continued that way. I raised young horses. I made money on my power by that. My power cost me only my feed. It took two acres for a horse. We had eight at one time.

Sometimes I long for those days. We thought we worried very little. If my father got pinched he didn't go to a bank. He went to his neighbors. One looked under the carpet on the stairs and got what he wanted. It was $300.

The disassociation began after the First World War. The factory seemed most attractive to the young men. When I was a boy, town boys made light of us. They thought us backward. Of course they had some of the conveniences. They had water under pressure, and lights. I think perhaps now city boys would like to get back to the country but it is an alien place.

I have been in the large cities and I am never happy there. I cannot imagine a boy growing up in these places. What does he find? Here he is among the animals in the fields and woods and growing things. When I was young a bunch of boys hoed in the fields and sang coming home.

Now there is so much propoganda by the big industries. We look up to the fellow in the office. Why is that? Well, crackers are not sold in a barrel anymore and young girls know nothing of lard. I do worry about the future. I say: I am glad I lived in my own time.

Ed Lane, 47

I remember once that my father went to Washington D.C., and while he was seeing the sights along Pennsylvania Avenue he went up to a guard on the steps of the White House and asked if he might see the president for a moment. The irony of this was that the president was Franklin Roosevelt and my father was a staunch Republican. His sister's husband was a labor leader and the family regarded him as a Communist. A further irony was that during the depression my father went to work for the federal land bank program which was one of those New Deal welfare programs. But it saved our farm and others in the community. There were Christmases when we got nothing but oranges.

The country life was comfortable enough. Unfortunately, I wasn't allergic to poison ivy and therefore got the job of cleaning out fence rows which I considered the worst job on the farm. Near the end of my years in high school the farmers began going to town. They were working an eight-hour day in the factory and made more than us who were working twice the hours. I objected to this. I objected to being tied down. We were tied so close, morning and night. I resented never being able to go away. Of course, I had my father's pig farmer bias—the pig was the only animal to make money on.

We had Major Grady, four other horses, and a small Farmall. At one time there were no rubber tires on the place, then I came back and counted fifty tires on the road. We had a 12-foot combine pulled by a tractor with cleats. But we had only 170 acres. You could not pay $12,000 for a cornpicker and farm only 170 acres. Our cousins, Ralph and Walter Baker, farmed with horses and went on in the old way. They cooked on a wood stove and had no plumbing. They had thought these things through and chosen. They were a bit intractable, too. Ralph was rather philosophical. He always quoted Emerson to me. They had a lemon tree with lemons big as grapefruit. And a century plant in a huge wooden tub. The century plant bloomed once in a hundred years and they got it to bloom. It was a big occasion.

In college, a professor named Samuel Marble told me something that influenced me a great deal: until you've lived in another part of the country you are so inculturated with the values and outlook of your community that you assume them to be the only truths. My father thought another farmer would deal honestly with him. But he saw city people as people who were out to take you. He saw them as people who made their money from such things as the manipulation of stocks. They didn't earn money by the sweat of their brow. Later, however, he invested in stocks, too.

Well, I look at that time rather positively because my bias is that technology has run away with us. When my father expanded production he grew out 800 feeder hogs a year. This required mechanization in raising corn, feeding, watering. One act required many changes. You either went all the way or remained primitive. I remember when we took the last hand pump out and replaced it with electricity. We worried because if there was a fire which cut the electric wires, then there was no water to fight it with. I regret the technological shifts but my lament of the simple life is personal. Perhaps there was never any choice, other than containing the population or, in moral terms, our greed. I'm not sure I'm a happier human being living the way I do now. But I would also be unhappy at giving it up. My house cost $80,000. I don't need to live in such a house. But I enjoy it. I do not discern in myself the fortitude to turn away.

The romantic sense is: one day I will be minister in a smaller church, living a simpler life. I say: *when my children are out of college.* I tell myself that I want a smaller church, that I would perhaps like to make furniture . . . Ministers, like farmers, are leaving their profession. So much effort goes into the maintenance of the institution and not into the maintenance of spiritual values. Many feel the structure of the institution is so much baggage. An English minister said to me once that an Englishman went to church three times in his life: when he was hatched, matched, and dispatched.

In spite of my romantic impulses, however, that life could not survive. I have no illusions about that. There is the nostalgic image: a garden. A cow. *I will live.* But there had to be a decline in independence. The farmer was becoming more intricately involved with a bureacracy. They complained of the records. But they traded in hardships. They traded in some of the work, some of the dying at an early age. The price was that fierce independence. It was an easier life but one directed by a bureaucracy. It is a question of to whom your servitude belongs—the dignity of wrestling with the elements rather than a structure. Worth of life came in a struggle with the elements. Dignity. Herb Donahue and I worked in the fields, going out to cut corn with a knife. He talked about shucking more corn than anyone in the neighborhood, which was true. He had a sense of pride in this personal skill. There is no pride in a cornpicker.

I find dignity in all things as long as the end result is not harmful. Even menial things. I liked making refrigerators on the assembly line in Dayton. I had a sense of pride in doing well. It was not boring. There was an element of challenge in the performance. I mounted cylinders on top of a unit. They were calibrated to seven ten-thousandths of an inch tolerance. Of course I may have looked at the assembly line differently if I had spent my life on it. I always knew I was going back to school. But there are very few tasks which do not have the potential for human dignity.

In New Burlington, the small system was not efficient. You paid an arm for the privilege of shopping at Blair's Grocery. We have become conditioned to options. Henry Ford said you can have any color you want as long as it's black. No more, no more. When my father went to work in Wilmington he killed the meat man and the bread man. He picked these things up in Wilmington because the automobile made his trip very casual.

But real life requires a certain tension which lies between the fun of doing things a more difficult way and the peril of doing them that way. Take all risks away and life is dull. Of course, I take the other side of this argument with my children. When I was in high school I drove across the country roads at 85 miles an hour in the middle of the night. I was not showing off because no one was with me.

In my shop I have furniture making tools but I prefer the hand tools. It requires skill and craft. The power tools tend to preclude this. Technology makes the groove, not me. There is distance and dilution. A thousand people are involved in the technology of cutting that groove and when it is done it is a groove undistinguishable from a thousand grooves. Being primitive means it is all me. By my hand, it is only me at work.

Russell Stingley, 77

Wonderful dirt. O yes. But my father, who was William, thought the tractors packed down the earth. Say 'Woah' and the horse stopped. The tractor didn't. He didn't like that. But if you wanted the corn in by the 20th of May, why, by God, you needed a tractor to do it. A tractor did what you told it. When I farmed I never knew about money until it was in my hand. I made $3,700 in 1917. In 1919 I took a $180 loss plus the feed. One year there was money for everybody. Next year nobody saw any. So I left the farm. My income went up. It was steady. My cattle didn't die. I'd take a salary everytime. My father used to say, 'Well, we can do this if we can pay this bill or that.' I was tired of hearing that as a child. Embarrassing. I pay my bills now. And it doesn't all go to one fellow. I pay everybody. I was tired of looking at a horse's arse. That's why I quit.

Ralph Baker's diary

February 10, 1906—four degrees:
The ice is 16 inches thick. The cold pierces to the marrow and icemen have a famous crop.

March 31, 1906—36 degrees:
From careful records it is seen that there hasn't been but 45 hours of sunshine during the entire month. Financial affairs are rather unsettled and subject to great change. The uncovering of graft in public offices goes on and almost every day brings forth some new case of robbery by a public official. What is agitating the people most is the control of corporations. It is said John D. Rockefeller has fled to New Jersey where he keeps an armed guard about the premises with orders to shoot any unknown person who may approach.

May 17, 1906—70 degrees:
It has been a cold, wet, backward spring and there is no fruit whatever. The first of the 17-year locusts have appeared and are very numerous. Their next appearance will be in 1923. Where will we be then and what will we be doing? That is a conundrum. The cut worms are very bad.

July 4, 1906—89 degrees:
Today the United States is 130 years old. What progress has been made! What would the framers of the constitution say could they be brought back to life and witness our complex, modern civilization? How they would stare at steam cars and trolley lines. The 130th year of our national life finds us at peace with the world and more prosperous than ever before.

July 12, 1908—100 degrees:
It is so hot and dry that the corn is rolled into knots. You can scrape grass off the ground with your foot. The cistern is dry. Three miles away people have corn in tassel and looking well. It is enough to disgust anyone in the business of farming.

May 14, 1910—50 degrees:
I saw Halley's Comet this morning. Its tail reached one-third across the heavens, a magnificent sight.

The Bakers

August 5, 1910—80 degrees:
The corn is in deperate straits. Great prairie and forest fires are raging all over the country. We need rain badly.

September 17, 1910—75 degrees:
It is disgusting to work like we have and then harvest such jackass fodder. It has been entirely too dry for us. This would not be so bad if it didn't happen three times to one. Everything else is a total failure except wheat which will make half a crop. 'Back to the farm' is the slogan—for newspaper writers in city offices who never saw the backside of a cow and hope not to. It is back to the farm for those who don't know any better and can't help themselves.

January 9, 1914—30 degrees:
I went nowhere today.

August 13, 1915—86 degrees:
There is lightning in all directions this evening. This is the season of screech owls, smelly cornfields, noisy cicadas, and hot restless nights.

May 28, 1916—88 degrees:
Today I picked strawberries and castrated pigs.

February 4, 1917—zero degrees:
Suffering among the animals is intense. It is almost impossible to breathe in this awful snow.

February 5, 1917—four degrees:
The United States has taken the first step in the direction of entering the awful European cataclysm. At 2 p.m. Saturday the German ambassador, Bernstoff, was handed his passport and the American ambassador, Gerard, recalled from Berlin. In my opinion this means war.

February 12, 1917—20 degrees:
It looks like there will be no wheat this year.

April 7, 1917—30 degrees:
The long expected has at last happened. The United States is at war against Germany. This became a fact yesterday at 1:11 p.m. when the president issued the formal declaration. Nobody can say where it will end or what horrors and bloody sacrifices we will be compelled to make. The world is about as bare and dead as it was in December. It looks as though spring will never come.

June 11, 1917—76 degrees:
I replanted corn today. It is the most discouraging prospect I have ever

seen. I can scarcely walk in the fields because of the water. Weeds are coming along something awful. I had just as soon be in Europe fighting as trying to farm under such unparalled conditions.

August 22, 1917—88 degrees:
There is an awful turmoil in the United States just now over the government's attempt to fix food prices. On one hand the government wishes the farmer to raise more stuff and on the other hand it is conscripting the best farmers into the army and destroying the markets by the devilish food control measures. It is a strange medley of contradictions. We are living in strange times. I pulled weeds today.

December 11, 1917—zero degrees:
The snow has drifted over fence tops. The stock is having a very hard time of it. Twenty below zero this morning. It is snowing again and birds are freezing to death.

December 19, 1917—15 degrees:
The war situation is the darkest it has ever been. We are up against the real thing. I husked three shocks of corn and hauled manure.

December 25, 1917—25 degrees:
It is a very cold raw day. I sat around the fire and did nothing.

February 20, 1918—27 degrees:
We devoutly wish for spring.

June 28, 1918—88 degrees:
I plowed some alleged corn today.

April 7, 1921—66 degrees:
I have heard the first purple martin of the season.

July 6, 1921—118 degrees:
It is so hot it is nearly impossible to live. Dry as Tophet and no relief in sight.

August 10, 1927—92 degrees:
All that today should have been it was not, and all that it should not have been it was.

January 27, 1931—46 degrees:
The well went dry today. That hasn't happened in 30 years. Drought conditions are as bad as anytime last summer.

February 17, 1931—44 degrees:
The price of all farm products is the lowest it has been for 39 years.
Business of all kinds are in desperate straits. No ordinary person has any
money. Bank failures are common. Farm conditions are at the limit of
our ability to stand.

June 18, 1931—86 degrees:
Today was clear with a light south wind. It was one of those rare June
days about which the poets rave. Clear and bright and radiantly beautiful. It is poor luck we are so crowded with work we have no time to admire such days.

December 16, 1931—50 degrees:
We are seeing the hardest times in a generation. Every day about a half
page in the county paper is devoted to bankrupt farmers. I wonder if it
will ever end.

January 25, 1932—19 degrees:
Herschel Hildebrecht shot himself through the body above the heart last
night on the church grounds.

March 18, 1932—50 degrees:
We have finished husking corn. It makes me feel as I imagine a pris-
oner might feel after being liberated from the penitentiary. This afternoon I cleaned out the chickenhouse.

May 15, 1932—62 degrees:
Colonel Lindberg's long-missing baby was found near its home with a
fractured skull.

June 18, 1932—80 degrees:
The wind blew down the lower Western Beauty apple tree.

July 17, 1932—95 degrees:
I spent the day lying around trying to recuperate from a week of strenu-
ous threshing.

September 5, 1932—86 degrees:
We sold three cows at two and half cents a pound. Corn is 25 cents a
bushel. A person at the present time can do the most work and get the
least I ever knew about. Everything is as dead as an anvil and nothing
worth the effort it takes to produce it.

November 8, 1932—78 degrees:
Today was the election. President Hoover vs. Roosevelt. I'm much
afraid Roosevelt will win. If so we are surely in for a bad time of it.

November 16, 1932—34 degrees:
The boat weighed 820 pounds and sold for $4.10
                                   freight was   2.00
                                    weighing   .12
                                  commission   .50
                                         net $1.48

September 9, 1933—83 degrees:
Ed Blatt and I went to Cincinnati in our auto where we went to the art museum and looked at pictures by Corot, Van Dyck, Dürer, Murillo, Sargent, and Reynolds.

August 5, 1934—109 degrees:
The sun shone today with a pitiless glare that defies description. Everything is perishing. At Kansas City it is said the thermometer has not been below 106 degrees for two weeks. Despair is general.

November 8, 1934—50 degrees:
King Edward VIII of England has developed a romantic yen for Mrs. Wallis Warfield Simpson, an American divorcée.

January 23, 1938—34 degrees:
I went to the woods today and got a redbud tree to set along the yard fence. Nothing is more beautiful than a redbud tree.

February 6, 1938—50 degrees:
There is water over the whole earth and the mud is unspeakably deep.

May 8, 1938—72 degrees:
The ground is desperately dry and there are wide fathomless cracks a week's rain would not fill. The pastures are dying. No corn is planted and prospects look gloomy.

May 12, 1938—50 degrees:
The temperature fell to 27 degrees last night and ice formed on the water troughs. It is the coldest May I have ever seen, and dry as the Sahara.

May 21, 1938—86 degrees:
An awful thunderstorm came and deluged the world. A lot of hail came, too. Chickens were drowned. There is everywhere mud, water, and misery.

December 25, 1938—38 degrees:
Today is Christmas. It is another drab, commonplace day. When I think of the joyous days and feasts and company we used to have in the long ago it is almost too much to bear. Would that I might bring them back again.

Syrup

When the trees are scratches against the surly February sky Charles McIntire goes into the woods where his breath hangs in balloons as if momentarily the balloons might fill with language. He drills small holes in the maples which he recognizes by the dignified bark which looks like marbled slate. And waits for the precarious succession of freezing nights and warm days which makes the sap rise in the irresolute veins of the maple. There is no clue that inwardly the maple seethes in the breaking up of winter. The world seems still and vague. It is as though color and motion have never existed except in the imagination. For Charles to come here is an act of faith in a dead season. The woods could be etchings.

In the cornfield behind the sugar house a bird cries a piercing, mournful sound. Neither Charles nor Judy has ever seen it but they hear it every year at the same time. Charles calls it the sugar bird. When he hears it in the cornfield he knows it is time to go to the woods. When the syrup season begins Judy has a dream. In the dream she finds Charles' body in the maple woods. It is full of spiles, his blood dripping slowly into a bucket.

There are fewer than six syrup makers in the New Burlington community now although at one time every country family had its syrup makers. All of the syrup makers except Charles are older men. Some of them remember hauling the sap with teams of horses, and boiling in huge iron kettles.

When the sugar camps open in late February people from the cities drive into the country in their station wagons looking for the high rolling clouds of steam from the syrup makers' pans. Most of the visitors are quiet and modest, as though they are watching the performance of a great and difficult skill. The syrup makers, however, know this is not true. Among themselves they recognize it not as difficult but exacting.

They see it as a sly craft, essentially unknowable. The maple is moved only by sun and light, thaw and freeze. No one is certain why the sap behaves as it does. The maple remains mysterious. It absorbs the qualities of the earth into its huge but imperceptible life. Two months before the revival of vegetation the sap moves dimly in the marrow of the maple. February is a pale month and the syrup makers wait for the weather. In February they assert themselves in the maple groves. Although they are living in a time of great technology it no longer applies. The maple is unmoved. The men contrast themselves with the season, an ancient gesture.

At night Charles listens carefully to the weather reporters although he knows better. Their important, authoritative voices sound like generals commanding troop movements. They sound as if they could be believed. Judy dreams of fields of wheat. The stalks of grain seem like tendrils.

When they are able to get out, the very old men who once made syrup like to visit the sugar camps where they stand near the pans and say, "When I used to make syrup . . ." Although many years have passed the old syrup makers find everything known to them. It is as though they see themselves as younger men doing familiar work. Occasionally Howard Leaming who is in his eighties will visit the sugar camp where he recalls a time fifty years ago: "We had three camps and tapped three hundred trees. We always tapped on the south side because experience told us the water would run better. Sometimes the season would be long and sometimes short. One year was not like the other. At first there was nothing but an old twist auger to tap with and wooden spiles. What was done you see was to take an elder and punch the pith out for a tap. Then they were made of oak bored out. Earthenware crocks were what was used then and set on the ground although the coon dogs were bad to come along and piss in them. We usually made 215 gallons or more and used all we wanted and sold all we could at a dollar a gallon. There was a lot of syrup made in this part of the country and it was really good on buckwheat cakes. What the old nigger woman would say: make you swallow your tongue. Now there are only a few sugar camps and the maples are not as they were."

It is snowing now. The temperature is down to fourteen but it will soon rise past twenty-eight. Buckets creak on trees. A dead walnut tree sways, its broken wood groaning. Although it is cold the sun is strong and

Lee Ames boiling syrup on the evaporator (PHOTOGRAPH BY DAN PATTERSON)

soon it will pull the sap into the buckets. When the wind stops the sap begins to slowly drip from the spiles and splash into the empty buckets where it forms perfect orchestral notes in the quiet of the woods.

Across the fields to the north Charles can see the steam from Carl Weinman's evaporator. Carl continues to collect the sap in buckets and boil it down over a wood fire. Some of the syrup makers use tubing which runs from tree to tree and to a central tank. Then they boil the sap over a fuel oil fire. In Carl's woods is a maple used as a survey marker in

1799. Someone has been tapping the maple for 175 years. When the Indians tapped such maples they danced under the trees calling the time "maple moon," which they recognized as a preface to spring. The countrymen of New Burlington built sugar camps within sight of each other and they, too, celebrated: community, craft, the breaking up of winter. They wrapped chickens in cloth soaked in the sap, baked them in the coals under the evaporator, and invited in their neighbors. Only Carl can bake chickens but he is old now and his health is fragile. Charles is glad when he looks across the fields at the steam rising above Carl's sugar house. Carl is well. Hope rises with the sweet water in this narrow season.

Junior Hormel lives down the lane from Carl. While tapping the DeHaven woods Junior drove a spile into a telephone pole and hung a bucket on it. "That damn idiot Junior Hormel," said the people of Buck Run, laughing. Farther south, old man Bash built his sugar house then added a bedroom onto it. Sometimes Carl Weinman while running his evaporator cooks himself a couple of eggs by boiling them in the sugar water which becomes syrup at seven points above the boiling point of water. Carl sells some of his syrup to a Middletown tobacco manufacturer who uses it to sweeten chewing tobacco but most of his syrup is sold out of his back door. This is the way the New Burlington syrup makers prefer to sell their syrup. On a good year Charles or Lee Ames may sell two hundred gallons each, most of it to people who come to the sugar house or to the kitchen door. Some of them buy ten gallons. For most of them it is not just another shopping trip but rather an event. They consider themselves connoisseurs taking part in something old and continuous.

The syrup makers themselves begin to consider their season in the summer when they can watch the foliage on the trees. To them this is an indication that the trees are manufacturing a great deal of sap. By late December the syrup makers have forgotten last season's pain. They are ready to go into the woods again. It is something they have known for a long time. Even the young man, Charles McIntire, began when he was a teenager, after his father and his grandfather. "I do not always have reasons for the things I do," he says. "But I do not think I could *not* make maple syrup."

Charles' son, Gregg, who is now seven, has been going to the woods with his father each February since he was three. When the two of them run the evaporator they are father and son studious, alert, constantly moving, watching. Gregg has a small ladder so that he may look into the pans where he checks to see if the sweet water is foaming too much. He knows when it is time to go to the woods and that it usually takes forty gallons of sap to make one gallon of syrup. He knows how to run all of the syrup operation but he is not tall enough to reach everything yet.

When Charles and Gregg go into the Mitchener woods to haul the sap they see Thurmond Mitchener's coon dogs running. The dogs seem old and morose. Gregg thinks that the dogs may be looking for Thurmond who is now dying in a rest home. The dogs look watchfully at strangers, peer out of ditches at late hours, stare into headlights. They run silently in fields. A jug of Charles' syrup sits on the breakfast table in Thurmond's old farmhouse which remains exactly like it was when Thurmond left it more than a year ago.

The air is sweeter now in March. It is not as painful. Tiny bell-like flowers appear under the light crust of snow. In one of the buckets is a bird's nest, perfectly formed. Tractors bloom in the fields.

The Operator

*She has heard there is a vacancy somewhere in the country. She sits at the
city switchboard dreaming. Of a big house with white pillars and a great,
winding stair. She will stand poised at the top looking down upon guests.
In her dream she is elegant. Through the switchboard she talks with Stanley Kirby about the vacancy. She thinks he must look like Abraham Lincoln. A voice of stature and size. And drives past cornfields and fat cows
to find New Burlington and Stanley Kirby a little fellow with big brogans.
And moves into the house with the telephone exchange to share a
bathroom with the village. And watches the weather by looking into a
puddle in the road. Rain in it or sky of some kind.*

Della Wilson, 46

I had been there a little while and felt very discouraged. But Arthur Tur-
ner, a one-armed man, brought me a bouquet of gladiolas. And Ray Carr
got us up one Sunday morning to give us a dozen eggs. I began to understand the old Quakers. One said, 'The only problem we have is my
mother listens in and we can hardly hear anybody we're talking to.' And I
said, 'Yes, it cuts the volume down. Why don't you talk to her?' And he
said, 'O no! We couldn't do that!' After a month I had all the numbers
memorized. Except Haineses and Joneses. There was Charles A. Jones
and Charles T. Jones. And Haineses everywhere. One hundred and seventy five families. My husband, Lee, called them out to me.

In the village were five-party lines. Ten-party lines outside. Everybody had his own code. Ten parties, ten different rings in each house. Farm houses sounded like fire stations. 'O no,' they said. 'We don't hear the other rings. If we are sleeping, only our ring wakes us.' I got a long-distance call for so-and-so on such-and-such street. I looked outside and found nothing but Route 380. 'Operator,' I said, 'you must have the wrong New Burlington. We don't *have* any streets . . .'

Once a receiver was off and Lee began to whistle into the line. Attract someone's attention perhaps. A whistling came back. 'I hear a *bird*,' Lee said. It was Mary Hyden. *She* had heard a bird, too. Not knowing her receiver was off and crawling around the house whistling. Weird New Burlington. 'That's George Arledge's extension off,' I would say. 'I can hear his cows.'

I took cow calls for Melvin Hollingsworth. He went away to school and studied artificial insemination. He called one day, hoo-hawing around, finally to ask, 'Della, I ain't home all the time and I might get a call and I wonder if you would take it down for me?' And I said, 'Well, yah.' And the farmers would call up when their old cow got in heat and say, 'I noticed 'er this morning,' or 'I noticed 'er this evening when I went out to milk.' And before long I was saying, 'Well, when did you notice 'er?'

I was always on the job, although people here thought of the time. No one called after 10 o'clock. If there was a call after 10, you could hear all the receivers go up. People calling from the outside often kept trying, and finally some neighbor would pick up and say, 'He's not home. He's gone someplace. Quit calling.' It changed some in later years, but not to extremes.

Whoever was closest worked the switchboard. I never knew if my egg was hot or cold. I had the company put a long cord on the board so I could walk in the kitchen and stir my beans. I was training Lee how to run the board and his hands got sweaty and it shocked him and he yelled 'GODDAMN!' into the open line and I thought, O my God, we'll be run out. But nothing ever came of it. When Lee answered, a male voice startled the other operators. 'We're taking over,' he said to them. 'Where's the operator?' they asked. 'Washing dishes,' he said. At noon I blew the siren and dashed into the bathroom. Before I was the New Burlington operator, there was nothing but an outhouse. Sometimes when the operator was out back, there'd be a call. 'Where have you been?' they'd ask. She told them in very certain terms.

When there was a fire, whoever was on the street just stuck his head in the door to ask where. I didn't know this. One day there's a fire and Ronnie Grooms sticks his head in the door and I'm sitting at the switchboard in my slip and bra. When the flood came, everybody called to check on people. I handled 345 calls in one hour. By five o'clock I lost my voice. I could have stopped all the calls by asking 'Is this an emergency?' But of course I didn't. During bad storms, lightning sometimes arced on the wires, which frightened me.

I learned to sew through the switchboard. Effie, the chief operator in Wilmington, told me how. She plugged in and she taught me about the tension on the sewing machine. Helen Stingley and I studied the Bible through the switchboard. I scratched my dog's stomach with my foot while I worked. Junior, the cat, slept on top of the switchboard. We had another cat named Sweetmeat. He had his eye put out by Gary McClure, who did it with a piece of asphalt. I asked him why. 'I felt like it,' he said.

When Alice Haines was doing her Masters Degree and writing a term paper on my daughter Kim, I said, 'She's an abnormal kid, brought up under abnormal circumstances. She bathes in the kitchen sink . . .' Lee said to Kim, 'Come on, Kim. Let's walk up to Greene County.' The county line went through the village, you see. We weren't even sure where the city limits were. Since the rates changed outside of the village, we figured out the limits for ourselves. We used the signpost at Pig Alley, the graveyard, over to Ruthie Conklin's and up to George Lovett's.

When I first went there I said, 'I'm going to be all business.' One night there was a bird flying around the switchboard. Sandy was working the board, and the bird is flying around and I'm flying around after the bird and a woman on Buck Run calls in and says, 'Honey, do you know how to make bread and butter pickles?' And Sandy said, 'No m'am, I don't.'

There were never any problems with the people. Although Mr. Reicker wanted his name spelled right on his bill. The old operators spelled it like it sounded. He said he wouldn't pay it because it wasn't addressed to him. And once a man named Wallace wanted his phone taken out, so he yanked it out and brought it into the office. My God, I thought. Where am I?

Shirley Lovett was the postmistress, and she could look out the back of the post office and watch the road from Wilmington. If she saw anyone who looked official, she told me and I got the cat off the switchboard. But I felt responsible for the village. I was needed. I listened to their voices to tell how they were. My switchboard was the center of the neighborhood. The heart of it. I was connected to them all, and all to each other.

> *Do you know so-and-so*
> *Yah, she's pregnant*
> *And how's your cabbage*

When we made the changeover to the dial system, we had a little ceremony at 2 a.m. The cutover was made after everyone was asleep. So we cut the wire and it looked like it was gasping for air. Alice Haines said, 'It's so sad.' She drove all the way home, then she turned around and came back. I am packing. 'Della! Della!' she said. 'We won't have you anymore . . .'

I made a tape for the dial system which announced wrong numbers. People found out they could dial a wrong number and get my voice. Jane Collett used to do it, and Opal Jasper said she did it when she got lonely. It lasted a month and wore out. The human voice that they had known, you see. When the new building came they brought in a bulldozer and it ran over our rhubarb. 'They cut our rhubarb down!' I said. By that time we had moved out on Brimstone Road. Through fire and flood, I said, then out to Brimstone Road. Maybe I just won't even have a telephone . . .

The Auctioneer

He has always been an auctioneer. When he was 10 he auctioned off a tomcat in his backyard. At 77 he retired to attend other mens' auctions. To listen to the sing-song rush of words off the crier's tongue. For a bargain under the warp and rust of used machinery. And secrets lying dull in boxes and barrels. By seven o'clock of this late fall morning frost underfoot and sun overhead Bill Conklin's sale has begun. An auctioneer's litany over buckets of bolts, nails, buckles, screws, washers, a thousand cunning shapes. And to a blacksmith's anvil which might have made them all. The old auctioneer follows along. To grin a sly grin behind the anvil and say: 'When I was an auctioneer we used to pick 'em up to sell 'em.' And the young auctioneer looks at the old man pausing only a moment before grinning himself to reply: 'Times change old man and water rolls on under bridges.' Tacit recognition between them in a nod from the old auctioneer who turns to the house for coffee. Behind him the auctioneer's chant is lulling. It could be an old song.

Jess Stanley, 80

When I was small, I was always selling. Walking home from school I'd see something in the fields, I'd sell it. Old sow across the fence. Cow in a pasture. Made no difference to me. I had heard the old auctioneers and I liked the voices. I began to mock them. I had a plain, strong voice. You could hear me for 30 squares. The week after I was 15, I was at a sale in

New Burlington and the auctioneer asked if there were any other auctioneers around. If there were, he said, they could sell awhile and he could get a bite to eat.

Well, my neighbors were there and said, 'Put Jess up there. He sells everything he sees along the road from chickens to tomcats.' I was in the haymow playing. Looked like a hayseed. 'A kid like me?' I said. I went out. There was a row of rakes and hoes, harness on a pole, stretching from the barn out to the road. Must have been 500 people there. I got up on a chair. They handed me the harness and I started in. The old man, who was Bill Mills, watched a minute and said, 'Gentlemen, that kid is alright. I'll have something to eat now.' He came back, I was in the barn selling hay and oats. I cleaned that barn out. I have been doing that since I was knee high to a duck. Bill Mills told me, 'All you have to do is keep on going . . .'

I think I was cut out to be an auctioneer. It seemed natural to me. Fifty-eight years and I never had a sore throat. When I was 18, I put on my button slippers and went to the Jones National School of Auctioneering in Chicago. We were there six weeks. It was 1914. We sold toys, pretending they were the real items. We had an auction and Mr. Jones called our numbers and I was first on the floor. Some there were 60. I was still a kid. 'Young fellow,' he said, 'do it like you were back home.' When I finished, he said, 'That kid has been selling the old gray mare out behind the barn.' I was the youngest there.

I sold it all, toothpicks to threshing machines. I sold good Belgian mares in the streets of Wilmington. That was 1918. A team went for about $500. Two fellows want something, the price tends to go up. Once a man and a wife, one on each side were bidding against each other. Couldn't see each other. I stopped the auction. 'What's the matter?' I asked them. 'Don't you two get along?'

Don Workman saw a coal oil lamp he wanted once and asked Martha to bid for him. I was selling. She was bidding. Clippity clip, the lamp went right up. It got to be about $25 and I said, 'That's my wife over there but I want you to know she's spending her own money.' She let it go at $35. I've seen horse collars go for $8. I sold them once for fifty cents. Once I sold a china slipper. Held it up and before I asked for a bid, the girls had it up to $18. I just let them go.

Once I was delighted to sell horses. When I was 16 I sold a gray mare for $281. I thought I had done something. It was a handsome price. I can still walk to the spot where that happened. It was a nice day in the spring. If anyone laughed at such a boy doing a man's work, it didn't amount to anything. Because I always did the job, and did it well. Everybody was satisfied. I had been selling since I was nine. In 1912, I sold a box social at Cornstalk School. I did 200 sales a year and missed two in my life because I was laid up. I have been on a wagon selling, my mind on something else, looking way off someplace. Being an auctioneer gave me freedom. I was as good as you can find.

Flood

The villagers are isolated by the countryside which sprawls around them. They, too, think of themselves as country people and like the farmers whose lives they share they are on intimate terms with all manner of disaster. It is a relationship in which they are stoic and resigned, like the relationship of an obdurate old couple that has kept faith for a half century not with each other but the years themselves. There are diseases in man and nature. Too much rain. Not enough rain. Hog cholera and hailstones, maladies of mortgage and inflammations of debt. And foreclosures on the insolvencies of the human condition.

Fire, 1916: Wayne Smith running from his house carrying a lantern yet the whole earth bright as judgment day. He looks first at the fire then at the lantern. To pitch it in the street where it becomes a miniature fire mirroring the village. And Mr. Wilson late to help with his trousers on backward and the suspenders between his legs. The fire is mostly out by dawn and the new light fills the street revealing the firefighters in gowns and pajamas and underwear. And they look quietly at each other to walk back to their homes feeling exposed, slightly embarrassed.

Fire, 1939: Hazel Reeves down the street yelling, "Firefirefire!" and Burwell Miller out to see his grocery store burning and the house next door. And Leona watching her father's face, like something grown under moonlight. So pale strained suddenly old. From the store they save only the loafer's bench.

Afterward they begin to talk of a fire department. But country people are very conservative. Seeds of caution are sown genetically in the austere marriage of men and fields. They will have a fire department but it will be 20 years and another disaster before they do. In this interval of 20

Flood, 1913

years they will rely on the whim of Providence which they in their manner call "native ingenuity."

Most of the time whatever catches on fire burns. The firemen are farmers armed with sap buckets. They refer to themselves as foundation savers. This is a joke among themselves but not for others. They know they are in a precarious business; fire creates a vacuum, a loss which pulls in the vast country distances which in turn feeds the flames.

Houses burn and barns with livestock inside and in the spring the high water comes as if the polar manifestations of fire and flood neatly balance. The floods have occurred in this century with some frequency, behaving in accordance with certain unwritten rules: they occur usually in the spring, they rise to the cross streets, and soon they peak to leave the cellars filled with mud.

These are known traits and soon the villagers come to regard the water not as malevolent, the floods not as disasters, but rather an observance, like the preparations for Decoration Day or some other communal event. Sometimes there is present a quaint, festive air. Jumbo Reeves, who lives beside Anderson's Fork in the low-lying place, is always the first to know. When the water begins to rise in his yard he stands on his doorsteps and yells across to the villagers: "By God, you're fixing to get your asses wet!"

Vernon Stiles never even bothers to leave his house although in 1968 the water will chase him upstairs. "When it peaks," he explains to his up-town neighbors, "it will fall within the hour. If you aren't in here to begin sweeping with the water you'll have mud left on your doorknobs."

Just below the cross streets Louie Wills gets up and finds a boat at her front door. "I can't go now," Louie tells her rescuers. "I'm fixing Maude Hurley's breakfast."

Maude has the men row her to Louie's house where Louie puts the breakfast in a basket and the men are waiting outside to help the old ladies into the boat. They use the fireman's carry. "Put your arms around my neck," one of the men says to Louie. "You take care of that end and I'll take care of this one," says Louie.

She looks back to see Maude where she sits rigidly in the mens' interlocked arms as though she might be sitting in her pew at the church and Louie begins to laugh.

She goes to her daughter's house to spend the night where she lies awake and wonders what is happening in the village. Below Louie the rescuers find a pig with only its snout above the water. They lift the pig into the boat where it sits humbly among the men as they row through the cross streets.

The water rises above the hardware store and into the post office. Three doors above the telephone exchange Marie Blair finds her canned tomatoes floating in the cellar. Frank Lundy's tractor is in the bottomlands with only the top of its exhaust showing above the waters. To one of the villagers who is acquainted with the ocean, Frank's tractor exhaust resembles a periscope on an underwater vessel navigating New Burlington's personal sea.

Some the water drives insane: one man is found in his kitchen sink. When the rescuers wade into his house he warns them to get out.

"You'll all drown," he tells them. "Only I am safe. When the water rises up to me, I'll pull the plug . . ."

The next day when the water falls a rainbow forms in the dark clouds over the village. The rainbow curves into the farmland exactly where Graveyard Road begins and ends. Cornstalks hang from the telephone wires along Caesar's Creek. The villagers begin to clean up. They pour hot water through their radios, then cook them in their ovens.

They have not been prepared for the extent of this flood. It is as though nature has dealt them a final indignity. They will no longer be forbearant. They will render the surrounding universe, faulty in design and method, impotent by a pronouncement: they will *organize*. *Organization* will deal with the burning of houses and barns, midnight illnesses and sudden water. They will make a force of themselves to counter the capricious force without.

In the curve above New Burlington they build a firehouse. The farmers and villagers sign one-hundred dollar notes; the women make food to sell. Gladys Batson teaches the men to make coffee 20 gallons at a time. Soon the men have their first piece of equipment, a 1941 Chevrolet pumper. It is old but durable. It has switches, pumps, valves, couplings. These can be used to regulate calamity. In this truck, as in their ambulance, they will hound disaster. When they hear the siren on top of the firehouse it is as though something acute and pointed has run through the fiber of the village. As though such shrill vibrations whip through a single cellular column to which all the life of the countryside is connected. The sound of the siren is something close, intimate, and fearful among themselves. They know that when the equipment goes out it is to attend someone among them. It is to attend themselves.

By the time the Caesar's Creek dam backs water into the cross streets in that most final (and arbitrary) of floods, the village will have been gone for several years. This time, in 1968, the bottomlands are a flat sheet of water which stretches almost a mile east and west. It lies inertly on the cornfields as if it were a huge plate of steel. At one end it floods the cellar of Frank Lundy's farmhouse. At the other end it floods Bill Conklin's cellar. Below the Haineses, an uprooted sycamore slams into the double iron bridge ripping it partly from its abutments. Don and Mary Alice awake in the night and listen to the old bridge twisting in the water. Its noises seem to them articulate and protesting.

When the water peaks, farmer Phil Hartment drives his powerboat across the bottomlands towing his young son on water skis. The boy slaloms over Bill Conklin's submerged fence posts and up into New Burlington where he lands in Merle McIntire's peony bed. Four-year-old Gregg McIntire, watching both the water and the water skier, suggests to his great-grandmother that she not move from New Burlington as the Army Corps of Engineers demand rather remain and open a bait shop on her back porch overlooking the soon-to-be reservoir.

Gregg's mother, thinking this like him, laughs. Merle, almost 90, does not. Unsuccessful, at least for the moment, at willing herself to die, she soon meets the Corps deadline and moves into a trailer park.

And soon the fire department will be all that is left of New Burlington, Ohio. The village itself exists inside the minds of the firemen who gather at the firehouse on the second Tuesday of each month but they seldom talk of it. Occasionally they will recall the bad floods or laugh about the time the ambulance was at McClure's Garage for repairs and some of the village teenagers sneaked in and made love on the emergency cot. Or they will laugh about LaDonna Stanley who lives in the farmhouse across from the firehouse and the time she forgot her underwear which was brought to her by her husband, Charles, and she is riding in the back of the ambulance trying to pull her underwear on.

Mostly the men talk neither of solemn matters nor abstractions. When they do their language declines into vagueness and as if they themselves know how paltry it is they quickly begin to talk of the things they know: crops and tools and weather and machinery. And the village in their heads is like a filmstrip filed away in an archive.

Mary Robinson (PHOTOGRAPH BY DAN PATTERSON)

Depression

There once was a lady of fashion
who had a very fine passion.
To her boy friend she said
as they jumped into bed,
'Here's one thing Roosevelt can't ration.'
 —limerick in New Burlington
 during the depression

Mary Robinson, 75

Mr. Robinson and I rented some ground and sold melons and produce. We sold it up and down the street, right off the spring wagon. My father had taught me how to do that. When I was eight, I'd get up at two o'clock and we'd drive to Xenia. It took us an hour and 15 minutes. We went twice a week. We picked blackberries by the bushel and shelled lima beans all night. I've done that all night then dressed and drove to town with my father to sell them.

After the commotion on Wall Street, a farmer down the road came home and said, 'The stock market has crashed!' His little boy heard him and asked, 'Was any cows hurt?' That's all the stock market meant to any of us.

It was dry in 1930. We watered our limas. Kept them from going under when no one else had anything. Four of us sat up one night and shelled out 105 quarts. We took them to old Jake Hyman. He had a store in Xenia. I drove the machine up. He offered me 25 cents a quart.

'The only way, Jake,' I said, 'is to take them every one. Or I'll tramp the streets and sell them door to door.'

He said, 'O lady, that's a hellava lot of beans.'

I said, 'Didn't I find that out last night.'

We grew what we ate during the depression and husked corn in the flat land for six cents a shock. That was seventy five cents a day for two of us. A shock was fourteen by sixteen feet. We didn't give it much thought. There wasn't much we could do. We just sat there and lived.

187

One time we felt we were awful poor until the old bachelor next door came over to read our paper. Harold said, 'Harry, you had any dinner?'

Harry said, 'No.'

Harold looked at me and said, 'We got any beans left?'

I said, 'Yes.'

We gave old Harry beans and bread. No butter. We didn't have any butter. I had to cook another pot of beans for breakfast. I learned to eat muskrat. We called it the marsh hare. The meat is on the red order. Groundhogs, too, but no later than the 20th of June. As the old man says: it's a hell of a long time between the greens and the rabbits.

My parents had a little grocery store. Mother went by to see what had happened to one of her regular customers who hadn't been by in a while. The lady was cooking their little dog on the stove. She began to cry. I tell my kids, 'Don't waste anything.' They don't know what I'm saying.

We made use of everything we had. We raised geese and picked the feathers for our pillows. The feathers had to get ripe first. That was when they were ready to shed them in the spring. If they weren't ripe the old geese really squawked. We made our mattresses out of cornhusks. I still make my soap. Put water on wood ashes to make lye in the ash hopper up in the orchard. Six and a half pounds of grease to three pints of lye. Stir twenty minutes with a wooden spoon until it looks like strained honey. Pour it in a box lined with newspapers and muslin and let it age. It's better if it lays there about a month. Make it on a clear day or it won't set right.

There was even a use for manure. It was a hard life but we thought nothing of it. The depression was like an illness. It was something you went through and got over with. You don't miss things you've never had. I remember when cars drove with a handle. We had a house full once to listen to our new phonograph.

The world gradually grows on me but I go along with it. I nurse, cook, clean. It gets me out of the humdrum. It keeps me independent. I hope I am until I drop over.

God

The Quakers come first to New Burlington. They are farmers looking for freedom which to them consists of the absence of slavery and the presence of good topsoil. Their community precedes the existence of the village by 25 years. They build plain but lovely farmhouses of brick which are connected by orderly fields and forests which are not considered orderly. Needing something larger than the arrogant trees they begin in 1805 an indulged meeting. There are the familiar names: *Compton, Hawkins, Mendenhall, Wilson, Mills*. They build a meeting house on the banks of Caesar's Creek. It is a small blunt building in a forest clearing as if its presence is intended to be a statement in the face of God, man, and nature. Inside the building is a curtain which separates the men and the women although both sit upon the same stained oak benches. There is neither a piano nor an organ.

The Quakers pursue righteousness almost demoniacally. But they are good farmers and neighbors. They shake hands over business deals and keep their money under the carpet. Their faith is rigorous and severe. They adhere to a hundred rituals which serve to remind them that human equilibrium is poor and the fall from grace constantly imminent. A member is censured for playing a fiddle. Gravestones are removed from the churchyard because they are too high. The church states: "Tale bearing and distraction are discouraged."

Some perceive such a life as intolerably binding. Some who perceive this are Quakers who will become Methodists. The staunch old Quakers, however, immersed in an austerity of their own choosing, believe all things pinch and bind. They are therefore opposed to slavery, it being an unchosen austerity.

Jesse Hawkins's Sunday school class (Jesse at left, seated)

From the time Amos Hawkins spends part of his first winter in a lean-to above Caesar's Creek, the Quakers have been helping the black men escape. When they flee north through New Burlington the Quaker farmers treat them as kinsmen in need of shelter. They build homes with secret hiding places. Even the Methodist shopkeeper John Grant has a secret place in one end of a large upstairs cupboard. James Smith has a recess in the well wall at his blacksmith shop where the black men are lowered on the well bucket. It is not uncommon to see angry southern men with dogs stand in the cross streets and curse the villagers whom they suspect. They have, after all, caught Stephen Compton with his spring wagon loaded with escapees. And seen that he was fined $1,700, an awesome sum for even the village coffinmaker.

The ordinance of 1787 has made the Northwest Territory free of slavery but the Fugitive Slave Law of 1850 does not allow the villagers to aid the slaves. Neither Congress nor the slaveowners, however, consider the Quakers. "The freemen of Ohio will never turn out to chase the panting fugitive," declares Joshua Giddings. It is as though the Underground Railroad is an exercise in religious zeal for which they have been practicing all these pious, flinty years. As though this excitement is release from the decades of such a spare and narrow discipline.

They will hide the black men everywhere. They have cupboards, wells, and cisterns. The black men will be sanctified in the darkness of cellars, stairwells, and deep moonless nights. Where they will then be converted to freedom. Stephen Compton hides a slave in a newly made coffin while his daughters, Hannah and Rebecca, sit on the box and weep as they drive to the burying ground. On Sunday at the meeting house a slave hides under Lydia Jay's skirts as the owner passes by outside. A mother hides with her child in John Grant's cupboard and stuffs her skirt in the infant's mouth to keep it silent while the owner rages in the streets outside. To find she has accidentally smothered it. And the blacksmith buries it in an unmarked grave on the hill above the village.

The Underground Railroad begins on the Ohio River near Cincinnati and follows the Bullskin Trace north through New Burlington to Canada. This is the ancient trail made by animals traversing the great hardwood forests. It has since been usurped by men; first by Indians, later by the white men who brought commerce. Fifty thousand black men escape the South, most of them over the Bullskin Trace. The trail becomes consecrated; over it they will be made whole.

The Methodists are latecomers to the village, a fact which may cause them discomfort. Upon their hundredth anniversary a small history is written prefaced by the phrase: "We live in deeds not years, in thoughts not figures on a dial." It is as though the Methodists are defensive about being absent for twenty years.

They begin their worship in 1825 in the house of Alexander Jay. Later they move across the street and worship in the hardware store. The Methodists are, after all, shopkeepers: Hawes, .Grant, Smith, Collett. To the shopkeepers the transactions of both body and soul are sacred. What better symbol than Methodists meeting in a hardware store, joining geography, industry, and ritual in a trinity of worship?

Later, they, too, are not unmoved by slavery. By the 1850s the Methodist Church has lost half its membership because of its position on slavery. The Methodist abolitionists build a small building near the cross streets and begin their own worship which includes the prospects of servitude to the Lord but not to man. They are known politely as the "Wesleyan Methodists" and impolitely as "the woolly heads."

When the Republican Party is formed in 1854 by men opposed to the extension of slavery, the abolitionists—both Methodists and Quakers—embrace it as though it is sacrosanct. A hundred years later the descendents of these families, brought up in the old disciplines, will still cast unshakable votes for "the party of Lincoln." When the Civil War comes, it is considered by some of the villagers as vindication of a half century of active piety. It will be to them a Holy War.

Only a few of the villagers pursue other denominations. Some of the McKays, however, are Baptists who believe in foreordination. Sarah Harlan goes with them to church where she hears the minister say that there are infants in hell not a span long. When she returns to the village she tells the other ladies. "A span," she says, "is a man's hand. If that is so, what chance will Sarah Harlan have? It is not a religion for me . . ."

From 1805 until 1870, writes one of the Quakers, "Friends worshiped at Caesar's Creek in their usual programmed silent waiting upon the Lord which was the custom of Friends." The meeting house is as quiet and severe as ever. Only one thing changes: in 1868 an itinerant Irish stonemason stops long enough to build a stone wall around the old cemetery. Flat stone is hauled up the hill from Caesar's Creek and laid up without mortar. The Irishman works with the curious fossil-laden stone and a delicate sensibility. When he has finished an acre of the peaceful dead are enclosed with a thick four-foot high wall. Cost: $614.90.

To the Quakers who come to Ohio from New England and the East the stone wall is a reminder of oblique fields filled with rocks. Fields for stonemasons, not farmers. Stone fences (a harvest too) are repaired by custom: if you are climbing over and knock a stone off, put two back . . .

It is behind this wall that old Samuel Compton's—the original Quaker settler—grandchildren are buried, Sarah on top of Hannah to make room beside them for their black housekeeper. And old Samuel himself buried nearby, in the Jones's cornfield.

In 1870 some of the Caesar's Creek Quakers are restless in the ceremonies of abstention. Some of them are tempted by the looser pageantry of the village Methodists. They have passed by on warm days and heard them singing. The Quakers have converted by hand a thousand acres of forest into fields and they have abolished slavery and they, too, would like to sing.

Not even all the surrounding meetings are silent. The nearby Chester Friends Meeting has ministers, among them Jane Carey who is preaching one Sunday when her underwear falls down. When this happens Jane does not stop preaching and Ethel Hawkins Wall walks to the pulpit where Jane steps out of her underwear as if she were going to the wash house and Ethel folds the underwear and places it under her arm and returns to her seat. The Caesar's Creek Quakers do not, however, regard this as a sign.

When the Wesleyan Methodists return to the old church uptown—the war has arbitrated their position for them—they leave empty their tiny church at the cross streets. In the spring of 1870 Nathan and Esther Frame hold ten days of meetings in it. They do not sing but the traditionalists consider this an evangelistic meeting and they do not favor it. The older Friends warn their children not to attend. Soon, perhaps, there *will* be singing.

Alice Walton knows what will happen at such a time: the organist will work the pedals and the devil himself will be pumped into the atmosphere.

At the end of the ten days Jesse Spray stands upon a bench and says, "Friends, these are not drunken with new wine but the spirit of the Lord is here among the people." They buy the building from the Methodists for $400. When they seek a larger building, however, the Caesar's Creek Meeting sends them $551.37 for the building fund. The church is finished in January of 1895 and cost $4,500. There are 163 members.

One of the Quaker ministers is Jessie Hawkins who will be a minister for fifty years. Jessie is one of five brothers. All of them are ministers except Jehu. When this fact is mentioned in the presence of any of the brothers they say, "But he's a good man, Jehu." They are big men with big voices which are suitable for large greetings and enunciating The Word. Sometimes they shout greetings to each other from their houses about the village and their tolerant neighbors refer to this as "the Hawkins telephone."

When a very fat woman comes to Jessie to be married she gets stuck in a chair in his living room and he marries her while she is sitting there. He stands on the ground and marries a couple sitting in their spring wagon because they are in a hurry and do not wish to get out.

When Jessie's daughter, Isabel, is small her mother instructs her not to be too friendly with the daughter of the Methodist minister. "Remember your father's calling," her mother says. Most of the Hawkinses consider the Methodists worldly and they are polite but reserved with them. Jessie is not this way, however. He stops in the street to hold with anyone long, erudite conversations using a precise English which he has acquired from vast reading.

The Methodist minister, Reverend Amos Cowgill, like Reverend Hawkins, is not a reserved man. He is open, direct, and tolerant. When three of the village girls become pregnant at almost the same time, Dr. Whitacre stops Reverend Cowgill on the street to discuss the aspects of shame. But the minister will not censure the girls. "Some of us, Harry," he says, "have better luck than conduct."

Susan Morris Haydock, the schoolteacher, complains to Reverend Cowgill about Bill Devoe's profanity. "Yes, Susan," says the minister, "but have you ever heard him whistle? Like a nightingale . . ."

Susan fears profanity. To her it is a blasphemy which will summon the corrective hand of Jehovah. When W. B. Hamilton leaves the cobbler's shop to curse the minister, he falls in the street, rising speechless. He never talks again. Susan looks upon this as a sign. Several days later Phillip Lemar is cursing his horses while driving the coal wagon up the hill as Susan is cooling a prune pie on the windowsill.

"I'll drive you up this goddamn hill," says Phillip, "or I'll drive you straight to hell!"

Susan begins to tremble in the window. "Thomas," she says at dinner, "I think I'll move back to Harveysburg where it's quieter . . ."

Some of the village Quakers consider themselves mendicants living on the alms of piety. Horace Compton, in order to watch the side door of the pool hall, cuts the tops out of the sweetcorn in his garden. The villagers, even some of the Quakers themselves, enjoy Horace for he is a man in whom contradiction is firmly revealed. If Horace watches who comes and goes from the pool hall, he is also fond of watching the pretty village girls. "When Horace shouts 'Amen!' in church," says Ruby Smith, "it is for his eyesight." When Horace is working for one of the village groceries, the ladies ask each other, "I wonder which of us has bought Horace's thumb today?"

When the First World War comes, however, it is this time the Quakers who do not agree. Some of them, pacifistic and upset over

America's intervention in the European war, refuse to display the American flag in meeting. By late 1917 the Quakers have agreed to disagree. The pacifists are led by Jesse Hawkins. Those who are not pacifists walk up the street where they become Methodists, among them Jesse's daughter, Isabel, and her husband, Trevor Haydock. The children remain behind with Jesse. Quaker farmer Lawrence Mitchener refuses to serve at all and he is taken away to prison.

The churches are small continents where pieces occasionally break away and attach themselves elsewhere. It is as though the two are playing an odd match by rules which are not clear. There are also brief times when the two churches are angry at each other. Once the Quakers have Bernard McKay, Charlie Swindler, Carl Bangham and James Haydock, who will later call themselves "the ornery four," arrested for disturbing the peace. They are Methodist boys attending Christian Endeavor at the Quaker church and before meeting ends the boys shuffle their feet together and everyone, thinking the meeting ended, rises. The Quaker boys who participate with the four Methodists are not arrested. The Methodist boys are fined five dollars.

Normally the two churches live together, like in-laws resigned to each other's company. Once when the bell on top of the Quaker church fails to ring, an old Methodist up the street says, "Likely it is stuffed with supplication." In later years one of the sons who has left the village looks backward and considers the difference between the two churches. "The Methodists," he says, "sang a bit louder."

In the last days of the village both of the old churches are torn down. The timber from the meeting house is used to build a barn for Junior McCoy's hogs. Only the Caesar's Creek meeting house still stands. Even the land and forest around it seem ancient, silent, and unchanged. Although some of the younger Quaker farmers plant and harvest on Sundays the old ones still resist such a violation of the old discipline. In the March woods the Sunday sugar water runs out of the buckets and onto the ground. On Sundays in April Luther Haines' fields are quiet. "It is our custom," he says. But he belongs to another generation. The Joneses, of the newer generation, say: "We pay the preacher still . . ."

In the spring black snakes crawl dully from hibernation and rest on the stone wall of the cemetery where they allow the heat to stir their cold blood. Because the old church is isolated vandals occasionally topple the tombstones of the old Quaker farmers. This is where Luther Haines' brother, Everett, dies of a heart attack while he is trying to replace the stone on his uncle's grave.

The Ornery Four: Bernard McKay, James Haydock, Carl Bangham, and Charlie Swindler

The markers in the older section of the graveyard have been made illegible by the passing of seasons. No one remembers the stonemason's name but visitors still drive down the dirt lane to the churchyard where they photograph one another against the backdrop of creek stone which outlasts even the dead. Luther's wife, Edith, writes: *It is a compelling comment on the permanence of things, as against the impermanence of life, that the old books have lain on the shelf and the stones have kept their places on the wall* . . .

C. L. Wamsley, 76

John Wesley never intended to start another religion but he did. His followers were called 'Methodists' because they were methodistic. They proceeded with order. In a sense there is some derision in that. Everything a method, you see. John Wesley figured out that he had preached 42,000 sermons. In his eighties, he reflected upon this and said: "I am a wonder to myself."

America, however, was unlike England. It was the frontier. So the Methodists originated the circuit rider, a man who lived on horseback. This is why today you find little Methodist churches scattered among the country's crossroads and not little Presbyterian churches. It was said that a Presbyterian minister would go and ask how many Presbyterians were around. Methodists, however, never looked for other Methodists but for raw material. It was a very rugged life for the circuit rider. His life expectancy was in the upper thirties. Few lived to be fifty.

Zoar, Sharon, Harveysburg, New Burlington. That was the circuit here. I had two one Sunday, two the next. I came here in June of 1945. I had never been here before and knew no one. The wife of the previous minister said, 'It is there just where the road turns.'

Most of these villages, of course, are made up of farmers and their outlook is rural. I lean that way myself because I was raised on a farm. Rural people prefer a more informal service. They do not want too much ritual or form in their church activity. I think they do not want to carry the ritual of the seasons into their church.

These people were of my class. I felt I would not fit into a city church. Working among both, I have sensed a difference. The rural people are involved in life from its beginning to its end. They depend so much upon nature, you see. The storekeeper does not worry particularly in drought because his trade goes on. Because of this I think the farmer may be a more devout man. Of course, desperation drives men to inconsistency. There was a prayer meeting at the Methodist church during a drought. One lady complained of her garden drying up and asked if perhaps they could pray for rain. They prayed, yes, and there was a regular downpour, a washout. The garden went into the creek. 'You know,' she said to me the next day, 'that's just like those Methodists. They overdo everything . . .'

My own feeling of nature is that it is not tied closely to God. Nature is merely the working out of certain laws which are in operation in our world. A family was milking on a Sunday morning, a storm rising. Lightning struck the farmer's only daughter as she was turning the cows out. She was instantly dead. He was a devout man but he could not get over this. He became stoic. The child was 14, an only child. He could not reconcile this act with his devoutness. He saw this as God's caprice. But God did not design her death. It was an act of nature, operating in this world. Rain falls on the just and unjust, you know. God does not control every act of nature. Life and death is a natural process, and disease and affliction takes its course. A mile from home a boy was killed in an automobile crash. 'Well,' someone said, 'God took him.' I do not admit that. Predestination is for Presbyterians, isn't it? Peter Cartwright, a Methodist circuit rider, was eating dinner once with a Presbyterian. The Presbyterian minister served fried chicken. He stuck his fork into a drumstick and said, 'See, Peter, God from the beginning of creation predestined me to eat this drumstick.' And Peter reached across, grabbed it, and ate it himself—to prove *his* theory of predestination.

It is easy to forget perspective. Mine is that human nature remains the same everywhere, at all times. The nature of sin has not changed one particle. We have no new ways to sin. We can only   a little faster. We seem to be not as close to God. But, of course, I am getting along in years and at my age if not careful I tend to become a little pessimistic. They say to think young, be among young people. But to die young, try to keep up with them.

We resist change as we become older. It is the natural conduct of age. The condition seeks repose and familiarity. Energy dwindles. The body resists drastic change and also the mind. We are not able to cope. I retired at 65 because of the pressures of change and administration. I could not cope.

We are getting old when we feel every change is for the worse. Someone pointed out that I talked more of heaven than in the past. I had not thought of it but I guess this is so. I believe the world is getting worse, not better. We are not soon to be found beating our swords into plowshares and our spears into pruning hooks. God does not control man. Man must do as his will manifests. This is the design in the universe.

I also find the past is becoming more vivid to me. I cannot remember last week but 40 years ago remains very clear. In New Burlington I had a wilderness behind my house. So I bought four sheep for $5 to keep the weeds down and in two years I had a nice grassy lot. Once someone butchered an entire hog for me. I do not know whether this was a contribution to the church or not. It was quite a contribution to me. I never received a large salary. It began at $860 in 1931. I got two of three year's pay during the depression. I never considered that a debt. Legally, a minister cannot collect his salary, you know. The Kingdom of Heaven isn't built on that kind of economics anyway.

I can recall a time when an engineer was a man who drove an engine, and people were tied together by craft. There was a unity in knowing the fellow who made your shoes. And, of course, they did know each other. The folk of the rural churches talk together because they hold things in common. Everybody attended church because at that time there was no other place to go. If they had had other choices they would have taken them and not been in church. Presence in church does not assign us a religious nature.

At a meeting once in the summer when all the windows were up, a tall fellow stuck his head in the back window. Preacher said, 'Sam, you looking for salvation?' And Sam said, 'No, sir, I'm looking for Sal Johnson. I'm going to take her home after church tonight . . .'

New Burlington also had the Quakers, who were fine people, and the Nazarenes, who came out of the Methodist church. They thought we were a little broad-minded. To them, it was salvation, then sanctification. Sanctification was the *second* work of grace. But if sin is so crucified, how does it get back? If the old man of carnal nature is put to death . . . This is the way the Baptists think. Once saved, always. Rest on their oars, you might say. Well, I believe that God has never abrogated our will. I believe that life is constantly a struggle.

Luther Haines, 79

In 1650 George Fox was sentenced to prison in Derby Jail, six months for blasphemy. When he appeared before Justice Bennett, Fox had tried to convert the judge. 'Tremble in the name of the Lord,' said Fox. The judge replied, 'And quake thou quaker in the presence of the law.' After that, the term 'Quaker' was apparently in general use as a term of derision.

The Church of England wanted control, you see. So many of the Quakers came to America. When I visited England I was in the cells where they were imprisoned. Cold, clammy basements. No heat. I wonder if they lived.

When William Penn visited the court of King Charles II, he still had his hat upon his head since Friends refuse to remove their hats as a sign of acknowledging another person's superiority. So the king removed his crown. Penn said, 'Friend Charles, wherefore dost thee uncover thyself?' And King Charles replied, 'Friend Penn, it is the custom of this place for only one man to wear the hat . . .'

In 1861 Penn founded Pennsylvania as a home for all oppressed people. The land grant was provided by King Charles who asked from Penn in return one-fifth of any gold or silver mined there and two beaverskins a year. The Friends took advantage of his generosity and came by the hundreds. Philadelphia became the center of Quaker thought and activity.

Friends, of course, *were* friends and little by little the word became a proper noun. Rufus Jones said of Quakerism: 'In its essential meaning it is a movement and not a narrow sect with a static creed and an unalterable set of practices and testimonies.'

It only seemed unalterable at times. My great-grandfather was Zimri Haines—Zimri was one of the minor prophets—who was a cabinet maker. Some of his furniture is still in the community although not much. He began to see two of the young Compton ladies who were first cousins and both of them took a fancy to him. The fathers came to see Zimri and told him to choose one. Zimri said he thought he would choose neither. But after some time had gone by Elizabeth Compton's mother came to see him and said that her daughter was pining away. He must have been touched by her affection and so he married her. Of course, they had to secure the approval of the meeting and when they went there, Elizabeth's cousin objected to the marriage. So Zimri took Elizabeth to a justice of the peace and the Quakers disowned them. It didn't seem to affect them much, however, for they had 12 children.

The progenitor of the Compton family resided at Compton in Warwickshire at the time of the Norman conquest in 1066. He was a powerful nobleman and allowed to keep most of his land. When I visited England I learned that the present Lord Compton had had no children so he divorced and married a young girl who gave him two sons. It seemed very important to him. I don't know if his ex-wife found it as essential.

The old Quakers were very strict in their practices. Once a man was disowned for becoming drowsy in meeting. And once they censured a marriage certificate. It had a picture and under it the phrase 'boat of life in the current of time.' They found that superfluous and asked that it be stricken.

They also relied upon a man's word. No signed notes, just handshakes. This isn't to say they couldn't be sharp in a trade. A Quaker once traded his horse to a fellow and a few days later the fellow returned.

'What about that horse?' asked the Quaker.

'Well,' said the fellow, 'I was wondering if I could borrow your hat so I could trade him off . . .'

I remember once after a silent meeting at Caesar's Creek a man got up and said, 'Someone here has been thinking of how to beat a nigger out of a cow.'

'Friend,' someone asked, 'how doth thee know this?'

'Why,' the man said, 'because it was *myself* . . .'

The Quakers came here when the Philadelphia yearly meeting secured action against slavery. This began to exodus to the Northwest Territory. We've been here ever since and this is what our own Quaker poet, Whittier, has to say about it:

> *Our fathers to their graves have gone,*
> *Their strife is past, their triumph won.*
> *But sterner trials await the race*
> *Which rises in their honored place* . . .

❋   ❋   ❋

Notes on Methodists

❋ Damages allowed to Thomas Cottamin, a local preacher, because a disgruntled member shot small stones at his horse.

❋ On motion by John Sale, July 1825, a committee of three was appointed to consider the evil of our official characters and private members joining with and attending the Free Mason lodges and festivals.

❋ A sister has been arraigned before the quarterly meeting for indulging in too much jewelry.

❊ Elder John Sale reported that Adjil McQuire was no more fit to preach the gospel than his dog, Ranger.

❊ Reverend A. T. Spahr was licensed to preach at quarterly meeting held at New Burlington. He was quite young and timid. The presiding elder without any warning or mercy called on the young fellow to lead in prayer. Young Spahr was so frightened that he crawled under the seat and slipped out the door. After due trial and deliberation he became a force for good.

❊ Adjil McQuire has made wonderful improvement and become a power for righteousness.

❊ When the old church was outgrown the membership began a larger one in 1874. But not enough money was raised and the day of dedication came but the money did not. Moses, Jonathan, and Robert McKay left the crowd, deliberated a moment, and assumed the remaining indebtedness. Bishop Merrill preached that day as one sent of God.

❊ Item on a working consciousness: Margaret Jay Humston slipped from grace one Sunday morning and decided to miss class meeting in favor of a day of visiting with her relatives. As she was walking up graveyard hill she heard James Smith singing 'Must I Be To Judgment Brought?' Whirling on her feet she hastened back to church and found peace and favor ending with a shout of deliverance.

❊ Item of interest: Reverend George Maley in 1826 preached 262 sermons, received 100 members, traveled 2,928 miles, and received $200 in salary.

Picnic

Tradition says that it does not rain for the Collett-McKay picnic. Rain has fallen on the second Saturday in August several times since 1866 but there has always been dinner. For over a hundred years the two families have met in the picnic woods of Buck Run. There are no programs, no election of officers, no invitations. The men meet on the afternoon before the picnic and set up the 50-foot tables made of boards bought in 1879. For many years water was brought in a large hogshead, and coffee is still brewed in a huge iron kettle over a wood fire. The record of attendance is kept in large registers. The number attending has varied from the 111 people at the first picnic to 542 in 1888. The four-acre grounds, in an oak and sugar maple grove, is owned by the families who say it will always be a picnic ground for them.

An account of the Collett-McKay picnic, 1869

A notable event, differing from ordinary public assemblages, occurred on the seventh of August when the entire kith and kin of two celebrated families of Ohio, to wit: Collett and McKay, joined in the pleasantest manner possible, to entertain one another agreeably to their own notions of social enjoyment and propriety.

Why there have not been more of these social family reunions, after the toil of harvest is over, is one of those questions too subtle for analysis. An hour thus spent in perfect peace of mind and in easy, rollicking con-

Clemma McKay, fishing in Anderson's Fork

versation, flowing in fluent sympathy with all the aims, hopes, surprises and pleasures of life, away from the vulgar eye of the world, is worth a great deal in forming just opinions of the worth of social intercourse.

The manhood of the Collett and McKay families is to be measured only by the expressive word 'big.' Any other adjective would but poorly convey an adequate idea of the size of the men. Seven generations of sturdy farmers have gone before, and for them to lean upon: and there is no taint of weakness observable in their composition. Independence, courage, administrative talent, tact, and a likely taste for books, are the solid characteristics that distinguish them as a community of people.

More than two hundred years ago, husband, wife and babe, set sail from the coast of France to find a home in America. The wife, after a few day's passage, died and a famine having broken out on ship board, an allowance of one biscuit each day was issued to the adults on board. The children were doomed to starve. On this scant pittance the father and child survived and after a long voyage, reached their destination.

From the motherless babe, subsisted on half a biscuit and cradled in the arms of the sea, the hardy, loyal race of Colletts sprang. The sons and daughters are worthy to be the descendants of such a grand sire, as he, who in the midst of death, famine and storm, saved to the uttermost, the vine which has nourished a thousand branches.

There were present on the picnic grounds forty-one clusters from the original tree, numbering in all one hundred and eighty-five souls, all bearing the name of either Collett or McKay. Besides these, there were also present, those who descended directly from the parent stock but who, in consequence of marriage, have dropped one or the other of the pair of names.

The real estate owned by these two families amounts, in the aggregate, to three-quarters of a million dollars and comprises six thousand acres of cultivated land.

I undertook to count the actual number of babies present, but owing to the omnipresent ruffles and cloaks of similar style, color and fabric, and the ubiquity of movement by which they were transported from one pair of arms to another, occasioned me so much fatal reckoning as to cause an abandonment of the enterprise.

We, four of us, took our departure just as the eclipse grew thickest, the dusty roads flying under our horses' feet with the music of the stones and the spheres under us, and the wind whipping our coat tails into very whip-crackers; but ballasted with plenty of cake in the bottom of the vehicle, I rode home to find that I did not own the pretty word 'big' among my possessions.

—J. B. C.

Survivors

In warmer months when windows are open, the Nazarene minister's wrath floods the center of the village. The Nazarenes are newcomers therefore the old villagers find them somehow *novel*. Robert Shambaugh does not like the Nazarenes when he is trying to sleep late after drinking too much on Saturday night. But during the growing months he does not mind when they stomp and yell. He thinks they shake the earth and loosen the dirt and bring up the green things in his garden. The Quakers, meanwhile, isolate themselves across the street with old brick and older tradition; the Methodists by distance.

On Sundays Louie Wills sits on her front porch and listens to the Nazarenes cover the land with imprecation. At 94, she and her one-eared cat live in the tree-shaded lower part of the village but very near the cross streets. "Those Nazarenes get pretty high, I tell you," she laughs, courting blasphemy with a blush. She is beautiful; skin like parchment, hair a white that startles. What if she is carrying her kidneys in her pocketbook, attached by a tube? She has otherwise health, beauty, serenity. She is living forever.

Like most of the widows who live in the village, Mrs. Wills grew up on the farm. "There was ten of us and we were for each other, I remember that. We made our own clothes and raised our own food and after my mother died young, I saw my little brother stand on a chair to mix our bread. Before I was a grown lady, we lived four or five years around Port William and that was the way things were. I was 31 before I got married and nobody thought anything about it. I met Frank at the Rebecca Lodge. He was a schoolteacher down in Pike County and had a sister in Port William. He came up in the summer and helped run the threshing machine. I never went much with anybody else because I thought I had to like 'em well enough to marry 'em. I thought from the first that Frank was a mighty nice looking fellow. My grandmother said to my father, 'Si, if I were you, I'd take a shotgun to that buck.' But my father, of course, wasn't my grandmother, and Frank and I were married in 1907. She thought it would be bad to leave my father, but we took care of him. Whenever he took sick, we were there. He was 94 when he died."

Three years after they are married, Frank and Louie Wills buy a farm. It is 125 acres in a small valley east of New Burlington. The house and barns are grouped tightly together on the brow of a hill. Frank works with a team of horses. The fields surround them. They are less than two miles from the village yet it appears remote as an ocean. They speak of it as belonging to a life unknown to them. The children grow up and leave the farm. Years pass, and Frank becomes ill. His strength seems to flow into the fields he can no longer care for. He will, then, retreat from the land; he and Louie will move into the village. Eight months afterward, Frank is dead. Louie stays on in the small but adequate cottage. The grocery store is across the street. The post office is thirty yards farther, in case any of the children write from California. *Or wherever it is now.* Her sister, Abby, lives up the street.

Life, disease, death: each parallels the other. But New Burlington is a village where the pendulum is weighted. Here, people are as old as the village. Illness on the farm, death in the village. Those who are ill move into a house where someone has just died. In the last decade of New Burlington's life, only one new home is built, a brick ranch beside the old Methodist church. It confronts the rest of the old two-storied frame houses with its awkward new appearance.

Down the street, Louie lives on and on. Her neighbors are solicitous. Her daughter lives in the nearby country. Louie has lost her husband but she has gained centrality. She has become a *widow*. The summer she is 95, she is operated on and survives that, too. She has found a way to convert a horny patience (and other unknown properties) into an inner force. It is a force such as the vigor that drives the grain, the grass. She grows quiet, shy, girllike. She seems to blend into the seasons. When the summer sun pours into her side window, she twists imperceptibly toward it. She has less and less to say.

Louie's sister, Abby, lives in the middle of six widows, a sorority of imposed spinsterhood. And at the last, such a sorority suffers more than most because it has made of itself another community, complement to both family and village. Now the widows will pay for being so social. When the Corps of Engineers comes to build its lake, two widows are already gone. One has died. One has moved. One refuses to move. It is

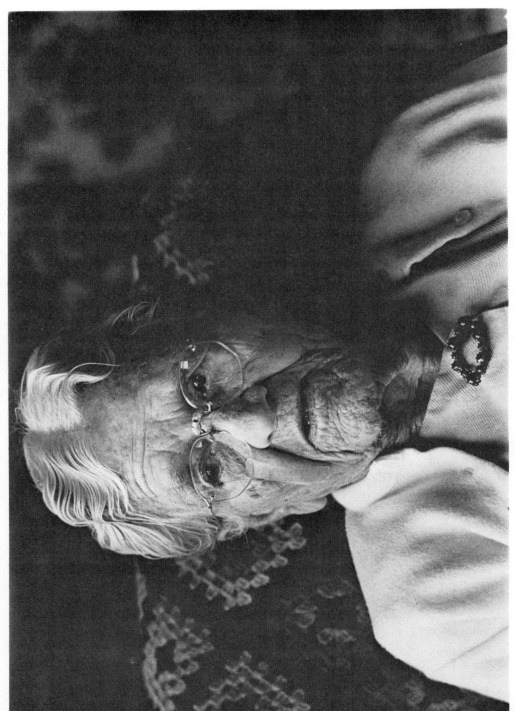

Louie Wills (PHOTOGRAPH BY KEN STEINHOFF)

known that she *will* go, but such protest serves for the moment and reality is tucked away in the attic rooms of the mind.

Next door to Abby, Merle McIntire, soon to be 90, prays to God that she may die before she has to move. "My great-grandfather," she tells Abbey, "died at 38, an effect of the war." She cannot remember which war. "My great-grandmother, however, lived to be 98. When I heard this I said, 'I'll live that long, too.' Now here I am, but life isn't the same when you're old. I have shaky knees. I want to die at home. That's what we all want. I have no place to go. In old Jerusalem, the children would sometimes take their parents in awhile and when they tired of them, they put money in the slot places, then turned them into the streets. Things change, and they do not change. Poor old Eve. She began it all."

In the summer, the sorority is together a final time. They place their belongings together and hold an auction. First, like honored guests at a buffet, the family picks through the houses. Then the outsiders come. Such an auction secretes an effluvium, of old lace, dark glass, the high and keening scent of ancient silver. Which like failure can be smelled for miles. Before the auction, Abby, who is nearly blind, walks carefully through her house, both upstairs and down, moving by the instinct which allows her grace in the growing darkness. She touches the pieces of furniture, old letters, glass. She pauses in each doorway, fixing her house forever in an interior vision. After the auction, the widows go away, to the side rooms of their children, trailer parks, rest homes. A veterinarian comes to put Abby's cat to sleep. The old cat fights wildly, clawing the veterinarian's arm and two days later, he finds that he has blood poisoning.

Below Louie Wills, five houses from the cross streets, Mrs. McClure begins to move, watching from her porch the commerce of bartered values. Her own commerce has passed quietly between herself and her granddaughter: how to make the plants grow. They have experimented on every inch of yard and when the space grew full they moved cuttings to the porch, kitchen, and living room. The house is on the lowest ground in the village and floods have left rich soil from higher ground.

"That's so very pretty," the lady next door tells Mrs. McClure, looking at a plant coming to flower.

"The name of that plant is the Resurrection Lily," replies Mrs. McClure, touching the leaves as if to protect them. She worries that when she has to move, no other place will be moist enough. She thinks: will the Resurrection Lily live transplanted?

Louie Wills bears all such grief silently. She stays in more. She does not go to the Methodist Church. She says she can no longer stand to be in a crowd. At home, she sometimes thinks of the old services. She tells her daughter, Opal, about a revival. "There was snow on the ground a foot deep, but the crowds were awful. You were born in September, and Wayne was six. He disappeared and we found him in back, crawling under the pews and pinching girls on the leg. Frank took him down front to sit and while the preacher was giving thanks, Wayne jumped up and shouted, 'I'm thankful for a house to live in!' " The remaining neighbors sit with her sometimes, on her front porch. She still mends but she has stopped making quilts. She tells the neighbors that her quilts are all over the countryside. She says she has made 200 of them, mostly from old clothes. She laughs at the memory of Frank who often told her he was afraid to go to bed at night because his clothes might end up in a quilt.

Merle McIntire is living in a trailer park with her sister, where she feels confined, rootless, abandoned. Her future being desolate, she considers the past, recalling that her father was a miller. "He was one of four boys. Three became millers. He did so because he was raised a miller. When he began, there was only one stone on top of another. Later, there were other contraptions. The flour went through a bolting cloth, fine as silk. I was born in 1881, in a two-room house behind the millrace. My husband was James McIntire, an honorable man. I would see him go past our house. Our young people's meeting on Sunday nights had a picnic at the covered bridge, under the buckeye tree. He took me home that night. The next winter, he proposed. He wanted to get married not later than April because of the spring plowing. We were married in April of 1906. I was no spring chicken. We bought a farm that year they had the collapse in the nation. We couldn't make a payment that year. We only paid the interest. We had 87 acres and a fraction. Later, we burned the mortgage in the cook stove. I like the country yet. It is a peaceful place, and your neighbors are in sight. We grew corn and wheat and began an orchard . . ."

When occasional visitors from the old neighborhood find their way into the trailer park, she asks them about the orchard. "Have you seen it when it is full of fruit?" she asks. Her grandson lives in the old house now, and tends the plum and apple trees. When he removed the outhouse which sat in the edge of the garden, she was upset. "What if the new works break?" she asked. "Where will you be then?"

Around her in her new environment, she notices expense, new devices, and distance. "The television carries the news in, but what takes it out? People of old visited, and did not use the telephone. Now man works, woman works, and the children are kept someplace else. I have noticed, too, there seem to be so many *words*. I do not know if anyone else has noticed that or not . . ."

Soon, Louie Wills moves into the country to live with her daughter.

Her house is gone now, the house across the street empty. Only Louie's chimney remains, still shrouded in ivy although someone has clipped it off near the ground, taking the roots and leaving the waxy tendrils to wither. She does not look back, however. She has lived on the farm, in the village, and now she is back in the country. If the rooms seem smaller now, and the walls narrow and pastel, if the driveway is asphalt and the siding aluminum, then other things do not change: the sky is still wide and the garden is out back and in two months the asparagus will be tender.

Mrs. McClure, who has moved to Xenia, dozes in a chair in front of her window. When she wakes, she finds that she has been crying. "I don't know where I am," she says. "I have no idea. I don't see anything I know. Nothing at all . . ."

Early one morning, Merle McIntire walks out of her son's house on her way to the graveyard. She is found on the lane, lying on her back. Her feet are primly together, her hands folded across her chest. She explains in a note: "When we reach a certain age, we are expected to walk to the cemetery and die on one's place." The bus, which will carry her great-grandchildren to school, passes by the end of the lane. Her son, waiting for the coroner, covers her with a blanket and goes inside where he looks at her through the living room window. A light snow begins to fall.

The carpenter, 90

The carpenter is a religious man although he seldom goes to church. "Do you have to go to church to be a religious man?" he asks. "I consider myself a religious man because I say a blessing before my dinner," he says, offering himself proof. Sitting beside him, his son does not reply. The son is nervous, pale, visiting from another century. *Let him go on,* the son thinks. The television bumbles in a far corner, showing a space launch. The carpenter wants to talk, but his son studies the monotony of space. The carpenter was 24 when the Wright brothers flew. "If they'd busted up," he says, "we'd have none of this." At Sunday school, after the first moon shot, the children were fearful. They did not know where God was and thought the rockets were disturbing the heavens. "Who had those first thoughts of the moon?" a neighbor lady demanded almost angrily, talking to the carpenter over her fence.

The son, who regards his father's house as a church, expiates guilt by

periodically driving from a distant city to offer filial communion. The
house is old, and deep in the country. It was built by the carpenter and
his father in 1901. The furniture is dark, heavy, and vague. Although the
son grew up here he can never remember how the furniture looks except
that it is dark and heavy. The air, too, is heavy. The son's eyes begin to
water. He is afraid to breathe. There are invisible things in the air. The
son tells his father goodbye but the carpenter does not notice him leave.
Prompted by the television, he is talking about a trip to New York: "I
didn't think much of it. I'll tell you why. There were too many machines. I had to stand on the curb thirty minutes to cross a street. All of
the machines had been hit. I saw some tough-looking characters in New
York. Ahey!"

The clock ticks. The furnace hums. Sunlight crashes onto the lawn.
The carpenter sits in a corner chair, so that he may look equally over the
room. "Come in if I know you!" he shouts. His dogs do not look up.

When the weather is bad, so is the carpenter. Winter is a communica-
ble disease which fills the lungs. The winter he is 90 he enters a rest
home. The nurses are young, large, concerned. In the *Xenia Gazette* the
carpenter reads about a man who lived until he was 117. "Why did he
live so long?" asks a nurse. The carpenter is surprised. "Why," he says,
"he just didn't die . . ."

The son comes to visit. "Five years ago," the carpenter tells him, "I
could have walked home from here. If it was warm enough I could sleep
out and make four miles a day. It would take me three days. I think
there's only one thing wrong with me: I'm full of piss and it makes me
move fast. I've pissed 400 gallons. I can put it out for the nurses. How's
that?"

When the son leaves, the carpenter says to a nurse, "The old man is
left to root for himself." He outlines a new life to her: "When I get
home, I won't work anymore. I have relatives in two cemeteries and
pines on all their graves. I keep them up and decorate them on Decoration Day. I'm going to cut this down to my wife's grave because I've
decided the others don't know much about it. I won't mow the law, either."

When the nurse asks him how he feels, he says, "I'm tough as a
buffalo and I'll butt you about as quick." When the supervisor asks him
about the nurses, he says, "I fill them full of Texas bull in the Ohio manner." Each afternoon the carpenter walks in the corridor. He moves very
slowly, looking like a thin bird on precarious footing. He uses a hand-
carved cane which was given to him by Jemima Boots, who died at 91.
Before that, the cane belonged to Henry Spray. The carpenter tells the
nurses his cane is 200 years old. On his walks, he surreptitiously studies

all the doors and back in his room makes elaborate diagrams which he hides in a drawer under his chewing tobacco.

The chewing tobacco is a gift from a nurse. The nurses like the carpenter. Between their fondness for him and the spareness of his demands, they have given him corn flakes, tobacco, and clothes. "I have the nurses eating out of my hand," he tells a man in the hall. "They are nice girls. Some are single and some are married. I'm only afraid I'm walking around in a dead man's clothes. I don't know whether I like that or not."

Sometimes the carpenter thinks of the widows who live around him in the country. There is Mrs. Snook, Mrs. Lewis, Mrs. Starbuck. He tells the nurses about them. "Mrs. Starbuck," he says, "was handy with a corn knife. She and he, she eight rows ahead. I said to my wife, 'I'd work like hell before I'd let you pass me with a corn knife.' Mary Snook has 200 acres of land. 'I have a notion,' she says, 'to rent that all to some farmer.' I say, 'Then what?' She says, 'Get me a house trailer across from you.' I say, 'No use in that. Just move in with me.' She says, 'When I was raising my family alone I'da jumped at the chance. Now I don't have to.' The carpenter thinks a moment. "That Mary Snook," he says. "She always was a plain-talking woman."

The carpenter shares his room with another man who sleeps most of the time. He sits in a chair by the window, asleep in his own urine. The urine is the same color as the February afternoon sunlight. Next door, a man shouts incessantly at a wall clock. "I can still hear it!" he cries to the nurses, who grow impatient. "It has to be stopped!" Only he sees or hears the wall clock. His roommate is a farmer whom the carpenter has known for sixty years. The farmer is fastened to a chair, which is tied to the wall. His hands make arcane gestures. He is working in his fields. When the sun heightens, the farmer removes his pajama tops. Once he hit a nurse while he was working, in his chair fastened to the wall. He is still very strong. Although the old farmer is next door, the carpenter does not visit.

The carpenter tells the nurses limericks. "I saw this one on a tombstone," he says.

> *Here lies the bones*
> *of Marcy Jones,*
> *for her death held no terrors.*
> *Born a virgin, died a virgin,*
> *no hits, no runs, no errors.*

"Is that a little spicy?" he asks. He tells a man in the hall, "I've felt about ten nurses' butts since I've been in here." The man gives the carpenter a pamphlet answering the question, "If God is really interested, why do so many prayers go unanswered?" He is inexplicably depressed. He sits in his room all afternoon. At dinner, he says to the nurse, "As soon as my son comes, they told me. I don't know whether that will be this year or the next. I said, anyone's son will do to take me out of here, and if he's a good driver I guess they won't catch us."

When the weather is some warmer, the son comes and takes the carpenter to the country. "If I make it to May," the carpenter tells the son, "I may make it to December. Ahey!" On certain days, a lady comes to cook and clean. "At one time," he tells the lady, "I could have eaten a whetstone. I was alright until I was 80." Neighbors pass on their way to work and blow their horns. *I am not afraid*, the carpenter thinks.

Ada T. McKay, 85

Ada T. McKay sometimes shows visitors a photograph of her husband, Weldon. "His face tells you: honesty," she says. She regards the photograph as if it is a fragile heirloom thrusting itself into an incomprehensible future. Her summer kitchen is filled with utensils which are unaffected and forthright. In the house is a room she calls "the old room." A chest in the old room has a drawer filled with eyeglasses once belonging to the old McKays. The house was built in 1869 by Weldon's father, Robert Francis, who died later in his fields. His great-grandmother brought cut-glass candlesticks on horseback from Virginia. Ada T. loves the McKay house. The weight of tradition here is so immense her vision cannot expand to take it all in. Her pride is sometimes so large as to be measurable, like currents of electricity in the walls. "I cannot think of anything we needed," she says.

When she becomes very old she moves in with her sister. She becomes the first McKay to move out of the house; the others died there. This knowledge is somehow painful to her, as though she has been irresponsible. In her sister's house she looks for something familiar. The McKay tartan on her bed, worn by the McKay regiment of the 1600's, reminds her of Scotland which she has visited. In her mind Scotland is more familiar to her than her sister's house. She thinks of Scotland often.

"There were big homes, lovely. They were castles, you might say. The dining rooms were large and the stairways very wide. I know I was surprised. Glasgow and Edinburgh were not far by bus. We went along very nicely. Everyone was friendly and we were not strangers. I became as familiar with the McKays as could be. We stayed at the hotel but we were planned for. There was a picnic. That is how they spoke of it. But it was

Ada T. McKay (PHOTOGRAPH BY KEN STEINHOFF)

dinner in the hotel. Everything was so lovely and I was dressed properly. I kept in touch for a long time afterward but I had nothing to say and they had nothing to say to me. But I was awful glad to have been there. That was years ago and it seems so familiar. O if I could only go back and live. My time and life is now over. I live with my sister. She takes my arms and guides me. I want to go but she wants to live. I cannot remember any more and I wonder what has happened to my head. But everything gets over with. Weldon died and we had no children. Once we went places, my, my. Then we did not go anyplace . . ."

Ada T. does not leave her bedroom. Seasons wheel slowly, artfully past. She sits in a chair by her window where she mourns the view. It is alien, eccentric, inscrutable. "When you get older," she says, "things get dim. Take with me now. Those buildings there are dim. I *see* them well enough but they're dim. They tell me who lives there but it does not mean anything. Who are they, I wonder, and what do they want to accomplish? It has been a very long life. I was married in 1916. It seems all a dream."

In the country, it is spring although Ada T. does not notice. The maples anoint the yard. The place is breath-taking. *What year is this? What season?* thinks the passerby. The house stands as it has always stood, beside the barn with Weldon's name on it. Young David McKay, Weldon's cousin, lives in the house now with his bride who will soon have a child. The child will be the first McKay born there. *I am 85,* thinks Ada T. *I have been a McKay forever.*

Mary Adams, 70

The final illness: he fell in the barn and I thought he was gone. The snow was that deep. My throat was so dry when I called for help I gave a little squeak. Dr. Stoneburner came in the jeep. Hospital? He'll be better there, Stony said.

I'm not going to get well, he said.

Yes, I said, yes . . .

That was the first of December and the snow was that deep. The first of January he was gone. He used to shock corn without any breakfast. You shouldn't shock corn without any breakfast. After he was gone I didn't know what to cook. I bought like he was alive because I didn't know how to do any other way. I'll fix this, I said, and that. It didn't seem right to do any other way.

Afterward, Mary Adams remains on in the farmhouse on the hill overlooking Anderson's Fork. Although over a hundred years old, her farmhouse and barns could have been built yesterday. The few Sunday drivers who come past on Graveyard Road stop out front to admire. It is like looking into a painting suspended in the museum of its past. Nothing is out of place.

Mary sees townspeople build ranch houses on the upper end of Graveyard Road but her view, at the moment, is absolute. It commands her fields, neighbors (both old and new), the covered bridge to the south. She does not mind the new houses because they bring neighbors. "The old ones did not neighbor," she says. "With younger ones about I feel younger, not 150. I like people about. Once there were two families on this road. In the winter you saw nothing. There was no way to get out. You were here. Deep snow, cold and blowing. I got so despondent. I felt there was no one anyplace. I felt I was alone in the world."

There are cars and motorbikes up the road now and the new neighbors come and go, spending warm weekends in their yards with large and complicated machines. She is not lonely in the warmer months but she is uncertain whether it is because of her new neighbors or the farm which surrounds her. In the old barns and fields, the intractable process goes on. She is an old midwife at the birth of her livestock.

"My cattle," she says, "are so much company. You do not feel so alone with something alive around. I like helping at calf-birth. The cow has no pain pills and the calf is up in less than 15 minutes. When we get a pain crossways the doctor fixes us up and a human baby is the most helpless thing on earth. There is a reverence in knowing these things, calf-birth or chicken-dressing. It is the whole process, you see. Did you ever dress a chicken? A hundred eggs or better there inside some as tiny as pinheads. A chicken is born, all the eggs are in there that she will ever lay. To tell a good layer, you pick her up and hold her under your arm, her head behind you. Put three fingers between the bones between her her legs. If you can only put one finger there you want to let her go. Pale combs, too, mean they do not lay well. I have a hundred chickens and I get 85 eggs a day. A bright coat in the henhouse, drop a bucket, wind on the window—they go whoooo! But if things are right they sing until I can't hear myself think while I'm gathering eggs. I walk out, they quit. They never see anyone but me. Perhaps they're glad I'm here. A good, hot egg is a small miracle, I think. They've never decided which came first, have they? They've never made up their minds. I think of the egg, then the world. There are many questions surrounding both."

I know nothing but this. Dig your sweet potatoes, catch your chickens. I won't tell you the flavor. We fed corn and grass. Now everything is forced. There is poison everywhere. What does it do to the earth? What was any better than to smell a wood fire? There is too much to grasp. If all things are easy, nothing has any value. That's my opinion. Come easy, go easy. There are papers, bills, taxes, laws, new road signs. I don't like modern things. Before long, push a button, take a pill. No one will have to step into the fields. Well, I will be crazy in my own way. The essential things, you see. Am I queer? Why stay here and raise chickens, Mary? Simply because it is my place. I would like to die in my henhouse.

Sometimes, standing in her fields, the old farmhouse seems to stand like a mediator between the past and future, which are alive and intolerant of each other. At such times, she feels precarious. "Before I die," she says, "I would like one thing. I would like to take one buggy ride down this whole road and through the covered bridge. I have long had that desire. There has been much history here but my daughter says she doesn't want it. She wouldn't live here for nothing on earth. It makes me feel bad. Five generations! I say. Keep on with it!

Flossie Mitchner, 86

In my time we courted in buggies. Do you know what the whip in the socket was used for? Why, to wrap the buggy lines around. What do you suppose the beau was doing? Generally, the horse knew where he was going anyway.

When one girl was talking about me having never been married she said, 'She didn't have a chance.' I said, 'That's as good a reason as any.' The other children didn't want me to be married but to take care of our parents. There were no nursing homes then and they lived into their eighties.

I'm not bragging any on how many fellows I had but I went with four. All the fellows I went with are dead now. Perhaps we were rough on them. On Saturday nights Mellie Reeves took the chairs out of the barber shop and we danced. Then the war came and all the boys went away and things were never the same again . . .

Aurora Peterson, 85

Aurora Peterson lives behind a doorbell which has not worked in 33 years. Her friends know about the doorbell and those who do not know are most likely selling something for which she has neither desire nor need. She is 85, and the commodities of desire and need have largely dwindled. Her house is a dim vivarium, warm and moist. Plants climb and push against the south windows. The rooms are filled with dark, ancient furniture as if dozens of people were expected momentarily. There are sepia photographs depicting a stern and unfamiliar life. One of the photographs shows Aurora on her 18th birthday, seated at a piano. It reminds her that she was once young, pretty, perhaps desirable.

"I went with several boys," she says. "They were mostly nice. One you might call a boyfriend. He went with everyone in the neighborhood so he wasn't exactly mine. We went many places. At Clifton Park I fell into the water up to my knees. Once we went to the Sabina Camp Meeting in an automobile. 'Why did you not marry?' my nieces sometimes ask. 'O the right one never came along,' I reply. Being married? Would that have made my life different?"

Such a thing is imponderable to Aurora. Did it hold some real or imagined dread? Not even she knows anymore. For her, such imaginings are like images of life in a small, distant country with an unpronounceable name. "My brother, John, hauled hickory logs to Dayton to smoke meat. He didn't marry until he cleared his land. 'Why not, John?' mother asked. 'You're married such a long time, mother,' he said. He saw it as a long-term investment, you see . . ."

Deeper into the family, a Peterson married an Indian. It is one of Aurora's favorite stories. "We came from Basel, Switzerland, to Chimney Rock, N.C. Martin Peterson and his two sisters were stolen by Indians and taken to upper Sandusky. Martin was a woodsman and got away. He lived on nuts and berries until he saw Chimney Rock. One sister married an Indian. I don't know about the other. My great-grandfather, was he in that bunch of Petersons, or not? I have to think and think. They were just young people. They had gone out to pick flowers . . ."

The Petersons become farmers. But becoming a farmer was like becoming a Peterson: some things, perhaps many things, are ordained. The land contented Aurora but not John. "He thought he wanted to do something. He didn't know what. *Something.* He took a course in Dayton. He thought of going on the railroad. Finally he became a farmer. Paul said,

Aurora Peterson, on her 18th birthday

'Father knows about farming. I will, too.' He was easier to persuade although no one was persuading. O we were farmers out and out. It might have been discouraging. But I never resented it. I never wanted anything else. Most farmers now go to town."

Aurora cleaned stables, cut wood, mowed the yard with a pushmower. In the early spring, when the feeble heat allows her new hope, she thinks of the pushmower. She would like to use it again in the yard. For a moment she forgets she is 85. *Such deceit!* she thinks. The mind after all can go anywhere while looking back to chide the reluctant body.

What day is this? What year?

There is a swing in the woodhouse. It is for her, Aurora. It is threshing season. Grandmother Peterson comes to the door.

Watch me watch me! shouts Aurora.

Umm-huh, yes, child . . .

There are 62 relatives at Grandfather Hurley's for Christmas dinner.

But what year?

Aurora is driving an automobile into New Burlington. An aunt is with her. "Don't hit that machine!" says the aunt. Aurora later explains: "So I hit the one at the barber shop . . ."

She is a young girl riding with her father and mother: "We began to go this way, then that. Off the road and down a bank. It broke all the glass jars of cottage cheese. Mother in the back hit her nose. O it was a scary time."

The past is an unexpected guest. It will be entertained.

"Each day I ask myself: will I go into the yard? Will I pick up walnuts today? What? Eighty-five, I say. I am eighty-five. I climb my stairs one at a time, one hand on the rail, one hand on the next step. The Methodist home, they say. Too far, I answer. I'm waiting for my time. I won't go as long as I can stay on top of the carpet . . ."

Two years ago she went to Missouri to visit her niece. "They wanted to show me a big time and they did. On New Year's Eve we went to see a three-hour show about Pearl Harbor. How much noise it made! I couldn't understand those Japanese at all and there were bombs and ships going down into the ocean. I knew the real thing was worse but it was all new to me. I looked at it all and was worn to a frazzle . . ."

It has been a simple life but even the awesomely familiar hides old and unanswered riddles.

What of such a life?

"Hard work, good neighbors," says Aurora. "I made 271 quilts on my great-grandmother's quilting frame. I did necktie quilts and a doctor's wife asked me to do her one. She gave me the doctor's ties. O how I laughed. It is the shape, you see, of the bow tie. Not the ties themselves.

Well, what else do I know? I know that I am giving things away but I find everyone has modern homes. There are no places for presses, corner cupboards, old things."

Aurora does not go out anymore. There are too many things to reckon with. She is tired very easily. "People invite me over and I say, 'I'm warm. I have enough to eat.' I prefer to be here. Although sometimes I say, 'O if only Effie Lane were here.' And my cousin says, 'Then what?' And I say, 'Why we could *talk*."

At night, in her upstairs bed, she asks herself: *will I get up in the morning? Can I? What will I do after I get up? What's to do? When I was 70 I walked to town pushing a cart. O there's Aurora, Indiana, Aurora, Illinois, the Aurora Borealis, and then there's Aurora Peterson* . . .

Sometimes her cousin visits and looks at the photograph of Aurora's father.

"Wasn't he a pretty man," she says.

Yes, thinks Aurora, *O yes* . . .

She tells her cousin of the time her mother was shaving him and accidentally clipped part of the mustache off. "Amos DeHaven didn't know who he was."

She tells the cousin, "I want to go to the family reunion one more time."

The cousin laughs. "That's what you said *last* year."

Aurora laughs, too. "Yes," she says.

Billy Hazard, 94

I was born in 1880 and became a blacksmith. I bought the tools and began to work and found I didn't know anything at all. I worked anyway. I got so I could see everything about a horse when it walked in the door. Then the auto came and took the driving horse and the tractor came and took the working horse and there I was. We don't know what to do sometimes.

I had four horses and a nice crop of corn. The next year it rained and rained and I had none. I plowed barefooted for $9 a month, bruised my feet and was paid off at $10. So I went to town and bought a suit, new shoes, and got my picture took.

I asked a minister once, 'Where are we going?' He looked at me a moment and said: 'That's a remarkable question.' I don't say much but I see things. I think the land is passing from us. I think it is getting harder to put the earth in order.

* * *

The widows are fiercely at peace. Elizabeth Beam, walking in the cemetery when she is 85, says, "I know more people underfoot than above." With fading eyesight she puts Jell-O in the skillet thinking it is liver. Jemima Boots sleeps soundly, a cow bell beneath her pillow for alarms. And down the street, Ellen Jenkins puts on her best dress when expecting the telephone to ring. Daisy Nash lives with her daughter where she sits in the front yard and watches the cabbage fields. "In November I will be 89," she says, "and I sleep more than I celebrate. Sometime, tell Ada McKay. Say 'Eighty-nine, Ada.' She would cry and cry." At the Reeves-McIntire reunion Hazel Reeves walks regally into the living room bearing a single ripe tomato on a plate which she intends to be admired as one she has grown. She walks around silently in the room until everyone understands what she wishes. And Margaret Starbuck alone in the deeps of Burlington fields. Margaret Starbuck who married into a whaling family which turned its back upon the sea. With whaling journals in the cabinet and a barometer up the farmhouse stairs to predict what turns of tide. "I like these stones, these fields," she says. "But every house has changed. Each has had its deaths. Now the evenings are so long. Perhaps just fifteen minutes of talk, I think. To be together is to be human. Once an old bachelor lived nearby. He played his violin in the evenings and we applauded across the fields. Do you notice the length of the evenings . . .?" She is stranded now on a great inland ocean, surrounded by the swell of fields and the great machines in them, big as ships.

The Children

The old man gives up the doctor's clinic for the deathbed, returns home. His wife raises the window. Outside, someone is yelling and swearing, an artful profanity. The old man sinks back into his pillow and smiles.

"I know I'm in New Burlington," he says. *"I know I'm home . . . ."*

—village story

She is up before first light, driving her father past the shrouded fields past the graveyard where the stones lean terribly (*No one I know will ever go there*). The hour before dawn is unfurnished and severe. She desires something she cannot name. It is vague but strong, something she has never had nor is likely to have. Her thoughts are extravagant: she wants to live in a huge house with chandeliers and sit in leatherbound chairs before a fireplace where her husband reads poetry to her.

Willie is not watching the road as Judy drives. He is looking at the faint outlines of the sycamores along Anderson's Fork where he likes to fish. His fishing weather has not been as good since the moon shots. He cannot depend any longer on weather predictions in the *Farmer's Almanac*.

"Listen," he says to his daughter. "They sent something up there and when it landed they said the moon shook for 45 minutes. Footsteps all over the moon. They said they wanted to go so they could find out how long it had been hanging up there. All they had to do was read *Genesis*."

He does not care what the photographs from space show: the earth is flat. He has read this in The Book.

"The Book says," he tells Judy, "that in the last days an angel shall come from each of the four corners of the earth and pour bile."

"Is it like a piece of paper?" she asks. "Do we sail off the edge?"

"Four corners," he says.

"I take *physics*," she says. "If the earth were flat it would be a cube. It would have *eight* corners."

"Flat," he says. "Four corners." He is still looking out across Frank Lundy's bottomlands where the huge sycamores are darker masses against the lightening horizon. Willie knows what he knows.

He gets out in the cross streets where the other men are waiting for their ride into the factory at Dayton. His cough seems to break the fragile dawn air around him. He has coughed since he was very young and working in the coal mines of Harlan County. When the factory workers from Kentucky talk of the old days in the mines they say to Willie, "Coal mining gets in your blood."

"Nope," says Willie. "It gets in your lungs."

Willie became a miner when he was 12. His grandchildren have seen pictures of miners but they are flatland Ohio children and cannot picture their grandfather in the awesome tunnels walking under mountains. Sometimes he tells them about mining: "We all went into the mines," he says, "because there was not enough land level for corn. I done robbing work, went in after the rooms were dug. It was easy pickings but dangerous. The mountain might come down on you. I've seen the mountain drive the timbers in, slate falling around me like black hailstones. In the Liggett Mines I cleaned out the last of the seams where the vein narrowed to four feet. It bent a man to work it so they called it the place where the monkey gets on your back."

The grandchildren picture Willie in the awful darkness something wild clawing his back. They find the stories delicious.

He tells them about the blind miner of Harlan County. "Once," begins Willie, "a new man was working and after he loaded his cars he went into the next room to see what his neighbor was doing. There was a guy shoveling coal to beat forty—and no light.

'What happened to your light?' the new miner asked.

'I don't use a light,' said the other miner. 'I been in here 20 years without a light.'

"The new miner," says Willie, "thought he was talking to a spook . . ."

Willie tells his flatland grandchildren about mountain wildcats and poisonous snakes. The children rarely see snakes in Ohio because the nearby farmers grow hogs which are immune to the venom and consider snakes a delicacy.

"In the woods," sayd Willie, "I could smell a copperhead 20 feet away. It's a sweet smell like a pomegranate. Once you smell it you never forget it. I had a pet blacksnake who would get under my shirt and wrap around my stomach. One day I was going to the creek to swim and a fellow in a big car stopped to ask what time it was. I reached into my shirt, pulled out the blacksnake's head and looked at it. That fellow dug off and threw dirt all over me . . ."

Sometimes Willie laughs with his daughter over his courting days. He tells Judy how her mother, Mary, brought him out of the mines. Judy has heard his stories dozens of times but she always laughs, too. She pictures him as a very young man living in the Kentucky mountains near the town which bears their family name—Hyden. In her picture of him he is strong and healthy. He does not have a cough. He brawls in taverns and makes whiskey. He is spontaneous, roguish. She admires this image of her father but she does not let her mother know that she does.

"When I was young," Willie says, "and a woman just look like she wanted to get married I'd run like a turkey. I'd take a girl to church then I'd sneak a look over at her and think: 'What am I doing here?' My grandfather lived at Hyden on the Middle Fork River. My grandmother lived 20 miles away on the Redbird River. This was before she was my grandmother. He rode a mule to see her. I've ridden that far and didn't even like the girl. I met Mary on a blind date. I was 29. I decided to get married and that was the end of my rowdy days and I made a husband for my wife. I can't explain it . . ."

Mary recognizes that nothing is safe in the backward mountains. The men try to grow tobacco on the ungovernable hillsides and some of them make whiskey in the sheltered coves and those who are left go into the mines. Mary acknowledges this as a perverse but realistic condition. She and Willie head north, to Dayton, where the factories stand against the flat, treeless horizon and union scale tempers the endless timecard weeks. "I lived in Kentucky 29 years," Willie tells Judy, "and after 29 years the only thing I had that I wasn't borned into it with was the black lung."

In the long summer afternoons after Willie has returned from the factory he and Judy fish off the double-iron bridge below the village. She loves him but she is angry and impatient: *My father believes that the earth is flat . . .*

In time Judy reconsiders castles and aristocratic buildings. She does not consider herself a wholly practical person but she has practical thoughts: she wonders how a castle is heated. She imagines bathrooms made of stone, 30-feet ceilings, and corridors like mining shafts. Considering aristocracy a perspective, she trades images of mansions for a farmhouse.

In her courtship she explains to Charles McIntire, a young engineer who lives above the village, that FM stands for frequency modulation.

"Yes," says Charles, "but what does that mean?"

"It means," she replies, "the modulation of the frequency of the transmitting wave in accordance with speech or a signal. This is contrasted with the modulation of the amplitude of the transmitting wave. Which means that FM is mostly static free."

Impressed, Charles proposes. He goes to Kentucky with Judy and Willie and Mary to meet the rest of the family. Aunt Jane likes Charles and laughs with him: he goes around barefooted while all of them wear shoes.

Soon Charles and Judy are married. Charles invents complicated electronic machinery for a Dayton company which sends him west. In California they take their tiny daughter, Cherie, to Disneyland where she shakes Captain Hook's hook. When Cherie is older she finds the moment is her earliest memory. "I can see the picture in my mind," she says, "but I do not know how I felt about that . . ."

They have no desire to live in California. It seems transient, kaleidoscopic. Even the California ground is unstable. In Lovelock, Nevada, they drive up to a hotel where they intend to spend the night. The hotel is not a hotel, however, but a whorehouse called La Belle's. It has a huge graveled parking lot for truckers. For six weeks Charles works out in the desert. Judy finds the land harsh and insupportable. Nevada, she thinks, might be purgatory. She dreams of rows of green Ohio corn growing in the alien red deserts. They spend Thanksgiving in a mobile home in Lovelock. *We must be home for Christmas;* they think.

Charles' grandmother McIntire who is very old writes to them offering them her farmhouse above the village, above the graveyard. It is across the field from where Charles was born. They come home in a Thunderbird. The new highways obliterate distance. Charles and Judy know men in New Burlington who came this way in wagons. Their neighbor, Lester Lane, has in his basement a hoop from a Conestoga wagon in which he rode to California. This seems to them somehow implausible although they know it is true.

Like many of the country people around him Charles lives in the country but drives to work near Dayton. His life, however, is bound to the old farm. He tends the orchard and garden and builds a sugar house where he temporarily abandons his company each spring to make maple syrup. The people at the company joke with him about the season: "No," they say to mock customers, "we can't build anything for you now. It's February and time to tap maples . . ."

Although the men tease him, some of them once lived in the country

Gregg McIntire (PHOTOGRAPH BY KEN STEINHOFF)

The McIntires, four generations (PHOTOGRAPH BY KEN STEINHOFF)

and they come out in the uncompromising February weekends to help
with the tapping.

In the woods after dark Charles says, "We will pay for using up all this
moonlight." He thinks each movement is linked inextricably to every
other movement. He perceives the world as a piece of living machinery,
biology and mathematics both systems of maintenance. Sometimes
Charles' hands seem like separate beings. They move wisely over broken
things: they can repair anything even certain examples of human pain.
They can make anything. They could, perhaps, *perform*. "Horsepower,"
says Charles, "is footpounds per minute."

He himself will not be catalogued. He is uncommon, complex. If he
shows in one moment some prejudice taught in the isolated years of
growing up in New Burlington, then in another moment he refutes it by
generosity. If he seems reserved and aloof then he will erupt in a moment
of spontaneity.

> *Charles, I've lost 22 pounds.*
> *That's . . . two gallons.*

Charles is not interested in the ambivalences of human character; he
prefers the more certain revelations of machines. He finds machinery
constant, implacable, predictable. Machinery can be known. Human
character is inscrutable, bedeviling. This becomes to him a fact, like
physics, like weather. *The proper response to politics and other malfunc-
tions of character is to work in the garden.* Charles is more Wilson than
McIntire; the Wilsons were among the early settlers of New Burlington,
farmers and syrup makers, silent as stones. He will make no statements
about himself. He is serene, temperate. To regard him is like looking into
an eighteenth-century landscape.

Together Charles and Judy seem antipodal; she is talkative, fat, undis-
ciplined, known. She embraces the universe: stray animals, Bible sales-
men, community disorders and disasters. She is spontaneous, earthy, un-
prejudiced. Friends laugh with her about her housekeeping which is
largely nonexistent.

"It is the only house I know," they say, "where the bathtub ring is
around the living room."

"Does your vacuum cleaner have a flamethrower attachment?" they
ask.

"But I'm a good person!" she cries in feigned insult, making hot choc-
olate on a stove piled with dishes, clothes, and toys.

She has friends who keep immaculate houses. One of them makes dirt
for her son to play in by crumbling up styrofoam. Her own son, Gregg,
plays in the fields, the barnlot.

"If Gregg becomes an astronaut," a neighbor tells her, "he will be the first one to return from the moon with grass stains."

When the destruction of the village begins Judy feels vulnerable although she and Charles live in the countryside above. She feels that the countryside is suddenly fragile and temporary. She is angry but she has no place for it. She does not know how to protest. The villagers she grew up with begin to move. The houses disappear and only the foundations are left to scar the passive earth.

She walks through the village to fix it in her mind: *A witch lives here behind the orchard. I know because she wears a long flowered dress, a man's dress hat, brogans, a sweater even in the middle of summer. Then one day she comes into the orchard behind me and begins talking before I can run. Afterward I know she is not a witch. She is a very old lady who lives by herself on the other side of the orchard. No one I know will ever become old. When you become old you change and no one recognizes you. Sometimes the horse that pulls the cornwagon eats the orchard grass. I worry about her because she is very old too. If she falls down and it rains in her ear she will drown. She will not drown in the summer though because the storms are loud but quick. My daddy says the noise is an old Irishman turning over a tub of potatoes. I know it is summer because I look beside the creekstone step at the back door. When the puddle dries up it is summer.*

Judy knows that what she desires is the persistence of known images. *I want something that doesn't change,* she thinks. She tries to explain her feelings to Charles. "I don't think I like things that are replacing what I have known," she tells him. "If developers took this farm I could not stand it. I am uncertain why. When I was growing up my friends had homes their fathers *owned*. Their grandfathers lived nearby. I want my children to belong somewhere. I felt I never belonged. No place, home, piece of earth. Always movement, nothing constant. I had *family*, I knew I belonged there, but no *place*. When we went to California I thought it was as far as anyone could possibly go. I couldn't *believe*. Oceans. Mountains. I was so frightened . . ."

She thinks of the New Burlington prejudice against outsiders, a bias so subtle as to defy language to capture it. Her mother suggested by behavior: she never attended school functions or church. Willie did not belong to the fire department. They were from across the Ohio River: renters, factory people, *Briars. They do not want us because we don't have what they have.*

Judy remembers her mother returning home from the canning factory

in the white summer afternoons, her glasses splattered with corn. *I belong
here,* Judy thinks. *This place. This time. But how long . . .?*

Willie's cough is omnipresent. As he gets older the Ohio winters become more painful. His breathing in February is like a rasp. He sits inside waiting for the sun to come and bake the illness from him. There are
newspapers in the trashcan soaked in blood. Judy recognizes that he is
dying. When he is in the hospital he has a dream. In the dream he is on
a creekbank fishing but the fish are not biting. When he looks across the
stream he sees his brothers-in-law, Travis and Arthur. They are sitting in
the sunlight but there is no sunlight on his side of the stream. "Come
over here," says Arthur and Travis in the dream. "The fishing is good
over here." Willie says, "I don't have a way. When I find a way I'll
come." The dream frightens him. He tells Judy not to tell anyone.

Halfway through her piano recital, Willie's granddaughter Kathy looks
at her wristwatch. It is 9:59. This is the time at which Willie dies in the
hospital.

Judy wants her father buried in his fishing clothes. "He didn't wear a
suit," she tells her mother. "He didn't even wear his *teeth.*" Her mother,
however, has Willie buried in his only suit, the one he bought for Judy's
graduation from high school. At the service Judy lays her hand on her father's hand. Touching the body is a custom in the mountains. It is an ac-
knowledgment of the finality of the grave. Willie's relatives have come
from Kentucky and they drive to the cemetery where they stand beside
the country people looking uncomfortable and afflicted. The noise of the
dirt falling on the coffin from the gravedigger's shovel echoes in Judy's
ears. It sounds to her like falling timber.

Her house, although filled with her own family now, seems empty and
airless. Her son, Gregg, who is five, becomes intermittently angry. "Pa-
pa told me he would teach me how to fish," he says to Judy. "Although
he can't talk now he promised me." Judy's mother tells her not to bring
home the flowers on the grave.

"If you bring home the flowers," she says, "you'll go back there soon."

In the autumn Judy takes one afternoon to drive slowly through the
countryside. This is something she does each year at this time. She drives
mostly on the old unpaved lanes—Graveyard Road, Buck Run, Inwood.
But even here the land is changing. People talk of asphalt, plats, water
lines. A mobile home has moved into the field below them. The land
seems: compressed. Judy sometimes thinks that her children are growing
up on an island surrounded by a busy sea.

In the afternoons when Gregg, who is now seven, gets home from school he looks to see if the McKays are out in their fields. Then he stands at the end of the furrows until the driver stops for him and he rides without speaking for hours on the fantastic machinery. He says to Charles, "I want to be a farmer."

The children are awesomely beautiful; they sometimes seem to be exquisite procelain figurines which may shatter into pieces under the weight of time.

The family crowds into the farmhouse kitchen. The yard outside is filled with cords of wood and syrup buckets. These are artifacts of Charles' passage into his own ancestry: he becomes less contemporary. He begins heating the farmhouse with wood.

> *How many cords today, Charles?*
> *O two or twelve . . .*

On early winter weekends he and some of his neighbors go into the woods together to cut the fallen timber returning in the dark tired but pleased to warm themselves by their own design. "I do not always have reasons for the things I do," says Charles. But such a statement has a resonance; it is to be carefully regarded. Charles is sly. At moments his life becomes sculptured, arrested in an artful statement.

In another month he and Gregg will go into the woods to prepare for the maple-syrup season. In December Charles begins to see in his mind the woods as a *design*. Gregg thinks of Christmas. "For Christmas," he says, "I want a disc, a plow, and my pa-pa back . . ."

Willie and Mary Hyden (PHOTOGRAPH BY KEN STEINHOFF)

Perspective:
Rudolf Howe, 69

I am not sorry to see New Burlington gone. Every spring the outhouses went into the streams. My little girl caught scarlet fever. My son, polio. Children who waded in the streams got boils on their legs. In Europe, human wastes are used in the fields. We did not put a little house over human fertilizer.

The people of New Burlington also thought that if you had a glass of beer you were not good people. For my son Rudy's birthday we invited thirty children. Two came. Bobby Carr and the Pickering child. Mrs. Carr said, 'Mrs. Howe, you don't have a good name. You drink beer.' They thought we were serving the children beer! I said, There will never be a party here again. We are German people. Having a glass of beer is part of our life.

Before Burwell Miller died, I took him a small bottle of schnapps. I thought perhaps it would help him in his illness. After he died the family sent it back unopened. It is the attitude that keeps a village down. I asked the minister of the Methodist church once—William was his name— why so terrible? He was preaching against smoking, beer. 'Is it a sin,' I asked, 'for an old man to sit in his chair and smoke his pipe?' This is his satisfaction. If we do something against our health it is not necessarily sinful. Christ's first wonder was making new wine. The people of New Burlington said: grape juice. But it was wine. When Dick Scammahorn, a day laborer, went to work in Xenia as a bartender he said, 'You should see the New Burlington people who come in.' They were not bad people but this narrowmindedness kept their village down.

In my estimation our creator is a reasonable God. I have always found Him reasonable. I read the Bible every day and always I learn a little more. But in New Burlington the people made Him unreasonable. In the old books, you were a crumb. People were controlled by superstition. In Daniel, the people left great bowls of food for their god. Daniel told the king this was not true. For speaking so his life was jeopardized. He put flour on the floor and the next morning followed the footsteps from the bowls of food to the houses of priests. We are still fooled by our priests. In churches, sometimes politics are made to seem like the hand of God.

I speak up in church. But they felt I was disturbing the lesson. I could feel how they resented it when I spoke. They felt: *you do not belong in the family.* Once I sat down and a woman moved away from me. I thought: *they don't even want to sit with me.* The Methodists have beautiful songs. I love them. My son played the piano and only played what I knew well. A lady once made a request to Gene and he said, 'But my dad doesn't know that one . . .' They knew I loved to sing but they never asked me. So I stopped. They never asked about me but perhaps they missed my singing. *My gosh,* someone says. *Such a contrary man.* So the man keeps his mouth shut. He does it to keep peace. He is, of course, dishonest. He has been dishonest from the first. He took the apple from Eve to please her. To keep peace.

There were never any leaders in New Burlington. Everyone was afraid to give an opinion. I am not that way. I have a voice to wake the dead. It flies right out of my mouth. The people of New Burlington attended meetings and no one said anything. Once outside they would chatter away. 'Why didn't they say this or that? And what about suchandsuch?' Well, we are this way. We want to be accepted.

I came to this country in 1928. My parents thought there was a better life here. There were also relatives already here. My grandmother was opposed. 'You have the bread in Germany,' she said. 'Do not go to America for the butter.' But my parents painted a very pretty picture. But it was not all like that. If something happened to the stove in the winter whole families died. In the Dakotas they strung lines from the barn to the house. They say: it is wonderful in America but don't get sick. They say: if you buy an automobile you don't need a bankbook.

Coming here on the boat the people were friendly and loving. The food was excellent and there were many pretty girls. But as soon as the boat landed it was everyone for himself. All at once the journey was over and I was in a new land. I could not speak the language and my heart was in my throat. Once in Dayton, however, I was not homesick one day for my cousins were there and they spoke low German.

I went all around to find a job. Those who hired liked the Germans because we were good workers. I worked as a busboy in the dining room of the Van Cleve Hotel. I was a hod carrier. Then I went to work in the factory, where I went through the depression. 'If it happens again,' I said, 'I want to be able to eat. A place where I can grow something.' In 1942 we came to the country. My Louise did not want to go to school because the children of New Burlington called her a Nazi. They said: *You have bombed Coventry and so many died.* I spoke to Marge Lovett, who was a teacher there. 'Say no more,' she said to me. She said to them, 'We are all people of foreign countries. I myself am German.' Then it was over. Of course, what happens between children comes strictly from the parents. The tongue is the dirtiest part of the body. In Germany we have a saying: birds sing and the young ones follow.

The farms here used German prisoners. They thought Rudy could translate for them. But he did not want to. He was afraid people would call him a Nazi. My children were ashamed and did not learn the language. The war, can it be described? There were prisoners in Wilmington. A camp. A high fence. They were wheeling sod. My heart knocked me under my chin. I thought: Maybe someone from my hometown. Perhaps even my own family. I spoke to them. But the guard came and said we were not allowed to talk. I said, 'Do you want to tear my heart out? I am German, too!' The guard said 'Never come back.' I cannot describe this feeling.

My wife was so homesick and she went back to visit later. She saw American soldiers in Germany and was very happy. 'I'm from Dayton,' she said. 'I am, too!' said the soldier. She said, 'Well, I'm not exactly from Dayton,' she said. 'I'm not exactly, either!' he said. 'I'm closer to Xenia,' she said. 'Me, too!' he said. They talked, and showed each other photographs. It took me ten months to save enough money to bring her back.

We simply wanted a place in the country. A serene life. We grew up when life was plain and simple. When you have such a thing you should never give it up. A garden and a cow. Food and drink. If I had a million dollars I'd buy a thousand acres and divide it into fifty-acre farms. We would farm with horses, butcher, and have a smokehouse. I believe a man can live on fifty acres. There is a song about a man who has a choice between the Kaiser's crown, a lyre to make him famous, or to know a small house on the Rhine and a virtuous woman. Of course he gives up the crown and the lyre. I sing this song often.

Shame

Even those who disliked Harvey admitted he was a handsome devil. Perhaps the mustardseed of envy in such admissions: Harvey could have sold a manure spreader to the Methodist minister. His territory was all of the countryside and moonlit nights with village girls in his buggy and salesmanship raised to a high craft.

Pretty Kate was not a day over 14 when she became pregnant. After the child died Kate did not leave her father's house for over a year. And the shades always down as if to prevent the villagers from observing her sorrow.

Harvey finally did marry, however. But his wife died after visiting the country abortionist nearby. At the funeral her mother cried, "I'm glad you have died! I don't want you back . . ."

Harvey's cousin, Charlie, liked the ladies, too. When Charlie's girl in Spring Valley got pregnant Charlie married her then left after the ceremony. In the front door, out the back . . .

Joshua Scroggy, 92

We have always had this body of curious information among us. I have known these things always. I heard them from the old men on the benches in front of the cobbler's shop and at family picnics when no one knew I was paying any attention. You know what they say: little pitchers have biggest ears. Of course these things didn't get into the family histories or the obituaries. In our obituaries we were all so upright we must have been buried standing up. And in the histories we fought bravely in the war and owned all the land we rented.

It is something about the way we use language, I think. Have you noticed the way men have a formal and an informal voice? It is this way with our events, too. The informal events we tell over the fence. The formal events are for public consumption. The problem is that the formal events are not nearly so interesting. And often as not they are lies. This is because living well—or badly—is determined not by yourself but by your neighbors: *did she marry beneath herself? Does he belong to the Masonic Lodge?* The credentials, you see.

Once a baby was abandoned on Ebenezer Lucas's doorstep. He was not a well-off man so he went to see John Hill, who was. The Hills took the child. Her name was Mae. When she grew up Pete Blair asked her out. She said, 'No.' Pete Blair said, 'Who are you? No one. You don't even know who you are.' Mae cried. Although she grew up in the Hill house she was being reminded that after all she still lacked proper credentials. She was very beautiful and died when she was so young. She was not over 30.

Some of the village ladies went to extravagant lengths to be included among the Daughters of the American Revolution, an organization formed to reward one for the accidents of birth. A genealogist told me once that if he searched as diligently in other directions he could find a horse thief or two. 'Never saw a family tree that didn't need spraying,' he said.

In the first years of this century I was just a young boy but I remember the villagers talking a great deal about 'illegitimacy.' I thought that perhaps it was an epidemic and that I might catch it myself. I asked my mother about it and she told me that only girls caught it. I was somewhat relieved but I worried for my sisters. I remember praying in meeting that my sisters be spared 'the illegitimacy.' A few years later when I was in the upper grades at school three girls came down with the illegitimacy at the same time. That was about a third of the class, I suppose, and could therefore be classed as an epidemic.

The girls were all fine girls and soon they were married and happily it seemed although each firstborn child died not long after and badly at that: one burned, another drank poison, and one was run over. The old villagers regarded these things as a demonstration by the hand of God. It was no such thing. It was merely a demonstration that life is not a little haphazard, and a lot curious.

In time I came to the belief that 'illegitimacy' was merely a definition placed upon a situation. And the definition was for the purposes of intolerance to a kind of behavior. The proper definition, you know, is 'unlawfully begotten.' The key word is 'unlawfully.' I prefer a secondary definition of illegitimacy, which is 'illogical.'

In the early 1900's, we were very rural. People who had just returned from a trip to Dayton or Cincinnati were regarded as *infectious*. The village was a cloister and the order protected itself by rather rigid conventions. This was both a blessing and a curse: The older ones regarded it as a blessing and the younger ones a curse. I was a teacher kept comfortably by my grandfather's land and a certain lack of classical ambition; I was also too timid for much vice so the village conventions did not bother me. In 92 years I've never seen a set of conventions that worked very well so one set seemed about as good as another.

One of the conditions in a village, of course, is adjacency. Everyone is *adjacent* to everyone else. Therefore the villagers watched each other closely because they didn't have much of a choice, living so close together. I remember once that Herman Jones said to Marianna Compton's mother, 'Does Marianna have a bad cold?'

'No,' said Mrs. Compton, 'Why do you ask?'

'Well,' said Herman, 'I was passing by your house Sunday night and happened to look in the parlor window and I saw Raleigh Bogan listening to Marianna's *lungs*.'

Marianna's mother and father were Horace and Lucy Compton, fine people and self-appointed chroniclers of the village's high moments. Lucy kept a diary in which she noted the times of people's weddings. She consulted it when the firstborn arrived so she could pronounce a proper benediction. Marion Colvin and his wife had their first child nine months and fifteen minutes after the ceremony.

There was enough to watch even in a place as small as New Burlington. Matthew Stewart, a fine Negro farmer, had a daughter who married a man who soon began looking after a white woman. The marshal came out and arrested the man, he received a stiff fine, and his wife took in wash to pay it. This says more about the divinity of forgiveness than the nature of adultery. One assumes forgiveness, of course, but it was an assumption based upon her oblations at the laundry tub.

Bert Bailey, a bachelor, admired the beautiful wife of Alvah Blair the barber and one day Bert stopped by for a shave and Alvah lathered him up and said, 'By God! This is the moment I've been waiting for!' Chester Haydock was just a little fellow waiting on a haircut but he was old enough to know the which and the why of it so he ran out of the barber shop yelling. He thought Alvah was about to perform surgery on Bert which is also what Bert thought. They seemed to have reached an immediate understanding and before nightfall everybody in the village had heard some version of what had happened in Alvah Blair's barber chair.

In one prominent family a man died of venereal disease and there were village ladies who died during abortions. We had chicken thieves and barnburners and once the body of a peddler was found stuffed in a well. About 1912 we had a shooting, too. It was on a Saturday night and Ora Wilson and Glyden McNeil began firing away at each other. When the glass began breaking Burwell Miller shut himself in his meat cooler and left Uncle Ira Scroggy outside banging on the door. When the smoke had cleared both Ora and Glyden were lying in the street but Dr. Whitaker soon fixed them up. No one ever seemed to know what it was about. It was quite a lot of excitement, I remember. There was nothing like bed for some time and the village was full of coal oil lamps and idle speculation. Shootings were not yet fashionable but highly entertaining.

Around 1900, sometime before Dr. Whitaker, the village had a doctor—known as excellent—who performed abortions. He was also a bootlegger. My father said he kept two horses worn out. I regarded his occupations an interesting contradiction in the village fabric. It suggested that his trades were considered serviceable.

In the old part of the graveyard there was a depression in the ground and each year at a certain time flowers would be left there. My grandfather said it was the grave of an illegitimate child who was stillborn and the mother secretly visited the grave each birthday. As a sentient young man immersed in 19th-century American verse I was considerably impressed and had many fantasies regarding the secret and sorrowful life of the parents.

Stories such as these were always an undercurrent of village life and as I recall they were told tolerantly for the most part, as if they were things that had occurred in the *family*. This is what the village was at that time: a family. Literally everyone in the village in 1900 was related by either blood or marriage. My grandfather said the McKays always married cousins to keep the land in the family. It seemed *everyone* was cousins. So we knew all these stories and spoke of them among ourselves but it was knowledge to be contained. There was a *manner* for it to pass among us, a way for things to be recounted.

Drink was another secret passion in New Burlington. It was regarded more shameful than illegitimacy. The villagers acknowledged gluttony as a condition but drinking seemed to be such a *continual* form of it. Too much pleasure, you see. A genetic implant from the Puritans. H. L. Mencken defined Puritanism as 'the suspicion that somewhere someone might be having a good time.' The hard drinkers were prayed for in meeting, and often the drinkers themselves were there praying, too.

We got our milk from the shoemaker below the cross streets and once my sister went to fetch it and found the shoemaker suffering the delirium tremens. He was crying and picking rats and spiders off the wallpaper. When his wife went to get the milk he was angry because she was not helping him with the wallpaper. It made quite an impression on my sister, who was perhaps 13. She said the shoemaker was why she never drank.

The coffinmaker was intimately acquainted with the bottle, also. He worked for the Colvins and they told him frequently that one day he was going to die drunk and wake up in hell. One day the coffinmaker passed out drunk in the carpentry shop and the Colvins found him and laid him out in one of his coffins and put the lid on. Then they sat down to wait. Soon the coffinmaker came to. He rapped tentatively on the underside of the coffin lid and began to moan. 'Just as I expected,' he said. 'Died and gone to hell!'

When Hettie Walton married George McPherson, Pete Blair spiked the cider barrel and the whole village got drunk. People who had never touched liquor before. It was quite a sight. Burwell Miller and Uncle Ira Scroggy were outside trying to uproot a sugar maple. 'Pull, Ira,' said Burwell. 'I think it moved a bit, Burwell,' said Uncle Ira.

The miller drank, too, and when the mill burned everyone suspected he did it. They said he sold the grain people had stored there and set the fire to cover the loss. No one ever knew. Such losses at that time were borne only by an unimaginable labor: men began over. This was true with buildings, crops, families, wives. Those who did not went mad. Mary Bailey was a young woman when her child died at birth. Then Mary's husband, James, died, too. She never recovered. She refused to leave her farmhouse on Buck Run and lived there the rest of her life. At night she rambled through the yards and fields. She struck trees and the side of the house with a club. In the next farmhouse the DeHavens could hear her cursing God. She never changed anything in the house after her husband and child died. Even the cobwebs remained. She lived to be very old.

Insanity takes many forms, more than a few being socially acceptable, even admirable. In 1900, however, mental problems were still regarded as more of a curse than an illness. One prominent family consisted of eight children and six of them committed suicide. One of the boys, Arthur, drank blue vitriol after there had been too much rain on his corn. My grandmother said each time Arthur's mother became pregnant she spent most of the pregnancy in an institution.

It was common for village men to commit suicide when their health failed. Such a thing did have its precedents. The Scythians, an ancient nomadic people, committed suicide when they became too old or ill to keep pace. They regarded suicide as an act which preserved their children from guilt. By the time of Plato, a suicide's hand was cut off, the hand that inflicted death, and buried separately. Plato himself, however, thought an irreversible disease provocation enough for suicide. The Christians, of course, found suicide completely unacceptable so in later times the bodies of suicides were mutilated and their property taken by the state.

I was a young man when John Lemar hung himself in his barn. Because of his health, they said. I remember that reactions to his death were *statements* of shock but without much belief in the statements. They were really quite calm about it, and empathic. Of course, he was one of us. From among us. The village family, you see.

We had all these things, all manner of pride and gluttony, and sins real and imagined, but the village life caused a tolerance among us. It had to. Everyone came face to face each day. This led in most cases to accommodation. Like a family, the village shifted, arbitrated, accommodated, and came to terms with the odd corners in its own life. I have witnessed these tolerances in otherwise intolerant people and I have marveled at it.

These things may sound like gossip and I have a certain fondness for it but such stories about my family will have to come from someone else. Gossip needs the perspective of translation to *become* gossip. The thing that must be remembered about gossip is that it encompasses the art of narration, and literalness should always be secondary to a good narration. I find my own explanations of why I am a peculiar man rather tedious and no more truthful than anyone else's explanation. I have grown to prefer the village stories. They are always more interesting. A story, you see, is ultimately not about facts but rather about how people *feel*. So even a libel tells one *something*. One of the advantages of being past ninety is that no one is left to dispute me. Oral narration at best has always been a precarious business.

Death

Cork on the horses in the rain,
pulling the hearse. Two horses
slipping on the ice. The hearse
lurched and the casket out and the
body, too. Into the road. John, John,
what was your name? Holland. John
Holland.

—the gravedigger

Frank Robinson's house is on one hill, the graveyard is on another al-
though half a mile away. To get to his work he walks but everyone knows
him and most of the time he is soon given a ride. When a familiar au-
tomobile passes him by, as it occasionally does, he forgives although the
driver is likely to feel he has behaved irrationally, on some vague and
quarrelsome instinct, and he is left with the cusp of guilt as the gravedig-
ger shrinks in the rear glass. One of the villagers, far into a solemn
moment, will tell of this as if ashamed and say: "I've done that." The
gravedigger, living alone, returns silence for silence. The moment is too
complicated, somehow past reckoning.

"There is something to a gravedigger being avoided," he says. "Yes,
there is something to that. I once had a good friend; he liked me and I
him, but I buried his father and for six months after he did not speak. He
had been an easy man to get along with but he just had nothing to say
and it was a case of the silence being louder than the words. It was very
plain to see."

The gravedigger accepts his portion of the silences but it is an uneasy
truce. To shove such uneasily tenanted spaces away he is a voluminous
talker. "I spent three years in the fifth grade, finished with the seventh and
have learned since from books because I wanted to be able to keep up my
end of the conversation. In history I could not say when the War of 1812
was begun but I was good in reading and geography. I walked to school
because I preferred to. I enjoyed it because I could talk my way through
town. I like to talk so much you'd think I was vaccinated by a phonograph

needle. Although I have only a seventh-grade education I know that the speed of light is 186,000 miles per second. I believe that is correct and if it takes that long, those stars are getting way out there. I know that air pressure is 14.7 pounds per square inch and that if a bomb blew out in the yard near that sugar maple, why, it would create such a vacuum that there would be nothing to hold your body together and you would explode like a balloon. I've read that . . ."

He has closed off the front rooms of his house which his father built three-quarters of a century before and walks to work in the graveyard regularly from April until September. The walls of the house turn bare. The gravedigger himself feels occasional pain but he does not see a doctor. "I have not been to a doctor in 17 years," he says. "I do no business with the middleman . . ."

Frank Robinson, 60

I've tended the cemetery for 23 years. I work there from April up into September and dig graves any time they need them. I make about $30 a week for the year, and I've never asked for relief. My uncle was the town clerk and one day while I was doing day labor here and there, he said, 'Frank, I need a little help for a few days.' Little did I think I'd be there 23 years. It seemed to suit my mother very well. She liked me to stay close to home, and I did. She and my brother, Harold, are buried in the Caesar's Creek Cemetery but I buried my other brother, Russell, myself. He said Caesar's Creek was too snaky for him and he wanted in this one. Even though we didn't like digging his grave. It shouldn't be that a man has to lay his own brother away. My uncle said I had to and that was that, but it didn't set right.

At first, being the grave-digger seemed strange. I did an awful lot of thinking. It didn't look right to take pay for digging a man's grave. I thought the money would do me no good, that it would just kind of get away from me. But I figured that someone had to do it. You don't let your mind dwell on it when you're covering a man up. Another person gone, right or wrong, and who's a man to judge so quick? There used to be a fellow, Ralph McGill, a very good friend. He was a little older than I and married my niece. We used to have a little drink together and I'll tell you something: he never condemned no man. He talked with good sense and had a good heart and burying him made me stop and think: the

Frank Robinson (PHOTOGRAPH BY KEN STEINOFF)

big name means nothing because six feet of earth makes all men the same size. There's no discrimination to my work.

Of course, some notice such things as others don't. I've noticed burials seem to come in threes. When there are no graves for a bit, there'll be one, then two more. Others have noticed it besides me. Roy Reeves has and he's a very sensible man. It makes you wonder. Most graves are 96 inches long and 40 inches wide and four feet deep. At one time, they were all six feet deep, then five, then when they stopped laying them out in pine boxes and went to vaults, they put them in at four feet. That's so there'd still be 18 inches of dirt atop.

It used to be that many boxes were made of pine and afterwards, the lid would sink and the dirt would follow and we would have to fill, but now it is almost a law that people use the vault although I think it is all about money myself. I've buried two in a pine box, and my mother was buried in one. She said no vault, just pine and that's the way it was done. Now they lay a frame and put four cement biscuits on it for the base and lower the casket, then put a cement vault over it which is airtight. Some are made of steel. Me, I don't care how it's done as long as they don't cremate me. Something doesn't seem right about cremating. I don't know. It makes no difference to me, a gold vault or a pine box. It's nice to be laid away well but some people even in death desire to be above other people.

I've seen all manner of things up here, I'll tell you. I've seen rain fill the grave within inches and us dipping with a bucket. Then we used a pump and ran the water away with a downspout. We were dipping it out once as the people came in. I have used everything in digging a grave but a screwdriver. I never saw but one open casket, however, and there was a reason for it. Graves was the man, strange, isn't it? He died in Indiana and was shipped here and some of his people wanted to take a look. It seemed strange to me. I was not used to seeing it open. This time, I had a look at the man I was covering up and it made a difference to me although it never has been just a job. I have never been just putting a box away because I've buried 150 people at the most and there have been very few that I haven't known and I think about all of them, even a stranger, although not so much as when I'm laying a friend away. I've always thought some about it and usually I think this: what was last in his mind?

My uncle Bill Moon and his friend, Bill Fletcher, dug up a man who was buried in the wrong place and after they got him up, my uncle said, 'What do you say we take a little look now that he's up?' and so they opened it and do you know what? His whiskers had grown like everything and he was lying on his side. It makes a man think. When I was in the war, we brought back a wounded fellow and he was pronounced dead and laid out with the others when someone chanced to see him move.

The last I heard, he recovered and was in good shape. It used to be they put a mirror in front of the mouth but today they as well as operate on a man before he is buried and no chance of him being put away alive.

On the east side was a child's grave and the trustees wanted it moved and my job was to get it ready. I had to dig out all around it. I'll tell you, when we took the vault away to get to the casket, there was nothing left but a few small bones. There was nothing wrong with it, I suppose, but there looking at what little remained, I felt lonely and sad. I've never had children, you know. It's better to have had it and lost it than to have never had nothing at all. I've been called sentimental but people would be better off with more of it.

I buried a man, a cold-shouldered fellow. He didn't hew very close to the line. And I buried three of his wives. His fourth asked to be buried at Caesar's Creek. She said she just couldn't stand being in a crowd.

Different people get different ideas. Don Mitchener raised race horses and when he died, they had me put a horseshoe in the cement of the base and if you can figure that out it is more than I can do. I'll tell you, I'm not a superstitious man. I also remember when it was a custom to keep the body home for several days and the relations would sit up with it. I never got it through my head why. It was not going anywhere.

On Decoration Day, I say, 'This is your day.' Only a few are persistent in coming here. I won't mention any names but the well-off decorate the least. One time I kept track of everyone I buried, then I said, why, it's a task for relations but then the relations would come to me and ask me about dates. It shows how much attention they're paying to such things as are so permanent.

The dead here are always buried with their head to the west, facing east like it says in the Bible, ready for the rising sun and the day of judgment. Undertakers know their directions and never ask and I learned quick. On Judgment Day the graves will give us up and provide us with a new body, the way I understand it. I hope I get a better one than this one because it's kind of beat up. I don't believe in reincarnation but if after I'm gone and you see an old jackass in a field, treat him kindly just to be sure.

It used to be I had a fear of dying alone. People hardly ever came about, and around the grave you're sensitive to it, not hardened as some would think. But death is not mysterious. It is going to a new place, of one kind or another. I can't say too much about it. A couple of years ago I went into the village and sat around downtown and scratched my head and said to myself that it seemed that the boys didn't come around as much. Then I thought a minute and said to myself, 'Wait a minute, Frank, it's because you've buried most of them up on the hill . . .'

Others

Some accounting occurred to the oldtimers of New Burlington when the transients arrived:

In times past, when death finally took a relative who had disgraced the family with his ingeniously evil ways (or by some odious vacuum in the brain), the keeper of the family Bible would cross his name off the page of record with strokes so heavy even the indentations in the paper revealed nothing. His image was torn from the family photograph album and only the slow process of forgetting remained of him.

And yet, the keeper would say in chastisement of himself, it takes all kinds. Or if he were truly philosophical he would dwell upon the motto: to each his own, everything in its place. Something like that, he'd think, remembering there were places he'd like to visit if he didn't have to stay, and that dogs were good friends but you didn't have to let them have the foot of the bed. Or maybe, on long winter evenings, the album on his knee, he would stare at the empty spaces and wonder what crossing of blood lines made by relatives living elsewhere produced such a mutation.

They came like gypsies, bringing cans of aqua paint and rusted cars to sit on cement blocks and a ten-year collection of beer bottles. They lived strangely, too, packed into houses that once held a reasonable-sized family of five. How they did it was obvious in some places, mysterious in others. On the outskirts of town, closer to the fields than the stores, they attached trailers to the porches front and back and lived in the yards and roads when the weather was warm. In the center of town they took what was once Trevor Haydock's store and made it an apartment building. The front door slammed open and shut as frequently as it had for customers in that time past. But, strange sight, children swung their arms from every unscreened window and family arguments vibrated through all the walls, exploding into the streets.

Inside, the boy lived across the hall from the retired farmer who moved among the furniture of his former existence, mental and actual. The antique dealer made forays into the farmer's territory on warm Sundays, trying to ply with dollars the last contrasts between him and the boy.

But Mr. Humphreys, too old to fight the changes of the times, made himself useful to his own fancies, not the times', and if it was a protest too subtle for the occasion, it was at least a motif of struggle. The boy considered him addled. The old townspeople even began to regard him as "touched." And how was he to say at his age that when he went outside to sit by the water pump he was catching on his unkempt head the same sun that blessed the land?

"It was real pretty there," Mr. Humphreys said. "I have pictures of it in my head." The boy sometimes raised a finger to his temple and tapped it, looking down on the dying breed. They went their separate ways, Mr. Humphreys to stand guard over Mrs. Wills' house when she was out, lest the antique buyers should come, and the boy went off to the pool hall with its creosote floors and pastel walls.

The itinerant youngsters rode motorbikes with accoutrements—helmets and peace symbols—and disturbed the sleeping, both in the homes and in the graveyard on the hill. Down the country road the children came, tearing down the middle of the road on hot summer days when the sun was in the middle of the sky, over the streams where the covered bridges had been, practicing now for their inheritance of motors and speed. The littlest boy couldn't talk plainly. His brothers said he was an idiot. But he drove his tricycle like a professional, one-wheeling around the gas pumps and making ordered furrows in the lawn of a vacant house. Like a farmer's wordless intelligence with animals the boy saw no need to articulate plainly his immersion in the language of bikes.

The accounting occurred. But all in ways as subtle as Mr. Humphreys'. It was not a slowing of the brain the other oldtimers could claim as cause when the town finally divided itself and split apart. The process that was theirs, however, was as slow and imperceptible as a hardening of the arteries. The Corps of Engineers began twenty-five years before making the first lesions into the body of the town, as quietly as chronic disease makes its place among healthy cells.

A lone surveyor came with his tripod, set up business in a field where grain grew, looked through the eye of his equipment, and found what he saw fertile for progress, just as the home office had said he would. At a window, there appeared the face of the printer's wife, and a hand holding back an edge of a starched curtain. "I wonder who that is?" she asked, turning away with suspicion.

That night at dinner she mentioned the intruder. Eventually rumors moved from house to house, and in the persistence of rumor which remained for years at the passive levels of speculation, the people forgot the initial alarm of the first woman at the curtain. She herself forgot that her fingers had strained the starched curtain in that initial moment of panic. Poachers! her brain said. But dinner was on, fields waited, and cattle with full udders.

So the town accepted the rumor, assimilated it into itself, and lived on, vaguely worried, the demanding moment absorbed by time and duty.

Overlooking Anderson's Fork (PHOTOGRAPH BY DAN PATTERSON)

Winter

It is a hard winter in New Burlington because it comes late. Autumn melts into Indian summer and the trees flare as brilliant as the village's failure. A reasonable warmth remains through December as if to stay the deep and natural chill of loss. The weather is gentle, lulling, and treacherous. The snow and ice come in January, late, and if New Burlington had not kept memories of other winters like this one perhaps it would have felt betrayed.

In late January only the post office is open. Three families remain, and Lawrence Mitchener, who is waiting for the water. "Big changes coming," says a man at the service station west of the village. He sweeps his arm in an arc over the land the water will cover. "People and buildings and big automobiles. They'll be stakes and string and caterpillers to come and houses with carpet and clotheslines and birdbaths. Five years from now nobody'll know it. Me, I'm going the other way. I'm going to Idaho. I hear there ain't enough people to bother anybody in Idaho."

His tone is sure, as though he is certain of an audience able catch the inaudible measure of an unspoken rage, and understand. In New Burlington in front of a house of boarded windows a dog howls at midday.

The Last Man

*They don't call it stubbornness when a
mule has got it.*

—Charles Stanley

Lawrence Mitchner, 87

*If he goes until the Fourth of July with corn still unplanted he will not ask
for help. He will ask for nothing. They would come of course. Their big
steel-wheeled tractors packing down the earth so he and his horses could
never work it up. And talking talking. He could hear their questions loud
as oaths in the empty spaces between their conversations about crops and
livestock. They want to ask him about prison. At threshing time he does
not eat with the other men. He works alone in his fields under the startling
sun.*

Kent Holland was the first to go. World War I seemed very real after
that. Even Kent thought it was a mistake. Right up until he got off the
boat and stepped into a trench somewhere in France. How could they
take someone who had lost his trigger finger in a wringer washer? No
mind, they said. No mind. They even took boys blind in one eye.
"You'll see enough out of your good one before you get back," the doctor
said.

Most of the old Quakers were opposed to the war but they had to
admit: their farm prices had never been higher. Arthur Hartman said if
the war lasted two more months he'd make enough to buy another farm.
Some of the villagers wanted to tar and feather Arthur for saying that.
They didn't but they talked about it. Simple truths are often the most un-
bearable.

Then finally it is only he, Lawrence Mitchner, who refuses to serve at
all. The Methodists say he is "a tool" of the old Quakers. He has two
years to consider his choice. Two years in Leavenworth Prison. When he
returns he walks with a limp. Is it something they did to him in prison?

He will not say. He will leave the room as if even memory has tiny thrashing nerve endings which of course memory does.

The fields, however, are peaceful. Lawrence follows his horses through the careful furrows and the earth lies in great coils. He will never use anything but horses. He ignores the new machinery. He fills the old Cornstalk schoolhouse with corn. The villagers watch him closely: is being a horse farmer another protest? There is another war and the village boys go away again but this time no one protests.

When Lawrence is too old to farm he and his wife move into the village. The farm on Cornstalk Road is no more than a mile away but he refuses to ever see it again. His wife dies. At Christmas he places a photograph of her against the glass of the door, facing out. The village children occasionally see him on his porch in his green underwear. His body seems small and shrunken. The children find this a curious image. "A spook," says one child. "He is one of those kind who'll be here when the world gets over with."

In the early 1970's, when Lawrence is an old man, the Army Corps of Engineers says it will flood the village to make a reservoir. Lawrence knows that he will not move. When his neighbors ask him he says he will stay on. The widows (they sympathized with his wife) say: that is *like* Lawrence. But they have premonitions of their own lives in exile and they soon forget him.

In the spring of 1973 all of New Burlington is gone except four buildings: the old cobbler's shop, the Quaker church, two houses. Lawrence's house is the small bungalow with the watering trough in front. This trough is perhaps a hundred years old. It once watered the Colvins' horses when Lawrence's house was their undertaking parlor. Knowing this explains the design of the house which is mostly two long narrow rooms. This is where Black Jane came to pack ice around the corpses. Where the friends of John Clippard sat through the night after his death, John so bent by age the undertakers could make him lie flat only by tying him into the coffin and in the early morning hours the rope slipped and the body sat suddenly up.

"How do, John," said his friends who remarked later that it was pleasant having John sit with them one last time.

Now the house sits in the middle of the empty bulldozed lots which fill with weeds and vines. The country highway in front, Route 380, is noisier to him now as the cars come down into the heart of what was once the village and turn sharply across one of the two streams. He knows that the other buildings helped absorb the noise.

He will seldom answer his door now. He refuses to see Corps appraisers and when they write him he takes the letters and tears them across and hands them back to the postman. The house is shuttered as if to stave off the future itself which threatens to leak in at door jambs and windowsills.

He has quarreled recently with his brother, Thurmond, but he has forgotten why. He thinks it might be something about going to church. He is in the backyard cutting weeds with his pocketknife when Thurmond walks into the yard. He is frightened at first because he has not heard anyone but then he is glad to see Thurmond and does not think about the argument anymore.

"My God," he says. "Not a day goes past I don't think of you."

"I hear you won't open the door."

"I have a way of seeing through the door. I let in who I want."

Thurmond's wife has been dead for several years and he lives alone in the old farmhouse a mile or so east of the graveyard. He tells Lawrence there is plenty of room.

"I think I'll stay here until they haul me out," Lawrence says. He says this as though he were reading an announcement. He is not affronting Thurmond, however; he is *explaining*.

The villagers, scattered now across the countryside, regard Lawrence's behavior as an infraction of artful movement. They seldom fail to mention in their conversations that he would not go to war, either. In their speech they link the two events even though they themselves are very bitter about moving.

"He has always been *Lawrence*," says one of the widows, rolling her eyes heavenward, innuendo heavy in the gesture. "Very *odd*," she says. All judgment suspended tactfully in the ice of implication. *I wonder what he does with his time?* they ask among themselves.

Sometimes he rides in Frank Compton's cattle truck to Cincinnati and back, perhaps not talking at all, serenely watching the fields as they flow grandly past. Sometimes he drives his ancient automobile into Xenia where he visits the funeral home that buried his wife, sitting through long afternoons in the wide quiet rooms and their sense of ungovernable resolution.

He tells his relatives that God created the village and now Satan is destroying it. Forsaking metaphor, the relatives say Lawrence is "bitter."

One night while Don Haines is plowing he looks across Caesar's Creek to where the village once was. He can find nothing familiar. There is only the dim light from Lawrence's rear windows in all the dark space which seems dense and congested over the ruined foundations of the old village. When Don sees the Corps appraiser he asks him about Lawrence.

"We'll leave him alone as long as we can," says the appraiser.

Lawrence Mitchner's grave (PHOTOGRAPH BY DAN PATTERSON)

"What you mean," says Don, "is that you know he's almost ninety and you hope he'll die before you get ready for his house."

"Well, that is one way of putting it . . ."

"And if he outlives that time, then what?"

"We'll have to go in and take him out, put him someplace . . ."

Mice run in Lawrence's silver drawers and milk sours in the refrigerator. Sometimes he puts water in the trough, for horses he remembers from long ago. And then he dies.

The death certificate says heart attack. Bill Neeld, his old friend at the funeral home in Xenia, says: "He just wore out." He is lying in a casket banked with roses. Cosmotology has straightened his face and his mouth is a lifeless unrevealing seam. There are less than thirty people in the room. The minister does not know what to make of either Lawrence's life or his death. *Now if Christ be preached that he rose from the dead how say some among you that there is no resurrection of the dead?*

Lawrence's sister-in-law peers into the casket where she regards him with her flinty survivor's eye. "I haven't seen him looking so well in years," she says. At the graveside, Lawrence's niece passes out religious pamphlets entitled *Out of Uncertainty and Doubt* which were written by a Baltimore gynecologist. And the wet earth turns off the shovel and strikes the lowered coffin.

The day after, a sudden storm comes with high winds and rain and tears apart the ancient, thick-trunked maples around Lawrence's empty house. The early summer is cold. The new growth seems thick and dumb.

ξPILOGUE
Village

The village is deserted now; that is to say, the people have gone. And during the harsh winter when the land turned inward upon itself, sheathing itself in ice, making its own bones go stiff, it seemed that the town and the land had conspired to entomb the town's passing in mystery. But as spring foliage wraps around the houses like bed covers, while glassless windows look as dark as the pupil of the eye, New Burlington seems still to be alive.

If its remaining life is symbolic, its last spring not rebirth but summation before death, that fact is now a challenge. Like the work of art released from the fury of the artist and declared finished, the town, its effect on its people, the method of the fatal wound, all stand released for appraisal. The process of summation is a manifestation of the tragic fact that we learn values from things lost, ourselves the wounded and the healer, caught between pain and prognosis. The town looks mean.

(PHOTOGRAPH BY KEN STEINHOFF)